D0599396

VISUAL QUICKSTART GUIDE

iPhoto 1.1

FOR MAC OS X

Adam C. Engst

Peachpit Press

Visual QuickStart Guide

iPhoto 1.1 for Mac OS X

Adam C. Engst

Peachpit Press
1249 Eighth Street
Berkeley, CA 94710
510/524-2178
800/283-9444
510/524-2221 (fax)
Find us on the World Wide Web at: http://www.peachpit.com/
To report errors, please send a note to errata@peachpit.com
Peachpit Press is a division of Pearson Education

Editor: Nancy Davis
Production Coordinator: Lisa Brazieal
Copyeditor: Tonya Engst
Compositor: Adam C. Engst
Indexer: Rebecca Plunkett
Cover Design: The Visual Group

ISBN 0-321-12165-1

9 8 7 6 5 4 3 2 1

Printed and bound in the United States of America

Dedication

To my son, Tristan Mackay Engst, the subject of so many of my photographs.

About the Author

Adam C. Engst is the publisher of *TidBITS*, one of the oldest and largest Internet-based newsletters, distributed weekly to hundreds of thousands of readers (see *TidBITS* at `www.tidbits.com`). He has written numerous Internet books, including the best-selling *Internet Starter Kit* series, and many articles for magazines, including *Macworld*, where he is currently a Contributing Editor. He has appeared on a variety of internationally broadcast television and radio programs.

His indefatigable support of the Macintosh community and commitment to helping people has resulted in numerous awards and recognition at the highest levels. In the annual MDJ Power 25 survey of industry insiders, he ranked as the second (2000) and third (2001) most influential person in the Macintosh industry, and he was named one of MacDirectory's top ten visionaries. And how many industry figures can boast of being turned into an action figure?

Please send comments about the book to Adam at `iphoto-vqs@tidbits.com` or post them on the book's Web site at `http://iphoto.tidbits.com`.

Other Books by Adam Engst

Eudora 4.2 for Windows & Macintosh: Visual QuickStart Guide

Crossing Platforms: A Macintosh/Windows Phrasebook

Internet Starter Kit for Macintosh

Special Thanks

No book is the work of a single person, and many people helped with this one, including:

- Tonya Engst (not only my wonderful wife, but also a great copyeditor)
- Nancy Davis (a great editor and an almost geographically suitable friend)
- Lisa Brazieal (who can spot a wayward pixel at ten paces)
- Nancy Ruenzel (for giving me the nod on this book)
- Paula Baker (for PDF and Web wrangling)
- Kim Lombardi and Scott Cowlin (for PR and marketing wizardry)
- John Santoro (for iPhoto)
- Chris Engst (for watching Tristan!)
- Alex Hoffman (for kibitzing)
- Glenn Fleishman and Marshall Clow (without whose help I could never have explained color management and resolution)
- Jeff Carlson, Geoff Duncan, Matt Neuburg, and Mark Anbinder (for helping keep *TidBITS* running).

Featured Photographers

I took most of the photos you see in this book, but I also included some pictures from friends and the folks at Peachpit Press. Some of these people are wonderful photographers and artists—although I can't identify each picture, if it's really well done, someone else probably took it. A tip of the lens cap to: Marjorie Baer, Trish Booth, Lisa Brazieal, Jeff Carlson, Doug Davenport, Glenn Fleishman, Chris Holmes, Tim Holmes, Suzie Lowey, Gary-Paul Prince, and Mimi Vitetta.

Technical Colophon

I wrote this book using the following hardware and software.

- A Power Mac G4/450 with two 20-inch monitors for writing and layout, a Canon PowerShot S100 camera, and an Addonics Pocket DigiDrive card reader.
- iPhoto 1.0 and 1.1.1, QuarkXPress 4.1, Snapz Pro X for screenshots, GraphicConverter 4.0, and the Peachpit VQS template.

Contents at a Glance

Table of Contents

INTRODUCTION

In late 2001, Apple realized the immense popularity of digital cameras meant that millions of Mac owners now use digital cameras in favor of their traditional analog counterparts. And yet, the camera is only part of the equation, and the other part, the software, is often incomprehensible to the average user.

Enter iPhoto, which helps users perform tasks never before possible in a photo management program, such as ordering prints from an online service and building and printing photo books—essentially customized hardcover photo albums. At the same time, iPhoto is easy to use, thanks in part to a simple interface, but also thanks to the fact that it doesn't attempt to compete with the big boys of the image cataloging and image editing worlds.

If iPhoto is so easy, why write this book? Three reasons. iPhoto is still wet behind the ears, and not all of its functions are clear. Even iPhoto doesn't succeed entirely at demystifying the process of taking a digital photograph, editing it, and presenting it either on paper or on the computer screen. And iPhoto comes with no documentation beyond minimal online help.

Read on, then, for the help you need to make the most of your digital photos.

Hardware and Software Requirements

Although iPhoto is a simple program, it has fairly significant system requirements thanks to the difficulty of working with large digital images.

To run iPhoto, you need:

- A Macintosh with built-in USB ports. A sufficiently souped-up older Mac with a PCI card providing USB ports might work, but Apple isn't guaranteeing it. iPhoto should work on any Mac that runs Mac OS X, but Apple recommends one with at least a 400 MHz PowerPC G3 processor and at least 256 MB of RAM. Realistically, the more CPU power and RAM you can throw at iPhoto, the happier you'll be.
- Mac OS X 10.1.2 or later. iPhoto will run on earlier versions of Mac OS X, but some features won't operate correctly. Besides, Mac OS X is still new enough that you should update it whenever possible to take advantage of Apple's improvements.
- A source of digital images, which could be a compatible digital camera, scanned images, Photo CDs, or a service that provides digital images along with traditional film developing. Apple maintains a list of devices that are supposedly compatible with iPhoto at `www.apple.com/iphoto/compatibility/`. Take that list with a grain of salt; early reports indicate that some devices on that list may not work entirely properly, and there are also devices missing from the list that work fine.

iPhoto disk image file. *iPhoto disk after being mounted.*

iPhoto
iPhoto

Figure i.1 When you download iPhoto, you'll end up with a disk image file. Double-click it to have Disk Copy mount it as a disk.

Install iPhoto 1.0
Authorization
You need an Administrator password to install the software.
Authenticate
You need an administrator name and password or phrase to make changes in Installer.
Name: Adam Engst
Password or phrase:
Cancel
OK
Click the lock to make changes.
Close

Figure i.2 When prompted, click the lock and enter your Administrator password.

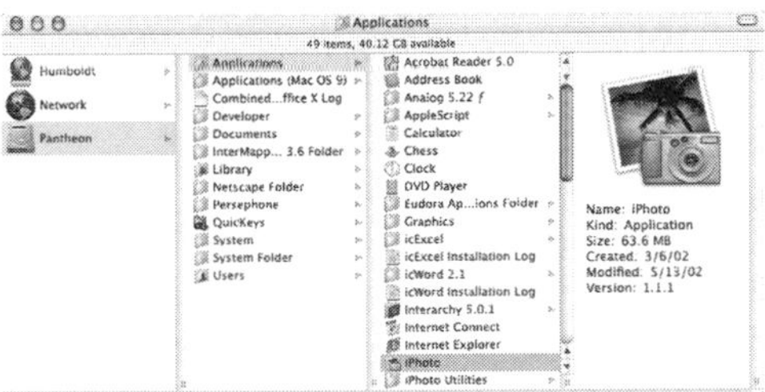

Figure i.3 When you're done installing, launch iPhoto by double-clicking its icon in your Applications folder.

Installing and Launching iPhoto

The current version of iPhoto might have come with your Mac, but if not, you'll need to download and install iPhoto.

To install iPhoto:

1. Visit Apple's iPhoto Web page at `www.apple.com/iphoto/` and download the latest version of iPhoto.

   You'll end up with an iPhoto disk image on your Desktop (or wherever your Web browser stores downloaded files).

2. Double-click the disk image file.

   Disk Copy launches and mounts the disk image file as a disk on your Desktop (**Figure i.1**).

3. Double-click the iPhoto disk to open it, and then double-click the iPhoto.pkg file to launch iPhoto's installer.

4. Click the lock icon in the installer window, enter your Administrator password (**Figure i.2**), and click OK.

5. Click through the Introduction, Read Me, License, Select Destination (select your hard disk here), Installation Type, Installing, and Finish Up steps.

   When you're done, you'll end up with an iPhoto icon in your Applications folder.

6. Double-click the iPhoto icon to launch the program (**Figure i.3**). If you plan to use iPhoto often, consider adding iPhoto to your Dock for faster access.

✔ Tip

- If you end up downloading iPhoto twice, the name of the second copy might end with a 2 rather than .dmg. Delete the 2 to make sure Disk Copy can open the file.

Updating from 1.0 to 1.1.1

In theory, updating from iPhoto 1.0 to 1.1.1 should be merely a matter of downloading 1.1.1 from Apple's iPhoto Web site and running the installer. However, a few simple actions can prevent future problems.

Tips when updating to iPhoto 1.1.1:

- Make sure to back up your iPhoto Library folder (located in your Pictures folder) before installing iPhoto 1.1.1. That way, if something terrible happens, you won't lose all your photos. I'm sure you have a backup anyway, but another one can't hurt.
- If you have installed third-party export plug-ins (see "Useful Export Plug-ins" in Chapter 5, "Sharing Photos"), make sure to remove them before updating to avoid crashes. To find them, Control-click iPhoto's icon in the Finder, choose Show Package Contents, and navigate to the PlugIns folder. Drag any third-party plug-ins you see to the Trash.
- If you want to be sure you're getting a clean installation, use Sherlock to search for "iphoto" and delete the com.apple.iPhoto.plist file, the iPhoto Cache folder, and of course, the iPhoto application itself. Then install iPhoto 1.1.1. Three other files necessary for the buttons in the share pane—BookService, HomePageService, and PrintsService—live in the System/Library/Services folder. You can't delete them without changing their privileges, but the iPhoto installer should update them to version 1.5 automatically.
- If you have trouble immediately after updating, delete the files mentioned above, then reinstall iPhoto 1.1.1.

Changes in iPhoto 1.1.1

iPhoto 1.0 came out at the very beginning of 2002; exactly four months later, Apple released iPhoto 1.1.1, addressing many of the initial limitations of version 1.0.

Major changes in iPhoto 1.1.1

- In the share pane you can now email selected photos using Apple's Mail program, make a photo into your Desktop picture, and turn an album into a Mac OS X slide show screen saver.
- In the edit pane, the redundant Rotate button has been replaced by controls for adjusting brightness and contrast. Yay!
- When you import photos by dragging them to iPhoto, iPhoto now preserves their filenames and names the film rolls to match folder names. If you drag a folder into the album pane, iPhoto imports the photos and creates the album in one step. You can also add photos to albums by dragging them in from the Finder. Last, you can now import directly from Kodak Photo CDs without locating the photos manually.
- In organize mode, you can now enter comments in the organize pane, plus search for text in titles, comments, and keywords.
- You can now modify certain things that were unchangeable in iPhoto 1.0. You can rearrange the order of albums, choose what information you want displayed in a photo's title, change the names and dates of film rolls, and even change the dates of photos (handy if your camera became confused about the date at some point). Perhaps most helpful, your iPhoto Library folder can now live anywhere as long as there's an alias called "iPhoto Library" in your Pictures folder.

Updating via Software Update

Although Apple initially released iPhoto 1.1.1 as a manual download, future updates will likely come via an Internet utility called Software Update that does most of the work for you once it's set up properly.

To set up Software Update:

1. Click the System Preferences icon in your Dock.
2. In the System collection of preferences panes, click Software Update to display the Software Update window.
3. To set Software Update to kick in on its own, click the Automatically radio button, and from the "Check for updates" pop-up menu choose how often you wish Software Update to check for updates (**Figure i.4**).

   or

   To invoke Software Update manually, make sure the Manually radio button is selected. To check for an update, click the Update Now button.

   Whether invoked automatically or manually, if Software Update finds updated software appropriate for your computer, it presents you with a list. If not, it tells you no updates are available.

To install an update:

1. Click the checkbox next to the update you want to install (**Figure i.5**).
2. Click the Install button.

   Depending on the update, you may need to enter your administrator password and restart the Mac. In that event, Software Update will prompt you as necessary.

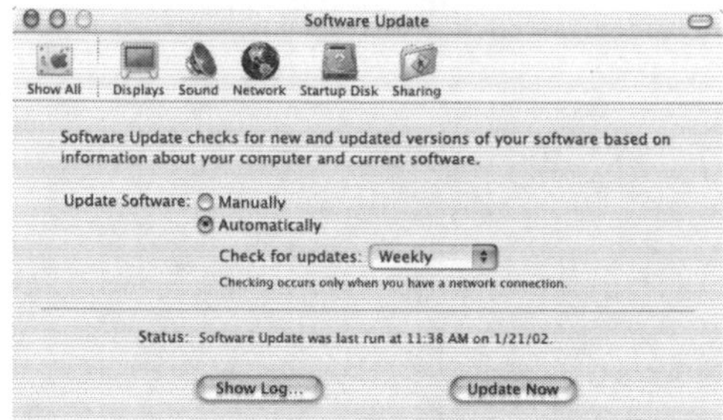

Software Update
Show All
Displays
Sound
Network
Startup Disk
Sharing
Software Update checks for new and updated versions of your software based on information about your computer and current software.
Update Software: Manually
Automatically
Check for updates: Weekly
Checking occurs only when you have a network connection.
Status: Software Update was last run at 11:36 AM on 1/21/02.
Show Log...
Update Now

Figure i.4 Choose between Manually and Automatically in the Software Update preferences panel, and choose how often you want Software Update to check for updates.

Software Update
Software Update found the following new or updated software for your computer.
Click the checkbox to select the software you want to install:
Install
Name
Version
Size
Brazilian Portuguese Language 10.1.2 6.1MB
Danish Language Support 10.1.2 6.2MB
Korean Language Support 10.1.2 40.0MB
Norwegian Language Support 10.1.2 5.8MB
Mac OS X is a multilingual operating system which allows users to use languages other than the one selected during installation. This update installs the additional fonts and resources needed to use Mac OS X in Danish in addition to any other language currently installed. After installing this update use the International preference pane to set your preferred order of
Status: Not installed.
Inactive Updates: 3
Updates to install: 1
Install

Figure i.5 To install an update, click the checkbox next to its name, and then click the Install button. This dialog doesn't show an iPhoto update because as of this writing, none have arrived via Software Update.

Apple's iPhoto Web Pages

Thanks to its status as one of Apple's high-profile "iApps," iPhoto boasts a number of pages accessible on Apple's Web site at `www.apple.com/iphoto/`. It would be a good idea to check those pages every so often for any news about iPhoto or updates that might not have been released via Software Update.

Interface Overview

Before we dive into the specifics of using iPhoto in the upcoming chapters, let's take a bird's-eye view of the main window so you can orient yourself and get a feel for the program's primary functions (**Figure i.6**).

I assume here that you already know about standard Mac OS X window widgets like the close, minimize, and zoom buttons, the scroll bars and scroll arrows, and the resize handle in the lower right. If not, let me recommend that you check out a copy of Robin Williams's *The Little Mac OS X Book,* also from Peachpit Press. It will help you with the basics of Mac OS X.

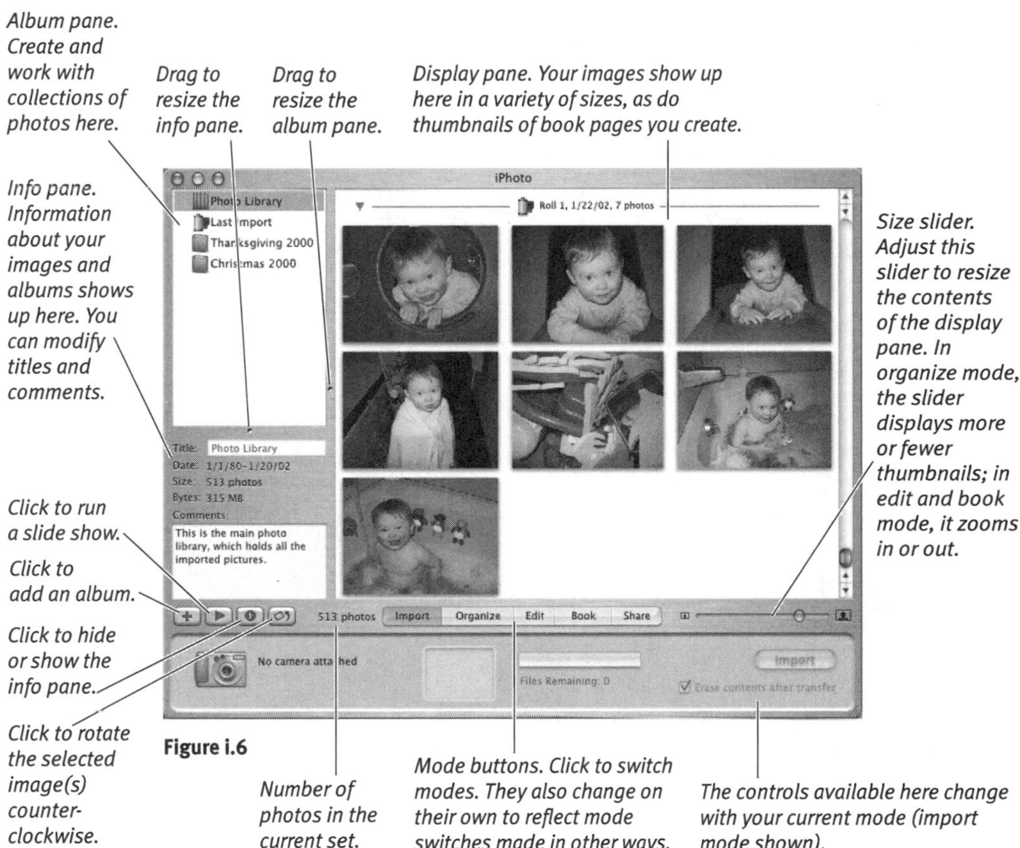
Album pane. Create and work with collections of photos here.
Drag to resize the info pane.
Drag to resize the album pane.
Display pane. Your images show up here in a variety of sizes, as do thumbnails of book pages you create.
Info pane. Information about your images and albums shows up here. You can modify titles and comments.
Size slider. Adjust this slider to resize the contents of the display pane. In organize mode, the slider displays more or fewer thumbnails; in edit and book mode, it zooms in or out.
Click to run a slide show.
Click to add an album.
Click to hide or show the info pane.
Click to rotate the selected image(s) counter-clockwise.
Number of photos in the current set.
Mode buttons. Click to switch modes. They also change on their own to reflect mode switches made in other ways.
The controls available here change with your current mode (import mode shown).
iPhoto
Photo Library
Last Import
Thanksgiving 2000
Christmas 2000
Roll 1, 1/22/02, 7 photos
Title: Photo Library
Date: 1/1/80–1/20/02
Size: 513 photos
Bytes: 315 MB
Comments:
This is the main photo library, which holds all the imported pictures.
513 photos
Import
Organize
Edit
Book
Share
No camera attached
Files Remaining: 0
Import
Erase contents after transfer

Figure i.6

iPhoto's Modes

When you use iPhoto, you'll find yourself in one of five modes at all times. The next five chapters will look at each mode in turn, focusing on the tasks you perform in each mode. Here's a quick summary of each.

Import mode

To add photos to your photo library, you import them, either from files or directly from a digital camera. iPhoto generally switches into import mode automatically.

Organize mode

Once you have images in iPhoto, you'll want to organize them into albums, assign them keywords, and delete the lousy ones. All that and more happens in organize mode, where you'll probably spend the bulk of your time.

Edit mode

Even the best photographers edit their images. iPhoto provides a few simple image editing tools in edit mode so you can crop pictures, adjust brightness and contrast, remove red-eye, and make them black-and-white. If you need more advanced tools, iPhoto can use another image editor.

Book mode

One of iPhoto's great strengths is the way it helps you design and print professional-looking hardcover photo albums. Book mode provides the tools you need.

Share mode

Most of us take pictures to share with relatives, friends, and colleagues. iPhoto's share mode provides tools for exporting photos, printing them, ordering high-quality prints online, printing books, running slide shows, creating Web pages, setting your Desktop picture, emailing photos, and more.

Importing Photos

1

The first thing to do in iPhoto is import some photos. iPhoto provides two basic ways you can import photos—from a digital camera or from existing files. Those files might be images you downloaded from your camera previously, acquired on a CD, scanned in from prints, or received from a photo processing company that provides digital images along with traditional prints. It's also possible to use a card reader—a USB device into which you put the memory card from your camera and which presents the contents of your memory card as files on a disk—with the twist that iPhoto recognizes some card readers and can import from them just as though they were cameras.

In this chapter, we'll look at both of these approaches to importing pictures into iPhoto, complete with tips, tricks, and advice for making sure your irreplaceable photos are protected from accidental modification or erasure.

Supporting More Cameras

Although iPhoto (via Mac OS X) supports a large number of cameras, many older cameras still lack support from Apple. Luckily, a small firm of driver gurus has stepped up to the plate—to add support for many cameras with similar guts, download a copy of the Mac OS X Driver for USB Still Cameras from IOXperts at `www.ioxperts.com/usbstillcamera.html`. A link on that page provides a full list of supported cameras. Kudos to IOXperts for bringing more cameras to iPhoto!

Entering Import Mode

It's easy to bring your photos into iPhoto no matter where they may originate because iPhoto offers four different importing approaches, all of which switch you into import mode automatically. The only time you need to switch into import mode manually is if you switch modes after connecting a camera but before clicking the Import button to start the actual import.

Methods of entering import mode:

- Connect your digital camera to your Mac's USB port and turn the camera on. iPhoto need not be running; it launches automatically if necessary.
- Insert your camera's memory card into the card reader. iPhoto need not be running; it launches if necessary.
- From iPhoto's File menu, choose Import. iPhoto displays an open file dialog from which you can select a file, a folder, or even multiple items before clicking the Open button.
- From the Finder, drag and drop one or more files or an entire folder of images into the iPhoto window or onto the iPhoto icon in the Dock.
- Click the Import button that's always present under the display pane (**Figure 1.1**).

✔ Tips

- iPhoto remembers the last set of images you imported in the Last Import album in the album pane. Click it to see just those images (**Figure 1.2**).
- iPhoto tracks every import as a separate film roll. Film rolls are a useful automatic organization tool (**Figure 1.3**).

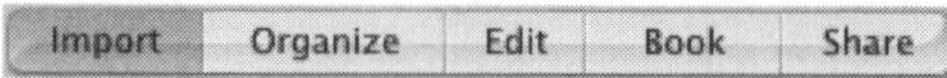
Import
Organize
Edit
Book
Share

Figure 1.1 To switch into import mode manually, click the Import button under the display pane.

Photo Library
Last Import
Thanksgiving 2000
Christmas 2000
Best of Tristan
Seattle Pigs
From Chris Holmes

Figure 1.2 To see the last set of images you imported, click the Last Import album in the album pane.

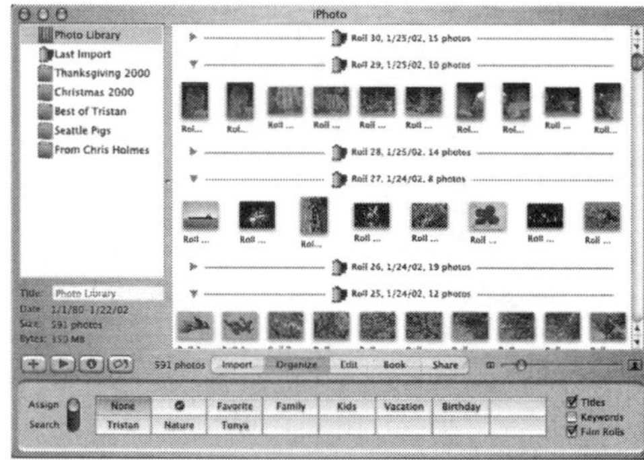
Photo Library
Last Import
Thanksgiving 2000
Christmas 2000
Best of Tristan
Seattle Pigs
From Chris Holmes

Figure 1.3 For best use of iPhoto's film rolls as an organizational device, shrink the thumbnail size using the size slider, then click the triangle next to film rolls you don't want to see to hide all the images inside.

Launching Automatically

iPhoto launches automatically only if you allow it to do so. The first time iPhoto runs, it asks you if you want it to launch automatically from then on. If you say yes, iPhoto takes over for Image Capture as the Hot Plug Application; see "iPhoto and Image Capture" at the end of this chapter for more details.

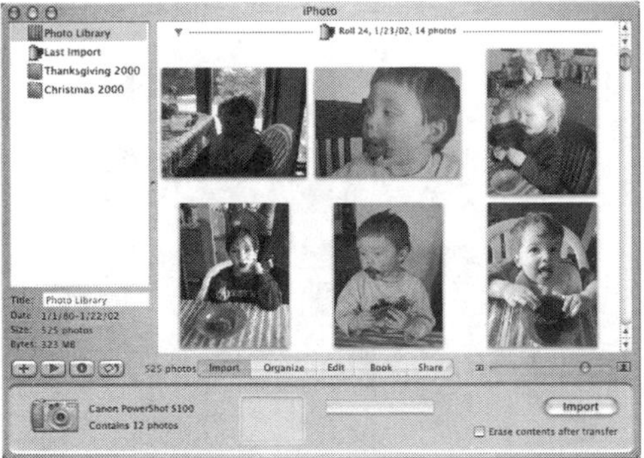

Figure 1.4 When you connect a camera to your Mac and turn the camera on, iPhoto launches and switches into import mode. It also identifies your camera and tells you how many images it contains. To start the import process, click the Import button on the right side of the import pane.

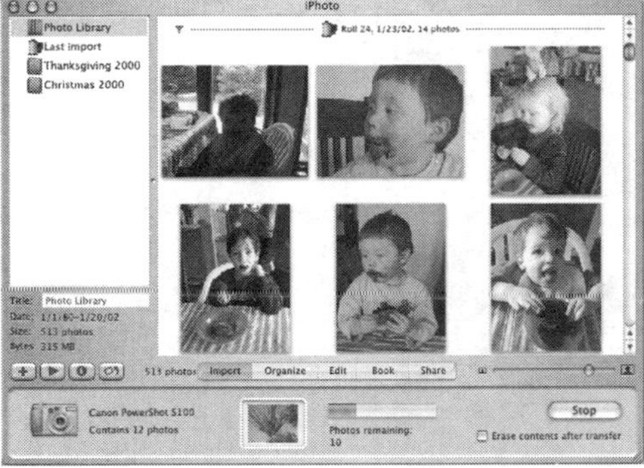

Figure 1.5 While iPhoto imports photos, it displays a thumbnail of the image being downloaded and displays a progress bar. To stop the process before it completes, click the Stop button.

Importing from Photo CD

iPhoto 1.1.1 adds support for importing from Kodak Photo CDs; it works just like importing from a camera. To import pictures from a Photo CD, open iPhoto, insert the Photo CD into your optical drive, switch to import mode, and click the Import button on the right side of the import pane.

Importing from a Camera

If you use a digital camera, it's easiest to import photos directly from the camera.

To import from a digital camera:

1. Connect your camera to your Mac using the USB cable included with the camera.
2. Turn on the camera. Make sure the camera is set to view pictures.
   iPhoto automatically launches and switches into import mode (**Figure 1.4**).
3. If you want iPhoto to erase the contents of your camera after transferring the images, click the "Erase contents after transfer" checkbox.
4. Click the Import button.
   iPhoto starts importing the photos, showing thumbnails and a progress bar. If you've made some sort of a mistake, click Stop to stop the import (**Figure 1.5**). When the import finishes, the photos appear in the display pane.

✔ Tips

- If you want to import only selected photos into iPhoto, either use Image Capture to transfer the files to your Mac and import into iPhoto from there (see "iPhoto and Image Capture" at the end of this chapter), or access the files directly using a card reader.
- Some digital cameras can record short movies, but iPhoto can't download them. (But it won't delete them either.)
- iPhoto can import either JPEG or TIFF files from cameras, but not RAW files. Any edits made to TIFF files will result in them being changed into JPEG format, which isn't generally as high quality. If you have trouble with importing TIFF files, convert them to JPEG first.

Importing from a Card Reader

Importing images via card reader works almost exactly like importing from a digital camera, except you trade connecting a USB cable for removing the memory card from the camera and putting it in the card reader.

To import from a card reader:

1. Connect your card reader to your Mac using the card reader's USB cable.
2. Insert your memory card.
   iPhoto automatically launches and switches into import mode (**Figure 1.6**).
3. To have iPhoto erase your memory card after transferring the photos, click the "Erase contents after transfer" checkbox.
4. Click the Import button.
   iPhoto starts importing the photos, showing thumbnails and a progress bar. If you've made a mistake, click Stop to stop the import.
5. To remove the memory card from the card reader, drag the card's disk icon to the Eject icon in the Dock (it replaces the Trash icon when you have a disk selected), and then eject the card from the card reader (**Figure 1.7**).

✔ Tips

- When using a card reader, you may be able to preview your pictures in the Finder's column view (**Figure 1.8**).
- You can delete pictures from the memory card in the Finder before importing into iPhoto, but eject and reinsert the card before importing to avoid confusing iPhoto about the number of images to import.
- Never eject the card while importing!

iPhoto
Photo Library
Last Import
Thanksgiving 2000
Christmas 2000
Best of Tristan
Seattle Pigs
From Chris Holmes
591 photos
Import
Organize
Edit
Book
Share
Pocket DigiDrive
Contains 14 photos
Import
Erase contents after transfer

Figure 1.6 When you insert a memory card, iPhoto launches and switches into import mode. It also identifies your card reader and tells you how many images it currently contains. To start the import process, click the Import button on the right side of the import pane.

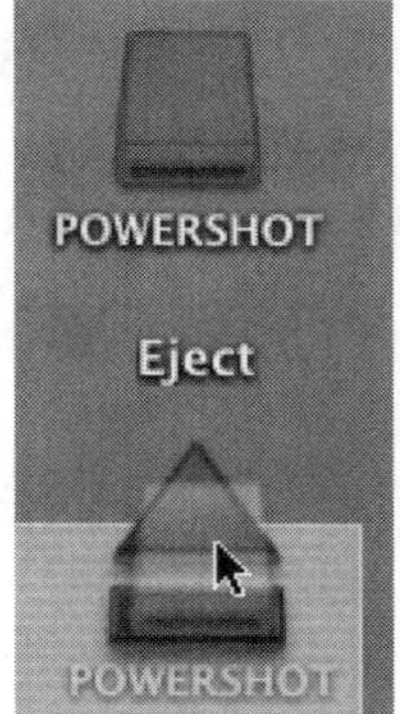
POWERSHOT
Eject
POWERSHOT

Figure 1.7 To remove a memory card from your card reader after importing, first drag the memory card's icon on the desktop to the Eject icon in the Dock, and only then eject the memory card from the card reader.

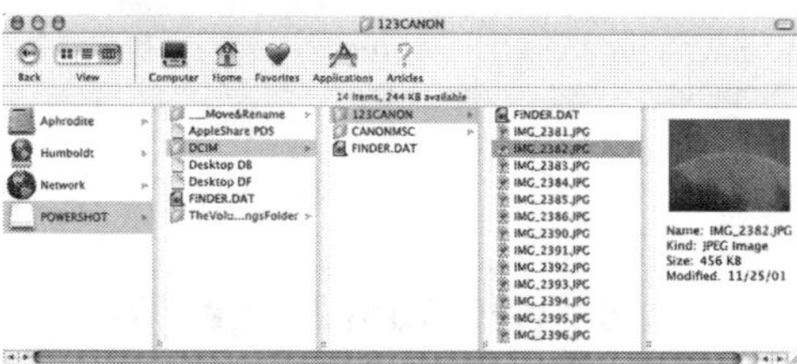
123CANON
Aphrodite
Humboldt
Network
POWERSHOT
DCIM
CANONMSC
FINDER.DAT
IMG_2382.JPG

Figure 1.8 For a quick look at a photo on a memory card, make sure you're in column view (the rightmost of the View buttons), navigate to where the images are stored, and select one to see a preview.

Import Photos
From: Photos from Chris
adam
Shared
tonya
backup.pdf
Classic Menu 2.5
Desktop
Documents
Downloads
Incomplete
Library
Movies
Music
Pictures
Public
Photos from Chris
Photos from Glenn
Photos from Jeff
Photos from Tim
Pictures of the Trol
Rug samples
subscriptions.pdf
Go to:
Add to Favorites
Cancel
Open

Figure 1.9 To import existing image files into iPhoto, choose Import from the File menu, navigate to your images, select the desired files, and click Open.

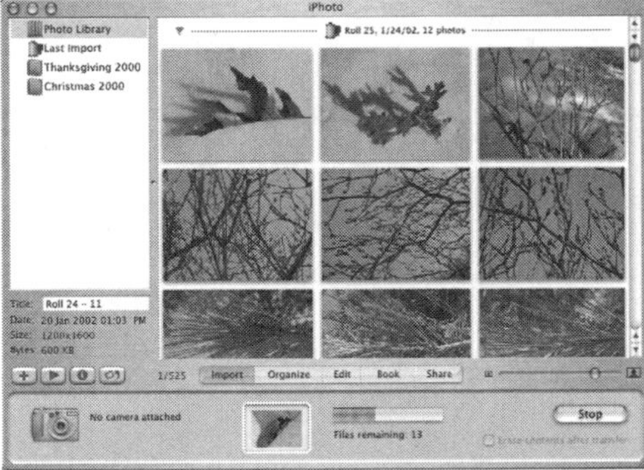
iPhoto
Photo Library
Last Import
Thanksgiving 2000
Christmas 2000
Import
Organize
Edit
Book
Share
No camera attached
Stop

Figure 1.10 iPhoto proceeds to import the images, showing a thumbnail of the current photo and a progress bar of how many remain to be processed. If you need to stop the import, click the Stop button.

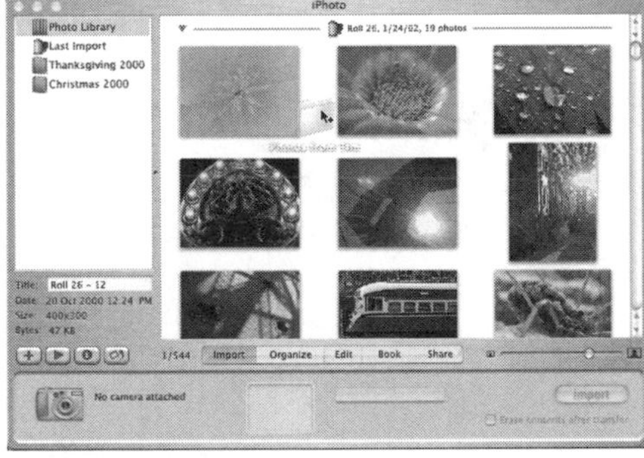
iPhoto
Photo Library
Last Import
Thanksgiving 2000
Christmas 2000
Import
Organize
Edit
Book
Share
No camera attached
Import

Figure 1.11 Alternatively, just drag the desired file(s) or folder(s) into iPhoto's display pane or album pane to start the import process.

Importing from Files

If, like most people, you used a digital camera before iPhoto was released, you probably have a collection of photos already on your hard disk. iPhoto can import these files in several ways.

To import files into iPhoto (I):

- From the File menu, choose Import. In the open file dialog, navigate to your images, select the desired file(s) or folder(s), and click Open (**Figure 1.9**).

  iPhoto starts importing the images. If you want to stop the import, click Stop (**Figure 1.10**). When the import finishes, the photos appear in the display pane.

To import files into iPhoto (II):

- From the Finder, drag the desired file(s) or folder(s) into iPhoto's display pane or album pane (**Figure 1.11**).

  iPhoto imports the images just as in the previous approach.

✔ Tips

- Hold down Shift or Cmd to select multiple files in the open file dialog.
- iPhoto copies the files you import, so make sure you have enough hard disk space if you're importing a lot of images.
- If you drag a file or folder into the album pane, iPhoto imports the photos and creates an album. You can also drag photos directly into a specific album.
- iPhoto retains the EXIF camera information stored with images along with filenames you've given the images.
- If you import folders, iPhoto creates and names a new film roll for each folder.
- You can also drag photos in from some other image cataloging programs.

Deleting Photos

We just finished importing photos, so why are we suddenly deleting them? Many of the pictures any photographer takes are lousy. Since iPhoto doesn't let you choose which photos to download, you'll need to cull out the ones of your spouse wearing a stupid expression.

To delete photos:

1. Make sure either Photo Library or Last Import is selected in import, organize, or share mode.
2. Select one or more photos (use Cmd-click and Shift-click to select multiple photos), and press Delete or choose Clear from the Edit menu.

   iPhoto warns you that proceeding will permanently remove the selected photos from the Photo Library and all albums (**Figure 1.12**). It's not kidding.
3. Click OK to agree that you really do want to delete those photos.

✔ Tips

- Deleting photos from any other album does not delete the original image.
- Be careful selecting images to delete.
- You cannot use Undo to recover from deleting photos.
- iPhoto really does delete the images—it doesn't just move them to the Trash.
- If you accidentally delete an important photo, stop using your Mac immediately. Any actions that write data to the disk could overwrite portions of the deleted file, which a data rescue tool like Norton Utilities may be able to recover.
- Backups are your friends!

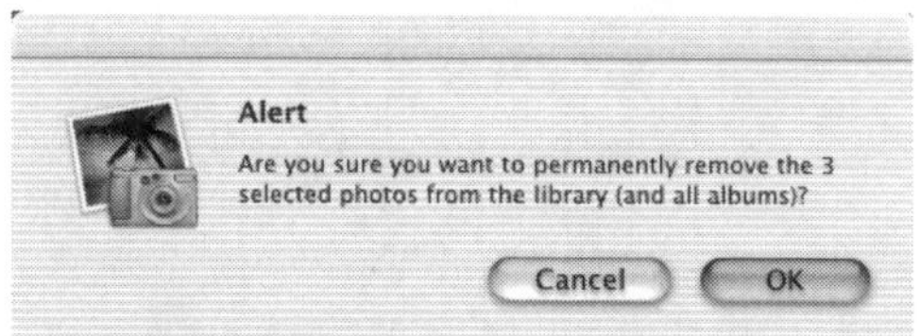
Alert
Are you sure you want to permanently remove the 3 selected photos from the library (and all albums)?
Cancel
OK

Figure 1.12 To delete images permanently, select them in the Photo Library and press Delete. Using the dialog above, iPhoto warns you it will delete the images for good; if you did indeed mean to delete the images, click OK. Otherwise click Cancel.

Figure 1.13 iPhoto uses a date-based directory structure that starts in your Pictures folder.

iPhoto Library Manager and iPhoto Librarian

Although iPhoto 1.1.1 lets you store your iPhoto Library folder wherever you want, maintaining multiple iPhoto Library folders is still tedious and prone to error.

There are two free utilities that let you switch between multiple iPhoto Library folders—iPhoto Librarian from `http://homepage.mac.com/scrufmeister/` and iPhoto Library Manager from `http://homepage.mac.com/bwebster/iphotolibrarymanager.html`.

Why might you want to use one of these utilities? You might want to keep multiple iPhoto Library folders as a way of keeping certain photos separate or handling a very large number of photos.

iPhoto Directory Structure

You might be wondering where iPhoto stores all your photos. Look in the Pictures folder inside your user folder. iPhoto creates an entire directory structure there, starting with a folder called iPhoto Library. Inside it, iPhoto creates folders for each year (along with support files and folders), inside each year folder are folders for months, inside those are folders for days, and only then do you get to the actual files, which are named with sequential numbers (**Figure 1.13**).

✔ Tips

- Do **not** move, rename, or delete anything inside the iPhoto Library folder in the Finder or you'll risk confusing iPhoto!
- With iPhoto 1.1.1, you can move your iPhoto Library folder to another location and put an alias to it (also named "iPhoto Library") in your Pictures folder. This lets you share your iPhoto Library folder by putting it in a public folder that multiple users of your Mac can access or on a server for different people to access over a network.
- If you need to locate a particular image in the Finder, drag and drop the photo from iPhoto's display pane onto the Show Image File AppleScript script, which you can download from Apple's Web site at `www.apple.com/applescript/iphoto/`. Again, beware that any changes you make inside the iPhoto Library folder can cause problems for iPhoto.
- If you drag photos from iPhoto to the Finder, it makes a copy of the original files in the destination.
- It's always a good idea to back up data like irreplaceable photographs. At a minimum, copy your iPhoto Library folder to another disk every so often.

iPhoto and Image Capture

Before Apple released iPhoto, the way you transferred images from a digital camera to a Mac running Mac OS X was with an included utility called Image Capture (found in your Applications folder). Image Capture is still useful if you want to download your photographs to a secondary location as a backup, rather than making iPhoto the sole repository. Image Capture can also download movies from your camera.

Image Capture functions:

- Using Image Capture, you can download photos to any folder. Select one in the Download To menu, and then click the Download All button (**Figure 1.14**).
- You can also download only selected images in Image Capture. Click the Download Some button in Image Capture's main window, select the images to download, and click the Download button (**Figure 1.15**).
- Although Image Capture offers some options for making a Web page from the images you download and formatting them to different sizes, it's much easier and more reliable to do this in iPhoto.
- If you want to download images using Image Capture, and then import them into iPhoto, it might be easiest to set the Hot Plug Action pop-up menu to launch Image Capture, rather than iPhoto.
- To adjust Image Capture's preferences, choose Preferences from the Image Capture application menu. In particular, make sure it doesn't delete after downloading so iPhoto can download the images as well. It might also be useful to have Image Capture download everything automatically and set your camera's date and time (**Figure 1.16**).

Canon PowerShot S100
Download To:
Big Heap O' Photos — .../Humboldt/P
Automatic Task:
None
Occurs after downloading
Hot Plug Action:
iPhoto
Application to open when a camera is connected
Items to download: 11
Download Some...
Download All

Figure 1.14 Use the old Image Capture application if you want to download images from your camera to a location outside of iPhoto, particularly if you want to download only a subset of images.

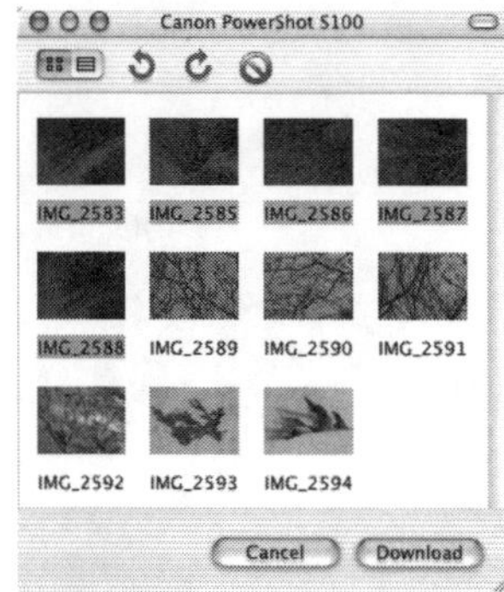
Canon PowerShot S100
IMG_2583
IMG_2585
IMG_2586
IMG_2587
IMG_2588
IMG_2589
IMG_2590
IMG_2591
IMG_2592
IMG_2593
IMG_2594
Cancel
Download

Figure 1.15 To download only some images, click Download Some in the main Image Capture window, select the images to download, and then click the Download button.

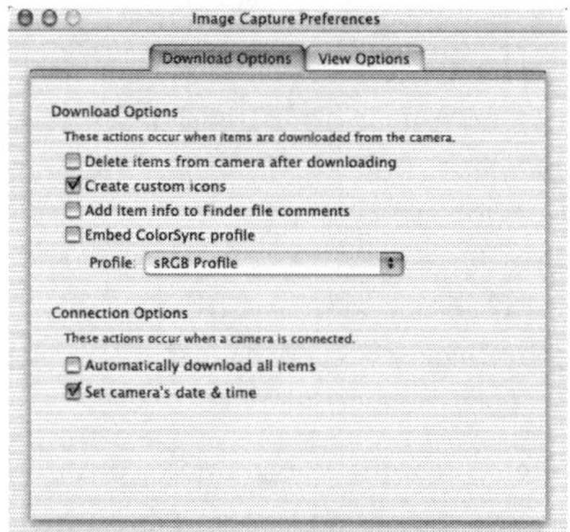
Image Capture Preferences
Download Options
View Options
Download Options
These actions occur when items are downloaded from the camera.
Delete items from camera after downloading
Create custom icons
Add item info to Finder file comments
Embed ColorSync profile
Profile:
sRGB Profile
Connection Options
These actions occur when a camera is connected.
Automatically download all items
Set camera's date & time

Figure 1.16 Image Capture has some options that may be useful; access them by choosing Preferences from the Image Capture application menu.

Organizing Photos

2

There are two types of people when it comes to photos. First are the Martha Stewart wanna-bes who manage to organize every picture into precious handmade albums constructed of used tissues and old grocery bags. Then there are the rest of us, who dump our pictures in a box, and that's if we remember to develop the film in the first place. We in the second group hate those in the first group (though we're sure you're actually very nice people).

For me, the promise of digital photography was a way not just to join that first group, but to beat them at their own game. I'm constitutionally incapable of cutting a print to crop it, and my miserable handwriting makes captions painful. I figured I could do it all on the computer with no trouble and make prints to boot. Unfortunately, it was just too hard—until iPhoto appeared.

iPhoto's editing tools are covered in a future chapter, so now we're going to focus on iPhoto's organizational features. Some require a little effort, but even with no work, your digital photo collection will be far better organized than the box in the attic.

And if you're one of those people who put together handmade photo albums before digital photography, well, you're still going to love what iPhoto can do for you.

Entering Organize Mode

For the most part, iPhoto makes sure you're in organize mode whenever necessary, but unlike with import mode, it can't do so automatically quite all the time.

Realistically, I don't expect you to do much more than click the Organize button when you want to switch into organize mode, but knowing the other methods may either prove useful as you become familiar with iPhoto or will at least explain why certain actions don't switch you into organize mode.

Methods of entering organize mode:

- At any time, click the Organize button under the display pane (**Figure 2.1**). No matter what mode you're in, iPhoto switches to organize mode and displays thumbnails of your photographs in the display pane.
- When you're in any other mode, click the Photo Library or Last Import in the album pane. One caveat: if Photo Library or Last Import is already selected, clicking it again won't switch you to organize mode.
- When you're in import or edit mode, but not book or share mode, click any album that isn't already selected to switch to organize mode.

Import
Organize
Edit
Book
Share

Figure 2.1 To switch into organize mode at any time, click the Organize button.

✔ Tip

- In addition to the scroll bar and mouse, you can use the arrow keys to navigate.

Organize Tools Overview

iPhoto's interface changes depending on what mode you're in, and some of the tools even offer different functions depending on mode. Here's a quick reference to the tools available in organize mode (**Figure 2.2**).

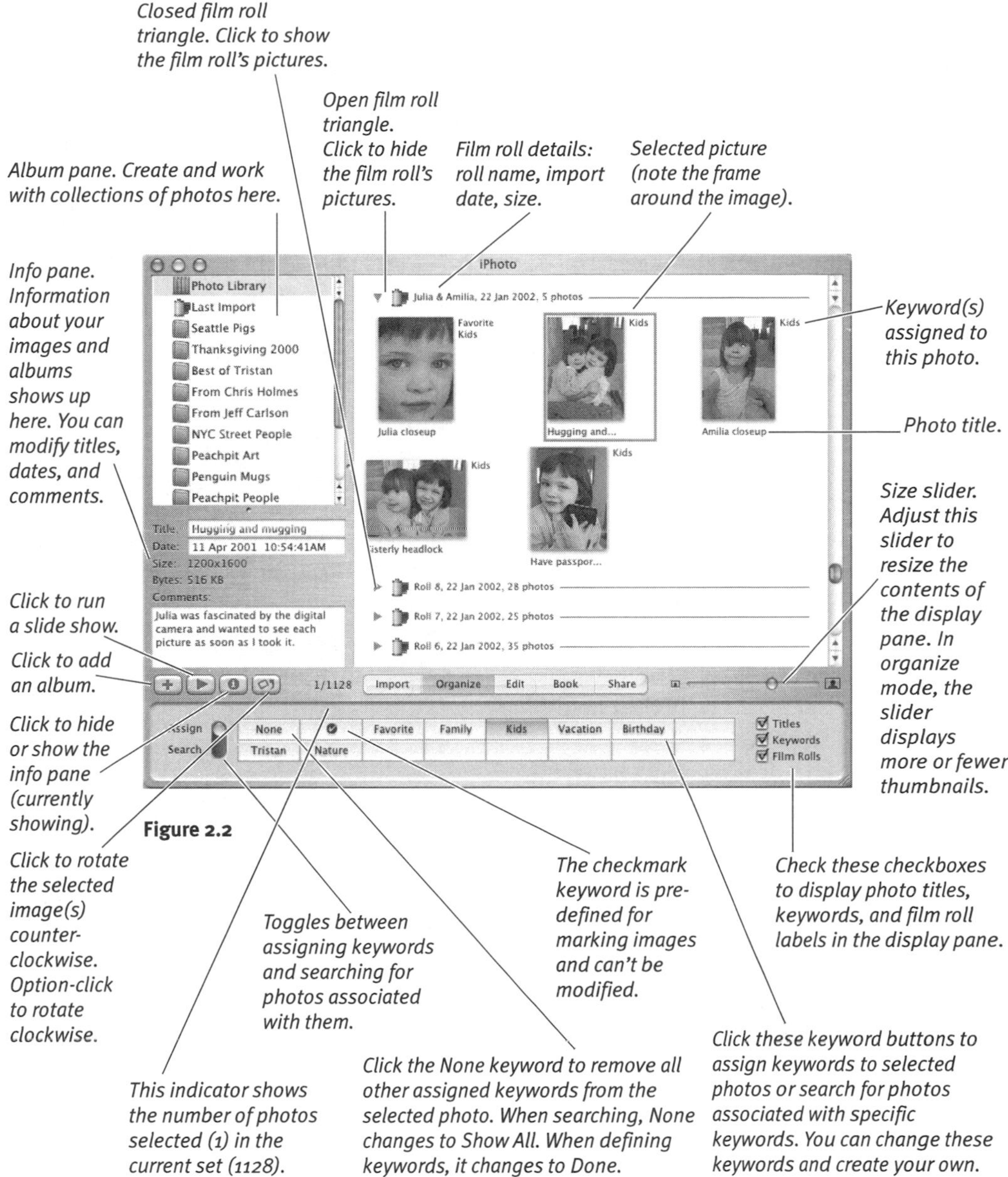
Closed film roll triangle. Click to show the film roll's pictures.
Open film roll triangle. Click to hide the film roll's pictures.
Album pane. Create and work with collections of photos here.
Film roll details: roll name, import date, size.
Selected picture (note the frame around the image).
Info pane. Information about your images and albums shows up here. You can modify titles, dates, and comments.
Keyword(s) assigned to this photo.
Photo title.
Size slider. Adjust this slider to resize the contents of the display pane. In organize mode, the slider displays more or fewer thumbnails.
Click to run a slide show.
Click to add an album.
Click to hide or show the info pane (currently showing).
Click to rotate the selected image(s) counter-clockwise. Option-click to rotate clockwise.
Toggles between assigning keywords and searching for photos associated with them.
The checkmark keyword is pre-defined for marking images and can't be modified.
Check these checkboxes to display photo titles, keywords, and film roll labels in the display pane.
This indicator shows the number of photos selected (1) in the current set (1128).
Click the None keyword to remove all other assigned keywords from the selected photo. When searching, None changes to Show All. When defining keywords, it changes to Done.
Click these keyword buttons to assign keywords to selected photos or search for photos associated with specific keywords. You can change these keywords and create your own.
iPhoto
Photo Library
Last Import
Seattle Pigs
Thanksgiving 2000
Best of Tristan
From Chris Holmes
From Jeff Carlson
NYC Street People
Peachpit Art
Penguin Mugs
Peachpit People
Title: Hugging and mugging
Date: 11 Apr 2001 10:54:41AM
Size: 1200x1600
Bytes: 516 KB
Comments:
Julia was fascinated by the digital camera and wanted to see each picture as soon as I took it.
Julia & Amilia, 22 Jan 2002, 5 photos
Favorite
Kids
Julia closeup
Hugging and...
Amilia closeup
Have passpor...
Roll 8, 22 Jan 2002, 28 photos
Roll 7, 22 Jan 2002, 25 photos
Roll 6, 22 Jan 2002, 35 photos
1/1128
Import
Organize
Edit
Book
Share
Search
None
Tristan
Nature
Family
Vacation
Birthday
Titles
Keywords
Film Rolls

Figure 2.2

Changing the Display Pane's Layout

One of iPhoto's slickest features is the slider that enables you to change the size of the thumbnails in the display pane, but there are other things you can do to change the way the display pane looks.

Changing the display pane layout:

- Move the size slider under the right side of the display pane to adjust the size of the thumbnails from a single image at the largest (**Figure 2.3**) all the way down to as many photos as will fit in the window at postage stamp size (**Figure 2.4**).
- To show titles, keywords, and film rolls, click their checkboxes in the organize pane (**Figure 2.5**).

✔ Tips

- Titles (and, to a lesser extent, keywords) aren't particularly useful at smaller sizes, although you can always see the title of the currently selected photo in the info pane.
- The film roll separators are a handy way to determine where you are in the Photo Library, so I recommend leaving them showing, particularly if you give them useful names.
- Play with different settings for the size slider and the three checkboxes to find a setting that fits your monitor size and working style. I personally like to see three thumbnails across—that seems like a good tradeoff that keeps the thumbnails viewable while still displaying a good number on the screen at once.

Figure 2.3 Move the size slider all the way to the right to view a single image at a time in organize mode.

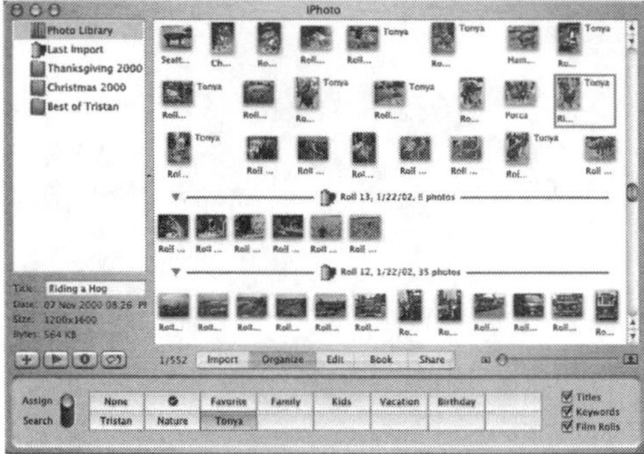

Figure 2.4 Move the size slider all the way to the left to view as many thumbnails as possible.

Figure 2.5 Uncheck the Titles, Keywords, and Film Rolls checkboxes for an uncluttered look.

Preferences
Photos:
Shadow
Frame
Black
Gray
White
Align to grid
Most recent at top
Rotate photos:
Clockwise
Counter Clockwise
Double-clicking photos opens them in:
Edit View
Separate Window
Other: PixelNhance
Set...
Assign/Search uses:
Keywords
Comments
Slide Show:
Play each slide for 2 seconds
Repeat slide show when finished
Music: Minuet in G

Figure 2.6 From the iPhoto application menu, choose Preferences to open the Preferences window, where you can switch between shadow and frame style, choose if you want your images to align to a grid, and decide whether to view keywords or comments in the organize pane.

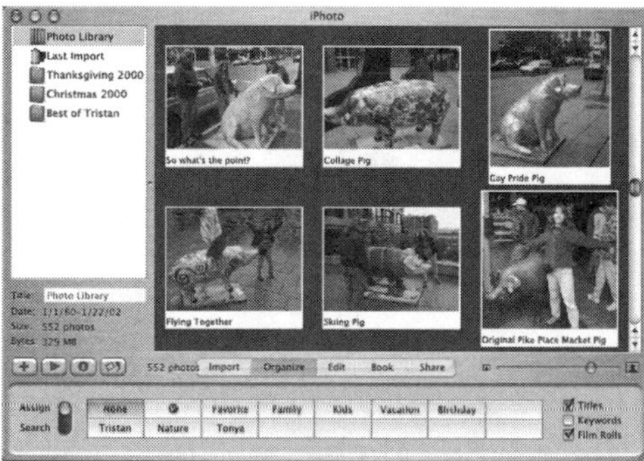
iPhoto
Photo Library
Last Import
Thanksgiving 2000
Christmas 2000
Best of Tristan
Collage Pig
Flying Together
Skiing Pig
Import
Organize
Edit
Book
Share
Assign
Search
None
Favorite
Family
Kids
Vacation
Birthday
Tristan
Nature
Tonya
Titles
Keywords
Film Rolls

Figure 2.7 Here how the display pane appears using frame style with a dark background—a significantly different look.

Setting Display Preferences

Along with the interactive methods that iPhoto provides for changing the look of the display pane, as mentioned on the previous page, you can set a few options in iPhoto's Preferences window that affect the way the display and organize panes look.

Changing display preferences:

- From the iPhoto application menu, choose Preferences (Cmd Y) to open the Preferences window (**Figure 2.6**). Choose between Shadow and Frame by clicking the appropriate radio button. To change the darkness of the background, click Frame and adjust the slider. The screenshots on the previous page use the shadow style with a white background; compare that to a frame style with a dark background (**Figure 2.7**).
- To align all your photos to a regular grid in which the width of the widest picture sets the width for all photos, check the "Align to grid" checkbox.
- To choose between viewing keywords and a large comments field (identical to the one in the info pane) in the organize pane, click the appropriate radio button.

✔ Tips

- The background darkness level you set applies even if you switch back to the shadow style, although you won't be able to see the shadow if the darkness level is too dark.
- The align to grid setting works poorly if you have keywords showing, since the keywords appear on the right side of the picture and expand its width by a variable amount.

Editing Film Rolls

In iPhoto 1.1.1, you can change the titles and dates of film rolls in the Photo Library.

To change the title of a film roll:

1. Make sure you're in the Photo Library with film rolls and the info pane showing, and then click a film roll in the display pane to select it.
2. In the info pane, enter a new title for the film roll (**Figure 2.8**).
   iPhoto changes the title of the film roll in the display pane to match.

To change the date of a film roll:

1. Make sure you're in the Photo Library with film rolls and the info pane showing, and then click a film roll in the display pane to select it.
2. In the info pane, enter a new date for the film roll (**Figure 2.8**).
   iPhoto changes the date of the film roll in the display pane and re-sorts the film rolls to put the one you edited in the proper order.

✔ Tips

- iPhoto ignores improperly formatted dates, so to avoid confusion, make sure you edit the date correctly, using the same date format iPhoto uses in the Date field.
- Remember that after you change the date of a film roll, iPhoto sorts it according to the new date, so it's likely to move to a new location in the display pane.

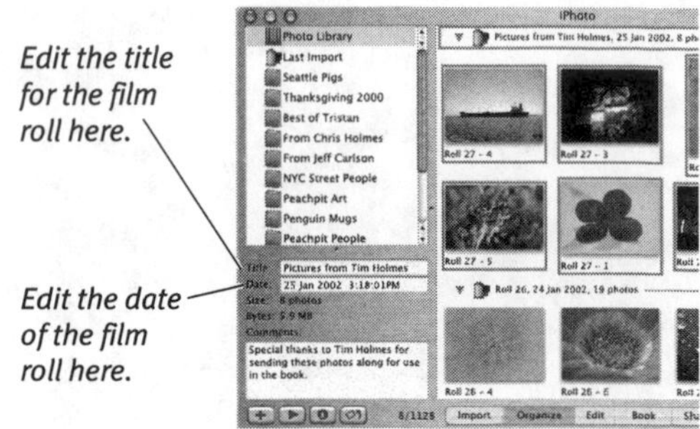
Edit the title for the film roll here.
Edit the date of the film roll here.

Figure 2.8 Use the Title and Date fields in the info pane to change the title and date of the selected film roll in the Photo Library.

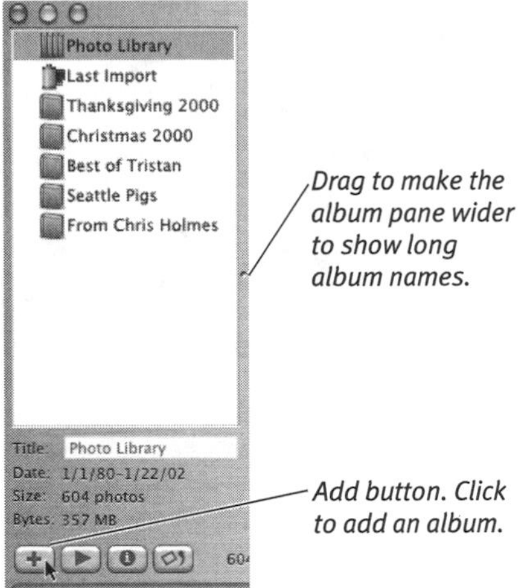
Photo Library
Last Import
Thanksgiving 2000
Christmas 2000
Best of Tristan
Seattle Pigs
From Chris Holmes
Drag to make the album pane wider to show long album names.
Title: Photo Library
Date: 1/1/80-1/22/02
Size: 604 photos
Bytes: 357 MB
Add button. Click to add an album.

Figure 2.9 To create a new album, first click the + button underneath the info pane.

New Album
Please enter a name for the new Album:
From Jeff Carlson
Cancel
OK

Figure 2.10 Next, name the album in the dialog iPhoto presents, and click OK.

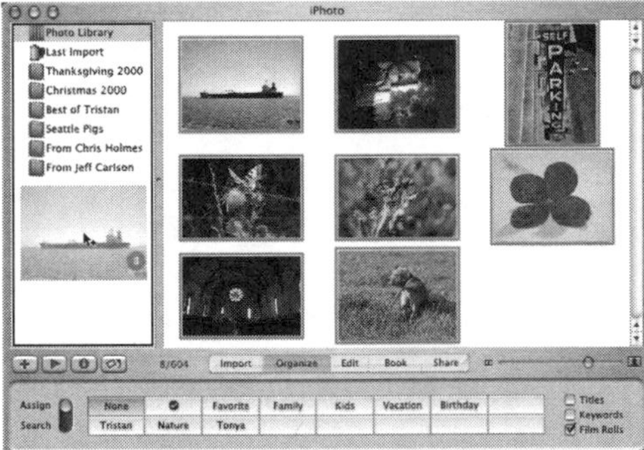
Photo Library
Last Import
Thanksgiving 2000
Christmas 2000
Best of Tristan
Seattle Pigs
From Chris Holmes
From Jeff Carlson

Figure 2.11 For another way to create a new album, select one or more photos, and then drag them to the album pane. Notice how the album pane gets a thick black border and your cursor changes from a plain arrow to one with a + badge. iPhoto also tells you, via a number in a red circle, how many images you're dragging.

Creating Albums

Most of us categorize our photos in our heads—these were from the trip to Hawaii, those were from Grandma's 80th birthday party—and iPhoto provides the concept of albums to help organize images and for working with books, as we'll see in Chapter 4, "Creating Books."

Use albums for unique categories of pictures that appear only once in your photo collection. In contrast, use keywords for categories that recur throughout your collection. Albums work well for a specific trip's photos; keywords work better for identifying pictures of your family members, landscapes, or recurring events.

To create an album (I):

1. Click the Add button below the info pane or choose New Album (Cmd N) from the File menu (**Figure 2.9**).

   iPhoto displays a dialog for you to name your album (**Figure 2.10**).

2. Enter a name for the album and click the OK button to add the album to your list in the album pane.

To create an album (II):

- Drag one or more photos, or an entire film roll, into the album pane, but *not* onto any existing album (**Figure 2.11**).

To create an album (III):

- Drag one or more photos, or a folder of photos from the Finder into the album pane, but *not* onto any existing album.

✔ Tips

- These dragging methods work only if there is free space in the album list.
- When possible, iPhoto uses the name of the film roll or folder as the album name.

Duplicating Albums

Another way to create a new album is to duplicate an existing one. Duplicating is useful for creating different versions of the same album quickly and easily, which you might want to do, for instance, to make similar books of baby pictures for two sets of grandparents or to customize a catalog or portfolio for different clients.

To duplicate an album:

- Select an album and then choose Duplicate from the File menu (Cmd D).

  iPhoto duplicates the album, giving it a generic name and putting it at the bottom of your list (**Figure 2.12**).

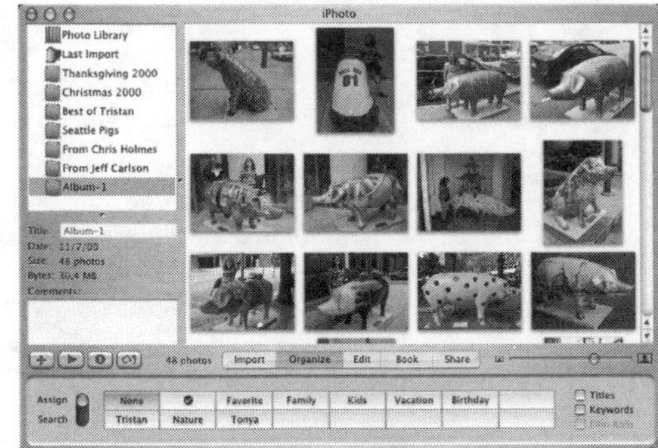
iPhoto
Photo Library
Last Import
Thanksgiving 2000
Christmas 2000
Best of Tristan
Seattle Pigs
From Chris Holmes
From Jeff Carlson
Album-1
Import
Organize
Edit
Book
Share
Assign
Search
None
Favorite
Family
Kids
Vacation
Birthday
Tristan
Nature
Tonya
Titles
Keywords

Figure 2.12 To duplicate an album, select it, and then choose Duplicate from the File menu, after which iPhoto creates a new, generically named album at the bottom of your list of albums.

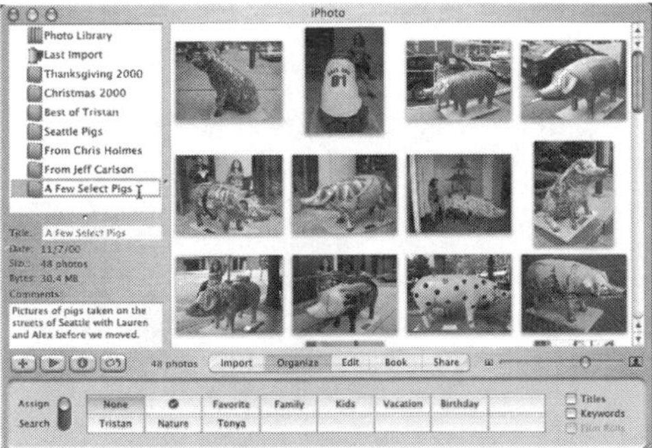
iPhoto
Photo Library
Last Import
Thanksgiving 2000
Christmas 2000
Best of Tristan
Seattle Pigs
From Chris Holmes
From Jeff Carlson
A Few Select Pigs
Import
Organize
Edit
Book
Share
Assign
Search
None
Favorite
Family
Kids
Vacation
Birthday
Tristan
Nature
Tonya
Titles
Keywords

Figure 2.13 To rename an album (such as one you just duplicated), double-click the album name and edit it. Note too that you can enter comments in the Comments field that describe the album but aren't used anywhere else in iPhoto.

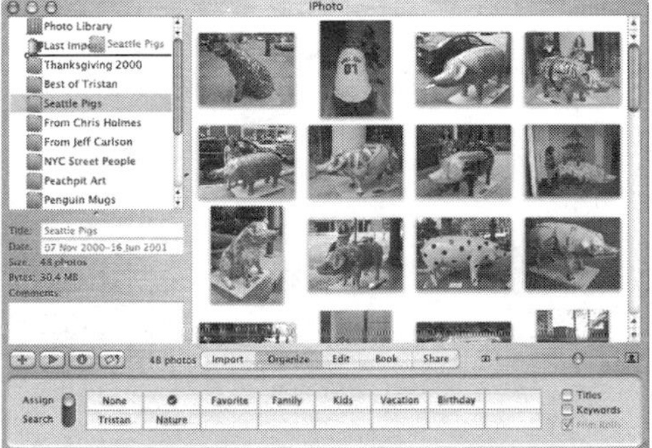
iPhoto
Photo Library
Last Import
Thanksgiving 2000
Best of Tristan
Seattle Pigs
From Chris Holmes
From Jeff Carlson
NYC Street People
Peachpit Art
Penguin Mugs
Import
Organize
Edit
Book
Share
Assign
Search
None
Favorite
Family
Kids
Vacation
Birthday
Tristan
Nature
Titles
Keywords

Figure 2.14 To move an album in the list, drag its name to the desired location. Note the black bar that indicates where it will appear when dropped.

Renaming and Rearranging Albums

You'll undoubtedly want to rename albums to give them more reasonable names than the generic ones iPhoto gives them. Plus, since iPhoto initially lists albums in the order you created them, you'll probably want to move them around in the list.

To rename an album:

- Double-click on the album's name, and then edit the name (**Figure 2.13**).

To rearrange the album list:

- Drag an album to the desired location in the album list. Note the black bar that indicates where the album will appear when you drop it (**Figure 2.14**).

✔ Tips

- You can enter comments about the album in the Comments field of the info pane (showing in **Figure 2.13**), but any comments are purely for your own use—they aren't used elsewhere in iPhoto.
- Although the name of the album shows up in the info pane's Title field, you can't edit it there.
- You're unlikely to need iPhoto's spelling tools in this context, but you can use them while editing album names. For more details on using iPhoto's spelling tools, see "Checking Spelling" in Chapter 4, "Creating Books."

Deleting Albums

Albums are easy to create, and luckily, they're even easier to delete if you decide you don't want one cluttering your list of albums.

Deleting an album containing photos doesn't affect the original photos in the Photo Library since the album merely contains pointers to the originals.

To delete an album:

- Select an album and either choose Clear from the Edit menu or press Delete.

  If the album contains photos, iPhoto prompts you before deleting; otherwise it just deletes the album (**Figure 2.15**).

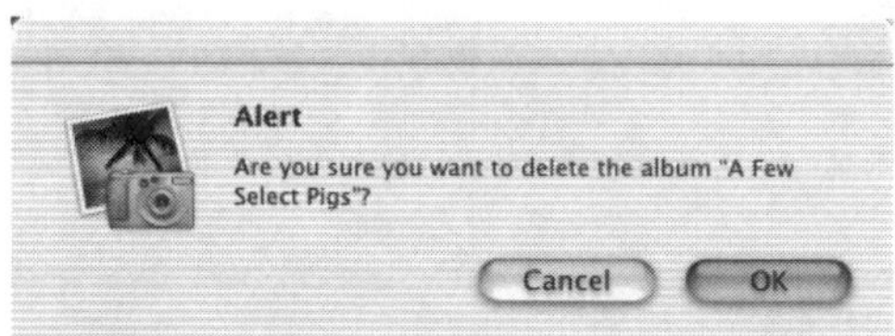
Alert
Are you sure you want to delete the album "A Few Select Pigs"?
Cancel
OK

Figure 2.15 To delete an album, select it and press Delete. If there are any photos in the album, iPhoto prompts to make sure you mean to delete the album.

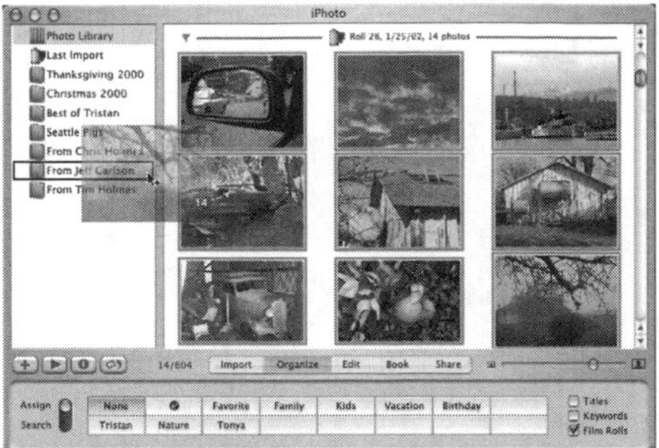

Figure 2.16 To add photos to an album, select them and drag them onto the desired album in the album pane. Note how the destination album gets a thick black border and how the cursor changes from a plain arrow to one with a + badge. iPhoto also tells you, via a number in a red circle, how many images you're dragging.

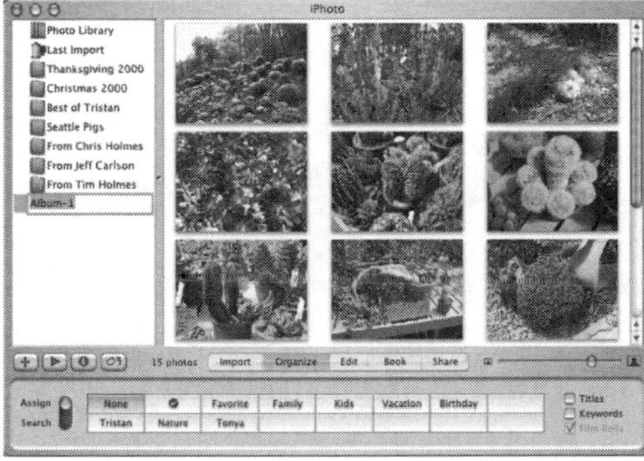

Figure 2.17 To create an album and add photos to it in one fell swoop, select the images and drag them to the album pane, but not onto any specific album. iPhoto creates the album with a generic name and adds the photos automatically. You'll undoubtedly want to rename the album, though.

Adding Photos to Albums

Now that you've made an album, the next task is to add photos to it. You may also want to remove images from an album.

To add photos to an album:

- Select one or more photos in the display pane and drag them onto an album in the album pane (**Figure 2.16**).
- Drag photos from the display pane into the album pane, but not onto a specific album. This technique creates a new album and adds the images (**Figure 2.17**).
- From the Finder, drag one or more photos, or an entire folder of photos, to an album. iPhoto imports the photos and then adds them to the album. Note that the photos will appear in the Photo Library also, not just in the album.
- Select photos, choose Copy (Cmd C) from the Edit menu, click the desired destination album, and choose Paste (Cmd V) from the Edit menu.

✔ Tips

- You can add a photo to an album only once; if you try to drag a photo to an album that already contains that photo, the photo snaps back to its original location when you drop it. To put a photo in an album twice, you must duplicate it—see "Duplicating Photos" in Chapter 3, "Editing Photos."
- When selecting photos to add to an album, you can be either in the Photo Library or in an album.
- There are many ways to select photos; see "Selecting Photos" at the end of this chapter.

Removing Photos from Albums

You may decide, after adding some photos to an album, that you don't want those particular images in the album. No worries—they're easy to remove.

To remove photos from an album:

- Making sure you're in the desired album, select the photos you want to remove, and press Delete.
- Select the photos you want to remove, and choose either Clear or Cut (Cmd X) from the Edit menu.

✔ Tips

- Removing a photo from an album does **not** delete it from your Photo Library or from your hard disk. However, removing a photo from the Photo Library does delete the original from your hard disk.
- iPhoto doesn't ask for confirmation when you remove photos from an album; if you remove the wrong photos accidentally, you can either choose Undo from the Edit menu (Cmd Z) immediately or add the photos again from the Photo Library.
- There are many ways to select photos; see "Selecting Photos" at the end of this chapter.

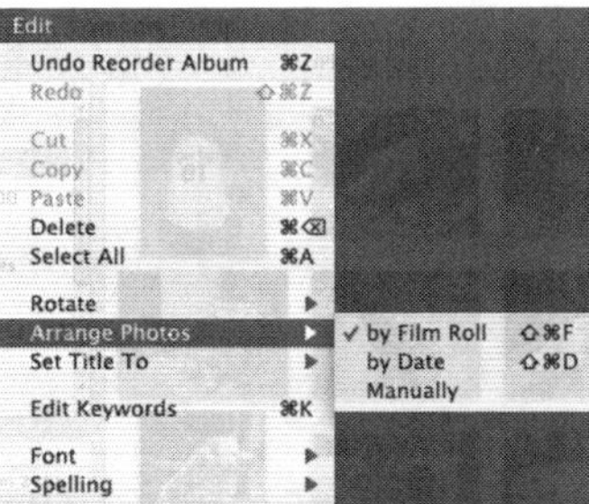
Edit
Undo Reorder Album ⌘Z
Redo ⇧⌘Z
Cut ⌘X
Copy ⌘C
Paste ⌘V
Delete
Select All ⌘A
Rotate
Arrange Photos
Set Title To
Edit Keywords ⌘K
Font
Spelling
✓ by Film Roll ⇧⌘F
by Date ⇧⌘D
Manually

Figure 2.18 To arrange photos in the current album, choose by Film Roll, by Date, or Manually from the Arrange Photos hierarchical menu in the Edit menu.

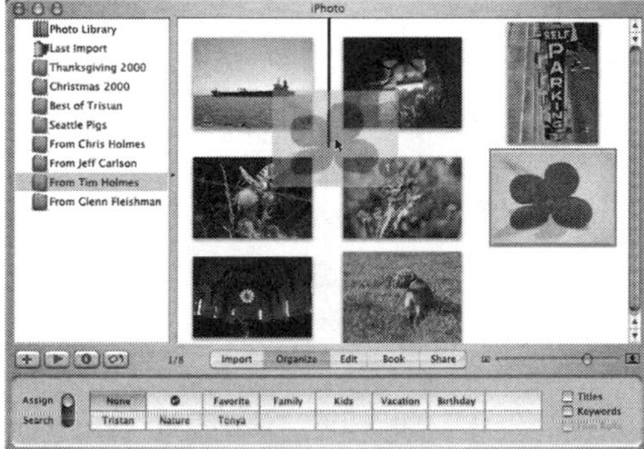
iPhoto
Photo Library
Last Import
Thanksgiving 2000
Christmas 2000
Best of Tristan
Seattle Pigs
From Chris Holmes
From Jeff Carlson
From Tim Holmes
From Glenn Fleishman
Import
Organize
Edit
Book
Share
Assign
Search
None
Favorite
Family
Kids
Vacation
Birthday
Tristan
Nature
Tonya
Titles
Keywords

Figure 2.19 To arrange photos manually, drag one or more photos to the desired location, as indicated by a thick black line.

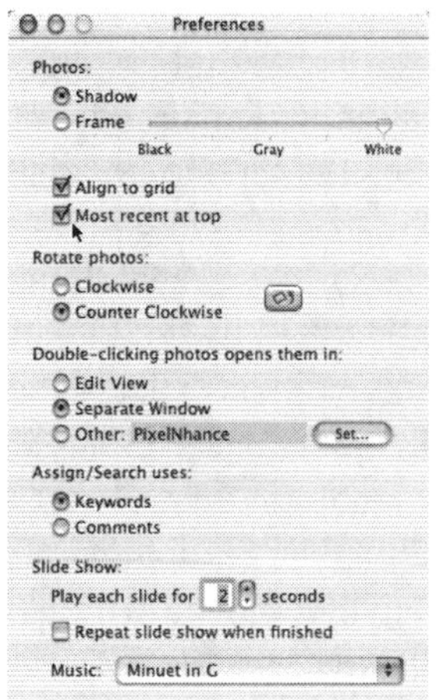
Preferences
Photos:
Shadow
Frame
Black
Gray
White
Align to grid
Most recent at top
Rotate photos:
Clockwise
Counter Clockwise
Double-clicking photos opens them in:
Edit View
Separate Window
Other: PixelNhance
Set...
Assign/Search uses:
Keywords
Comments
Slide Show:
Play each slide for 2 seconds
Repeat slide show when finished
Music: Minuet in G

Figure 2.20 To set whether newer photos sort to the top of your albums or the bottom, check the "Most recent at top" checkbox appropriately in iPhoto's Preferences window.

Arranging Photos

Once you've put your photos into albums, the time has come to arrange them. iPhoto can perform two simple sorts, or you can move images around manually, which is useful for books and slide shows.

To arrange photos by film roll:

◆ From the Edit menu's Arrange Photos hierarchical menu, choose by Film Roll (Shift Cmd F) (**Figure 2.18**).

iPhoto sorts images in the current album by film roll, which matches the order in which the images were imported.

To arrange photos by date:

◆ From the Edit menu's Arrange Photos hierarchical menu, choose by Date (Shift Cmd D).

iPhoto sorts the images in the current album by date, which corresponds to the order in which the images were taken.

To arrange photos manually:

◆ Select one or more photos and drag them to the desired location in the album, as marked by a black line (**Figure 2.19**).

iPhoto switches the Edit menu's Arrange Photos hierarchical menu to Manually.

✔ Tips

- To reverse sort order, set the "Most recent at top" checkbox appropriately in iPhoto's Preferences (**Figure 2.20**).
- Albums have individual sort settings.
- iPhoto remembers manual changes even if you switch to another sort order and back by choosing Manually from the Arrange Photos menu.
- You can't arrange photos manually in the Photo Library or Last Import.

Assigning Titles to Photos

Digital cameras assign sequential numeric names to photos, but iPhoto makes it easy to add your own titles. You can then search for text in titles, and iPhoto can use the titles when you design books or publish to Apple's iTools HomePage service.

To assign automatic titles to photos:

1. Select one or more photos, and then, from the Edit menu, choose Empty, Roll Info, File Name, or Date/Time from the hierarchical Set Title To menu (**Figure 2.21**).
2. If you chose Date/Time, use the dialog that appears to set the date and time format used for the title (**Figure 2.22**).

   iPhoto immediately changes the title appropriately.

To assign custom titles to photos:

- Make sure the info pane is showing by clicking the Information button below the album pane, and then select a photo and enter a title for it in the Title field (**Figure 2.23**).

✔ Tips

- Titles stick to their photos no matter what mode you're in. So, if you assign a title to a photo in an album in organize mode, that same title will show up in the Photo Library, when you're designing a book, and when you're preparing images for publishing to Apple's HomePage service. Plus, any changes you make to the title in one mode will be reflected in the others automatically.
- Unlike iPhoto 1.0, iPhoto 1.1.1 can use the names of imported files in the Title fields for those images.

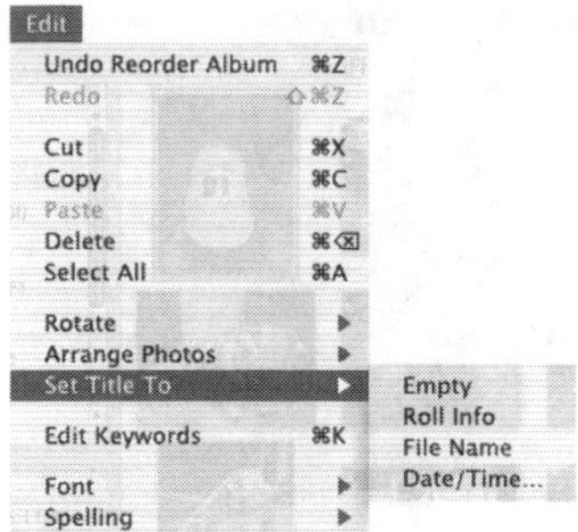
Edit
Undo Reorder Album ⌘Z
Redo ⇧⌘Z
Cut ⌘X
Copy ⌘C
Paste ⌘V
Delete ⌘⌫
Select All ⌘A
Rotate
Arrange Photos
Set Title To
Edit Keywords ⌘K
Font
Spelling
Empty
Roll Info
File Name
Date/Time...

Figure 2.21 Use the items in the Set Title To menu to set the title of selected photos automatically.

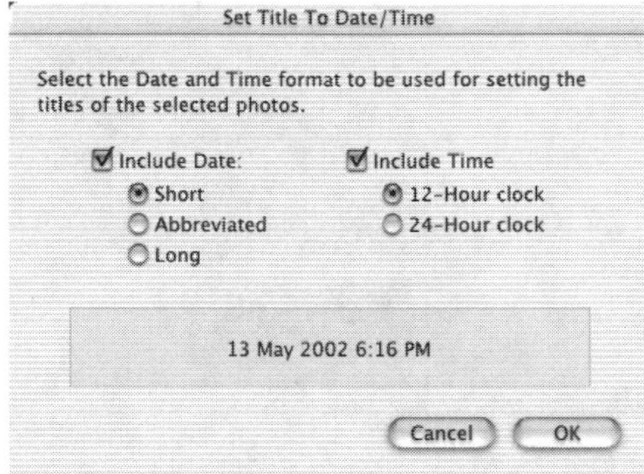
Set Title To Date/Time
Select the Date and Time format to be used for setting the titles of the selected photos.
Include Date:
Short
Abbreviated
Long
Include Time
12-Hour clock
24-Hour clock
13 May 2002 6:16 PM
Cancel
OK

Figure 2.22 When changing the title of a photo to Date/Time, use this dialog to determine the date and time format used for the title.

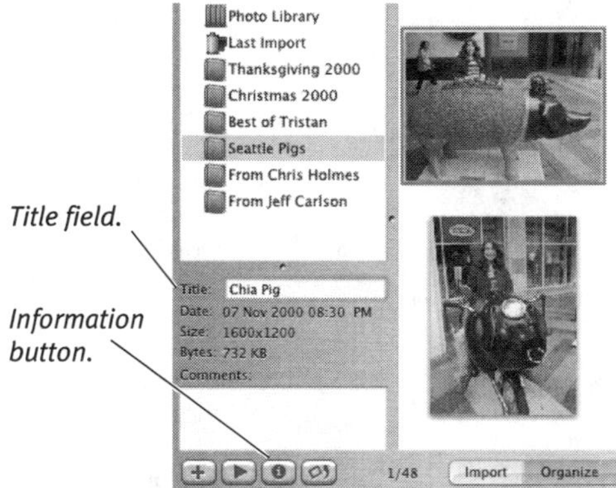
Photo Library
Last Import
Thanksgiving 2000
Christmas 2000
Best of Tristan
Seattle Pigs
From Chris Holmes
From Jeff Carlson
Title field.
Information button.
Title: Chia Pig
Date: 07 Nov 2000 08:30 PM
Size: 1600x1200
Bytes: 732 KB
Comments:
1/48
Import
Organize

Figure 2.23 To assign a title to a photo, select it and enter the name in the Title field. If the Title field isn't showing, click the Information button to reveal it.

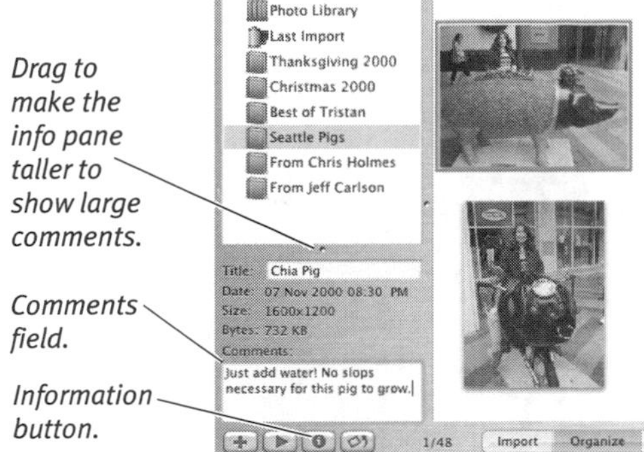
Drag to make the info pane taller to show large comments.
Comments field.
Information button.
Photo Library
Last Import
Thanksgiving 2000
Christmas 2000
Best of Tristan
Seattle Pigs
From Chris Holmes
From Jeff Carlson
Title: Chia Pig
Date: 07 Nov 2000 08:30 PM
Size: 1600x1200
Bytes: 732 KB
Comments:
Just add water! No slops necessary for this pig to grow.
1/48
Import
Organize

Figure 2.24 To assign a comment to a photo, select the photo and enter the comment in the Comments field. If the Comments field isn't showing, click the Information button once or twice to reveal it.

Assigning Comments to Photos (I)

It's often helpful to describe a photo briefly so you remember the original scene better. That's one good use for iPhoto's comments, but iPhoto also uses comments optionally in some of the book designs as descriptive text.

To assign comments to photos:

◆ Make sure the Comments field of the info pane is showing by clicking the Information button (once or twice, depending on what part of it is already showing), and then select a photo and type your comment in the Comments field (**Figure 2.24**).

✔ Tips

- You can resize the info pane by dragging the size handle at the top.
- Expanding the info pane is the only way to see more of the Comments field—iPhoto doesn't provide a scroll bar or even let you drag to scroll down through a comment that's too long to fit.
- You can put quite a lot of text in the Comments field, far more than will display. If you need very long comments for some reason, try creating and editing them in another application and pasting them into iPhoto.
- Like titles, comments stick to their photos no matter what mode you're in. So, if you assign a comment to a photo in an album in organize mode, that same comment will show up in the Photo Library and when you're designing a book. Plus, any changes you make to the comment while designing a book will be reflected in other modes automatically.

Assigning Comments to Photos (II)

With iPhoto 1.1.1, Apple provided an alternative way of assigning comments to photos.

To view the second Comments field:

1. From iPhoto's application menu, choose Preferences (Cmd Y).
2. Under "Assign/Search uses" click the Comments radio button (**Figure 2.25**).

   iPhoto displays a Comments field in place of the keyword buttons.
3. Close the Preferences window.

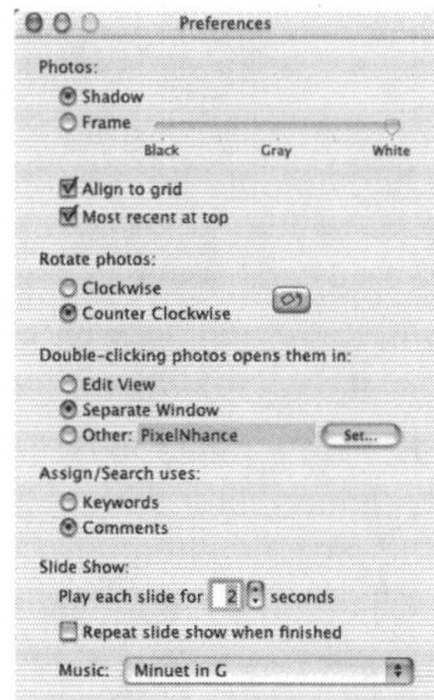
Preferences
Photos:
Shadow
Frame
Black
Gray
White
Align to grid
Most recent at top
Rotate photos:
Clockwise
Counter Clockwise
Double-clicking photos opens them in:
Edit View
Separate Window
Other: PixelNhance
Set...
Assign/Search uses:
Keywords
Comments
Slide Show:
Play each slide for 2 seconds
Repeat slide show when finished
Music: Minuet in G

Figure 2.25 In the Preferences window, click the Comments radio button under "Assign/Search uses" to see the Comments field rather than the keyword buttons.

To assign comments to photos:

1. Make sure the Assign/Search toggle control is set to Assign.
2. Type your comment in the organize pane's Comments field (**Figure 2.26**).

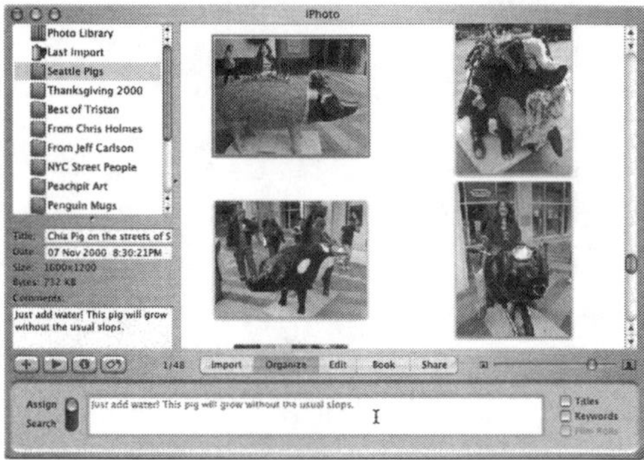
iPhoto
Photo Library
Last Import
Seattle Pigs
Thanksgiving 2000
Best of Tristan
From Chris Holmes
From Jeff Carlson
NYC Street People
Peachpit Art
Penguin Mugs
Import
Organize
Edit
Book
Share
Assign
Search
Titles
Keywords

Figure 2.26 You can also enter comments in the Comments field that replaces the keyword buttons in the organize pane. All changes show up in both Comments fields immediately—they're identical.

✔ Tips

- The contents of the two Comments fields are always identical—they're just different views of the same information.
- In the organize pane's Comments field, iPhoto doesn't wrap long lines of text or provide a scroll bar for viewing more text than fits, but you can drag to the right or use the right arrow key to see text that extends past the right edge of the field.
- Unless you plan to use the organize pane's Comments field for free text searching (see "Searching for Text" later in this chapter), it's easiest to use the info pane's Comments field and keep the organize pane showing the keyword buttons.

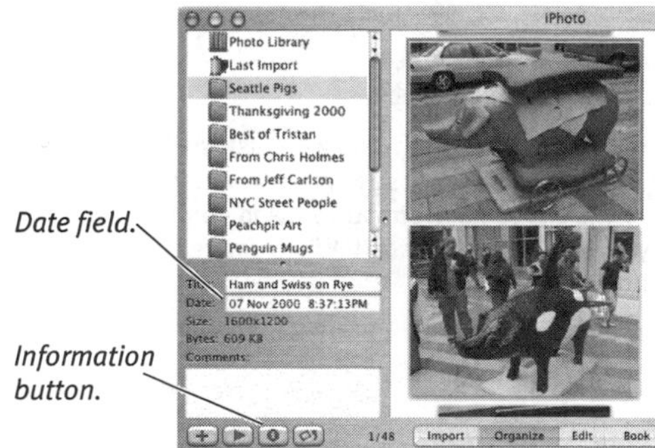
iPhoto
Photo Library
Last Import
Seattle Pigs
Thanksgiving 2000
Best of Tristan
From Chris Holmes
From Jeff Carlson
NYC Street People
Peachpit Art
Penguin Mugs
Ham and Swiss on Rye
07 Nov 2000 8:37:13PM
1600x1200
609 KB
Comments:
1/48
Import
Organize
Edit
Book
Date field.
Information button.

Figure 2.27 Edit the Date field to change a photo's date. If the Date field isn't showing, click the Information button to reveal it.

Editing Photo Dates

It's not uncommon for digital cameras to forget the date, which can result in a set of photos being imported as though they had been taken in 1980, for instance. You can edit photo dates in iPhoto to correct this annoyance.

To edit a photo's date:

◆ Make sure the info pane is showing by clicking the Information button below the album pane, and then select a photo and edit its date in the Date field (**Figure 2.27**).

✔ Tips

- iPhoto ignores improperly formatted dates, so to avoid confusion, make sure you edit the date correctly, using the same date format iPhoto uses.
- If iPhoto is set to arrange photos by date, changing a photo's date causes it to re-sort according to the new date. Keep that in mind if a photo isn't where you expect it to be after changing its date.

Editing Keywords

Along with titles and comments, you can assign keywords to your photos to help keep track of them. First though, you must learn how to edit the list of available keywords so it's relevant to your photos.

To edit the keyword list:

1. Make sure "Assign/Search uses" in iPhoto's Preferences window is set to Keywords, switch to organize mode if you're not already in it, and from the Edit menu, choose Edit Keywords (Cmd K).

   iPhoto changes the None/Show All button to Done, and makes the keyword button names editable (**Figure 2.28**).

2. Click one of the keyword buttons and edit as you would any normal bit of text. Repeat as desired.

3. When you're done, click the Done button, or choose Done Editing Keywords (Cmd K) from the Edit menu.

✔ Tips

- You're limited to a total of 15 keywords.
- You can't change the None/Show All and graphical checkmark keyword buttons in the top left.
- Photos inherit keyword changes, so if a photo has the Family keyword and you change the Family keyword button to Landscape, the photo updates to match.
- Use keywords for categories of pictures that recur throughout your photo collection. In contrast, use albums for unique categories that appear only once in your collection. Keywords work well for identifying pictures of your family, landscapes, or recurring events; an album would be better for a specific trip's photos.

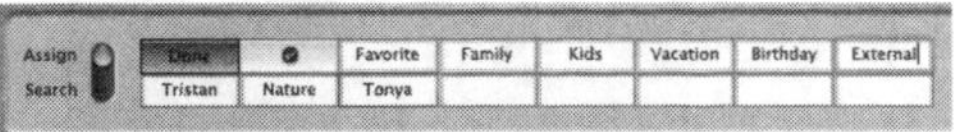
Assign
Search
Done
Favorite
Family
Kids
Vacation
Birthday
External
Tristan
Nature
Tonya

Figure 2.28 To edit the keyword list, switch into organize mode, choose Edit Keywords from the Edit menu, click a keyword button, and edit the name as you would any other text. When you're done, click the Done button.

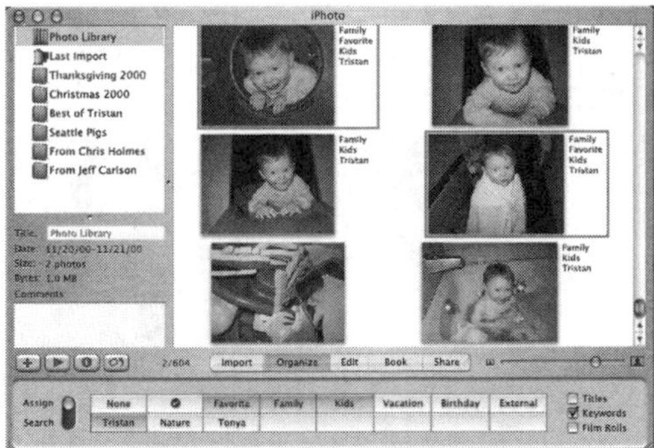
iPhoto
Photo Library
Last Import
Thanksgiving 2000
Christmas 2000
Best of Tristan
Seattle Pigs
From Chris Holmes
From Jeff Carlson
Import
Organize
Edit
Book
Share
Assign
Search
None
Favorite
Family
Kids
Vacation
Birthday
External
Tristan
Nature
Tonya
Titles
Keywords
Film Rolls

Figure 2.29 To assign keywords, make sure you're in organize mode, make sure the Assign/Search control is set to Assign, select one or more photos, and then click the buttons associated with the desired keywords.

Assigning and Removing Keywords

Once you've customized the list of keywords to those that are relevant to your photos, you can assign one or more keywords to individual images.

To assign keywords to photos:

1. Make sure the "Assign/Search uses" setting in iPhoto's Preferences window is set to Keywords, and switch to organize mode if you're not already in it.
2. Select one or more photos.
3. Make sure the Assign/Search toggle control is set to Assign. If not, click the top of the control to switch it.
4. For each keyword you want to assign to the selected photos, click the associated keyword button in the organize pane (**Figure 2.29**).

   iPhoto highlights the assigned keyword buttons and, if you have the Keywords checkbox selected, displays them next to the photos.

To remove keywords from photos:

1. Switch to organize mode if you're not already in it.
2. Select one or more photos that have keywords associated with them.
3. Make sure the Assign/Search toggle control is set to Assign. If not, click the top of the control to switch it.
4. For each keyword you want to remove from the selected photos, click the associated highlighted keyword button.

   iPhoto removes the highlight from the assigned keyword buttons in the organize pane.

Searching via Keyword

Keywords make it easy to find just those photos associated with certain keywords. When you search for photos, iPhoto doesn't merely select matching photos—it hides those that don't match and displays only those you want to see.

To search for photos via keyword:

1. Make sure the "Assign/Search uses" setting in iPhoto's Preferences window is set to Keywords, and switch to organize mode if you're not already in it.
2. Make sure the Assign/Search toggle control is set to Search. If not, click the bottom of the control to switch it.
3. Click each desired keyword to find photos associated with that keyword.

   As you click each keyword button, iPhoto displays just those photos that contain the set of selected keywords (**Figure 2.30** and **Figure 2.31**).

To widen a too-narrow search:

- Click highlighted keyword buttons to deselect them.

  iPhoto displays the photos that match the current set of keywords.

To stop searching and see all photos:

- Click the Show All keyword button.
- Click the Assign/Search control to switch back to Assign.
- Switch to any other album.

✔ Tip

- To change keywords for the photos found in a keyword search, drag them to the album pane to make a temporary album, make the changes in that album, and then delete the album when done.

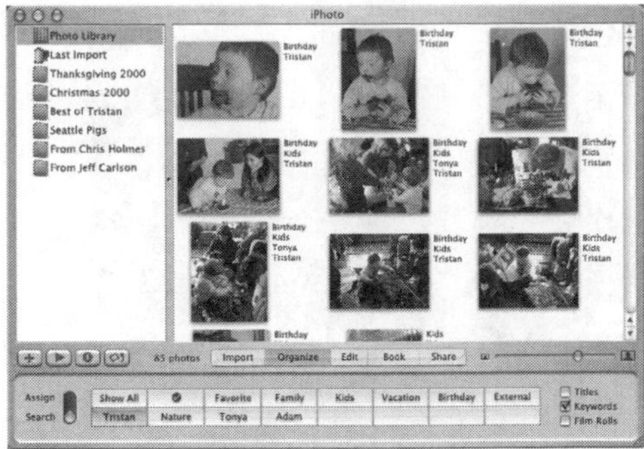

Figure 2.30 To search for photos using keywords that you've assigned, switch into organize mode, click the bottom of the Assign/Search control to switch it to Search, and click the keywords whose associated photos you wish to find.

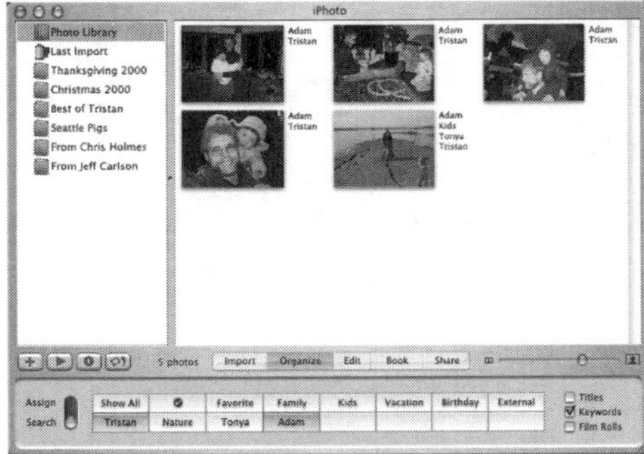

Figure 2.31 To narrow your search, click more keyword buttons. In the figure above, I searched only for pictures with the Tristan keyword and found 85 images. Here I've added the Adam keyword, and narrowed it to 5 images. To go in the other direction and widen the search, click a highlighted keyword button (like either the Tristan or Adam button above) to deselect it.

Figure 2.32 Enter text in the organize pane's Comments field when the Assign/Search toggle control is set to Search. Here I've searched for all photos with the word "pig" in their titles, comments, or keywords.

Figure 2.33 To narrow your search, enter additional search terms. In the figure above, I searched only for pictures associated with the word "pig" and found 21 images. Here I've added "Tonya," and narrowed it to 8 images. To go in the other direction and widen the search, delete one or more search terms.

Searching for Text

What if you want to find photos based on text that appears in their titles, comments, or keywords?

To search for photos via text:

1. Make sure the "Assign/Search uses" setting in iPhoto's Preferences window is set to Comments, and switch to organize mode if you're not already in it.
2. Make sure the Assign/Search toggle control is set to Search. If not, click the bottom of the control to switch it.
3. Enter the text you want to find.

   When you finish typing, iPhoto shows those photos whose titles, comments, or keywords contain the text you've typed (**Figure 2.32** and **Figure 2.33**).

To narrow a too-wide search:

- Add more words; iPhoto matches only photos that contain *all* the search terms.

To widen a too-narrow search:

- Delete some or all of your search terms.

To stop searching and see all photos:

- Click the Assign/Search control to switch back to Assign.
- Switch to any other album.

✔ Tips

- Be careful not to drag a photo to a new location in the display pane after finding it in a search; that action can crash iPhoto.
- You can't find text in dates this way.

Viewing Photo Information

iPhoto presents information about photos in two places: the info pane and in the Photo Info window that's new to iPhoto 1.1.1.

To view information in the info pane:

- With the info pane hidden, click the Information button underneath the album pane once to display the info pane, twice to display the info pane with the Comments field, and three times to hide the info pane again (**Figure 2.34**).

Info pane, with Title, Date, Size, Bytes, and Comments fields.

Figure 2.34 iPhoto's info pane displays some basic information about selected photos.

To view information in the Photo Info window:

1. Select a photo and choose Show Info from the File menu (Cmd I).

   iPhoto displays the Photo Info window with the Photo tab showing (**Figure 2.35**).

2. Click the Exposure tab to see exposure information (**Figure 2.36**).

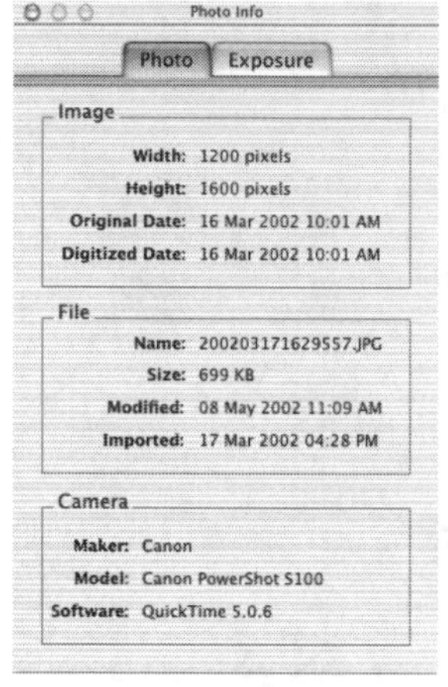
Photo Info
Photo
Exposure
Image
Width: 1200 pixels
Height: 1600 pixels
Original Date: 16 Mar 2002 10:01 AM
Digitized Date: 16 Mar 2002 10:01 AM
File
Name: 200203171629557.JPG
Size: 699 KB
Modified: 08 May 2002 11:09 AM
Imported: 17 Mar 2002 04:28 PM
Camera
Maker: Canon
Model: Canon PowerShot S100
Software: QuickTime 5.0.6

Figure 2.35 The Photo Info window's Photo tab provides detailed information about the image that was recorded by the camera.

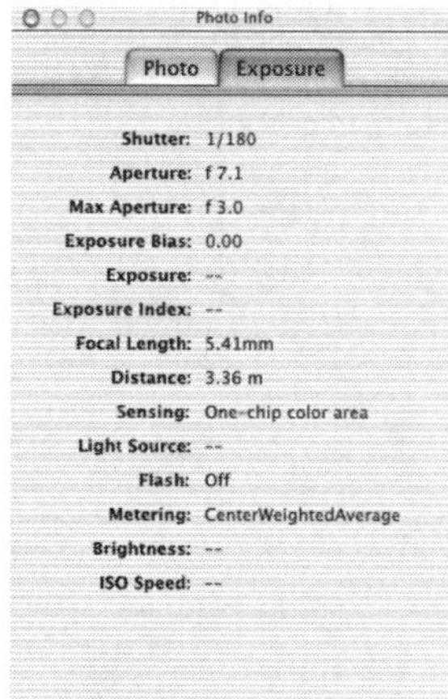
Photo Info
Photo
Exposure
Shutter: 1/180
Aperture: f 7.1
Max Aperture: f 3.0
Exposure Bias: 0.00
Exposure: --
Exposure Index: --
Focal Length: 5.41mm
Distance: 3.36 m
Sensing: One-chip color area
Light Source: --
Flash: Off
Metering: CenterWeightedAverage
Brightness: --
ISO Speed: --

Figure 2.36 The Exposure tab of the Photo Info window displays information about the camera's settings at the time it took the image.

✔ Tips

- You can change photo titles, dates, and comments in the info pane, but you can't make any changes in the Photo Info window.
- The Photo Info window picks up its information from the EXIF data stored by most digital cameras. EXIF is an industry standard that's designed to help interoperability between cameras, printers, and other imaging devices. In theory, EXIF support could help a printer produce a better rendition of an original image, although the theory appears to fall well short of the reality.

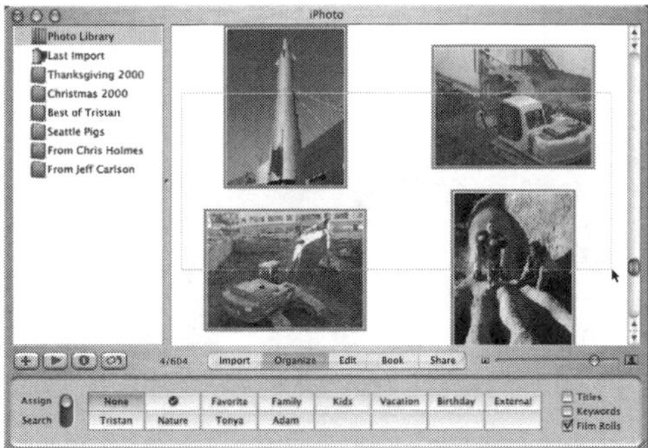
iPhoto
Photo Library
Last Import
Thanksgiving 2000
Christmas 2000
Best of Tristan
Seattle Pigs
From Chris Holmes
From Jeff Carlson
Import
Organize
Edit
Book
Share
Assign
Search
None
Favorite
Family
Kids
Vacation
Birthday
External
Tristan
Nature
Tonya
Adam
Titles
Keywords
Film Rolls

Figure 2.37 To select multiple pictures by dragging, click in an empty area of the display pane, and then drag a selection rectangle over the photos you want to select.

Selecting Photos

Throughout this chapter, I've talked about how you should select photos before performing some task. I'm sure you've all figured out the basic ways of selecting and deselecting images, but there are others that aren't so obvious.

Methods of selecting photos:

- Click a photo to select it.
- Click one photo to select it, hold down Shift, and then click another photo to select all the pictures between the two.
- Click one photo to select it, hold down Cmd, and then click additional photos to select them individually.
- Click in an empty area of the display pane, then drag a selection rectangle over the photos you want to select (**Figure 2.37**). If you drag to the top or bottom of the display pane, iPhoto scrolls the window and keeps selecting additional images.
- From the Edit menu, choose Select All (Cmd A) to select all the images in the current album.
- In the Photo Library, make sure the Film Rolls checkbox is checked to display film rolls, and then click the film roll separator to select all the images in that film roll. This works only in the Photo Library because film roll separators don't show in other albums.

Methods of deselecting photos:

- To deselect one of several selected images, Cmd-click it.
- To deselect all photos, click in the empty area surrounding the photos.

3 Editing Photos

If you're anything like me, not all of your photos come out perfect. In fact, lots of them are probably pretty bad, and those you can delete after import. No harm, no foul, and you didn't pay for developing.

What about those pictures that are okay, but not great? Most of the time they merely require a little work. Perhaps you need to crop out extraneous background that distracts the eye from the subject of the photo, or maybe you want to remove the red glow from your cute baby's eyes (it's the fault of the camera flash, not a sign of a demon child). iPhoto can help with those tasks.

I'm not suggesting that you whip out an image editing application, clip your cousin's ex-husband out of the family reunion photo, and use filters that sound like alien death rays (Gaussian blur?) to make it appear as though he was never there. If you can do that, great, and iPhoto will even let you use any other image editing application. But I can't do that, and I doubt most people can. For us, iPhoto provides most of the tools we need (not that it couldn't use a few more).

The main thing to remember is that there's no shame in editing photos to improve them. All the best photographers do it, and now you can do it too, thanks to iPhoto.

Entering Edit Mode

Since you can edit a photo in the display pane, in a separate window, or even in another application, it's not surprising that you can enter edit mode in several ways.

To choose how to edit photos:

1. From the iPhoto application menu, choose Preferences (Cmd Y).

   iPhoto opens the Preferences window (**Figure 3.1**).

2. Under "Double-clicking photos opens them in," select whether you want iPhoto to open photos for editing in the display pane (Edit View), in a separate window, or in another program.

3. To use another program, click the Set button, and choose a program in the open dialog (**Figure 3.2**).

4. Close the Preferences window.

To enter edit mode:

- Select a photo in any mode, and click the Edit button under the display pane (**Figure 3.3**).

  iPhoto switches to edit mode with the selected image in the display pane.

- Double-click a photo.

  iPhoto switches to edit mode and displays the photo according to the setting in the Preferences window.

- Option-double-click a photo.

  If iPhoto is set to display double-clicked images in the display pane, it instead opens the image in a separate window (**Figure 3.4**). If iPhoto is set to open images in a separate window, Option-double-clicking opens the image in the display pane.

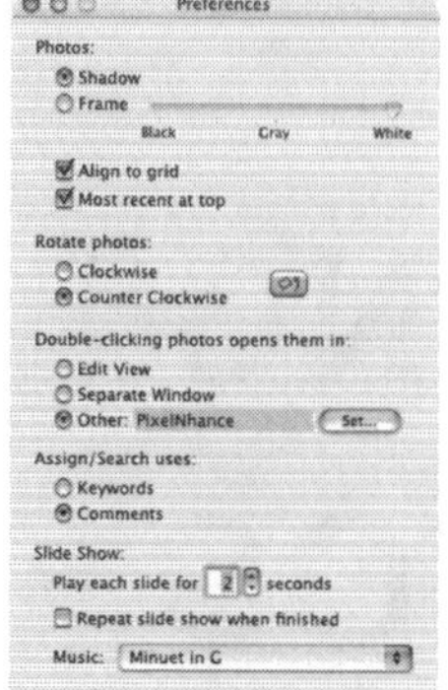
Preferences
Photos:
Shadow
Frame
Black
Gray
White
Align to grid
Most recent at top
Rotate photos:
Clockwise
Counter Clockwise
Double-clicking photos opens them in:
Edit View
Separate Window
Other: PixelNhance
Set...
Assign/Search uses:
Keywords
Comments
Slide Show:
Play each slide for 2 seconds
Repeat slide show when finished
Music: Minuet in G

Figure 3.1 In the Preferences window, select how you want iPhoto to react when you double-click a photo.

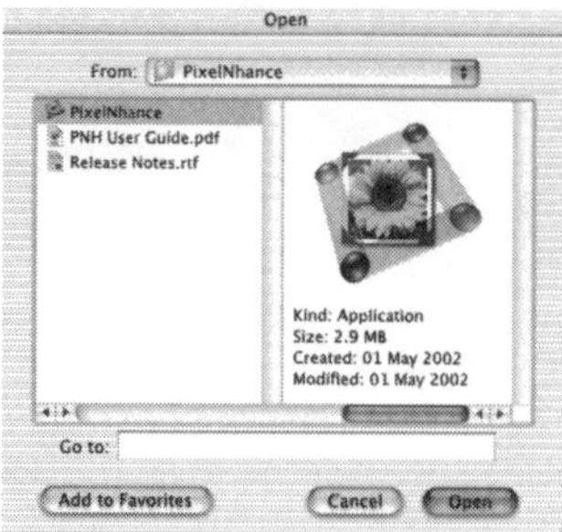
Open
From: PixelNhance
PixelNhance
PNH User Guide.pdf
Release Notes.rtf
Kind: Application
Size: 2.9 MB
Created: 01 May 2002
Modified: 01 May 2002
Go to:
Add to Favorites
Cancel
Open

Figure 3.2 To use another program for editing, select Other in the iPhoto Preferences window, click Set, and find your desired program.

Import
Organize
Edit
Book
Share

Figure 3.3 To switch into edit mode, click the Edit button underneath the display pane.

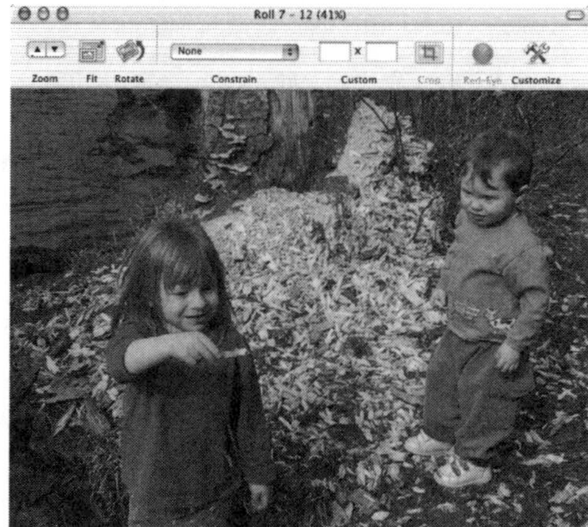
Roll 7 - 12 (41%)
None
Zoom
Fit
Rotate
Constrain
Custom
Crop
Red-Eye
Customize

Figure 3.4 To open a photo in its own window when iPhoto is set to open photos into the display pane, Option-double-click the photo.

Edit Tools Overview (Display Pane)

Here's a quick look at the tools available when you edit an image in the display pane (**Figure 3.5**).

Figure 3.5

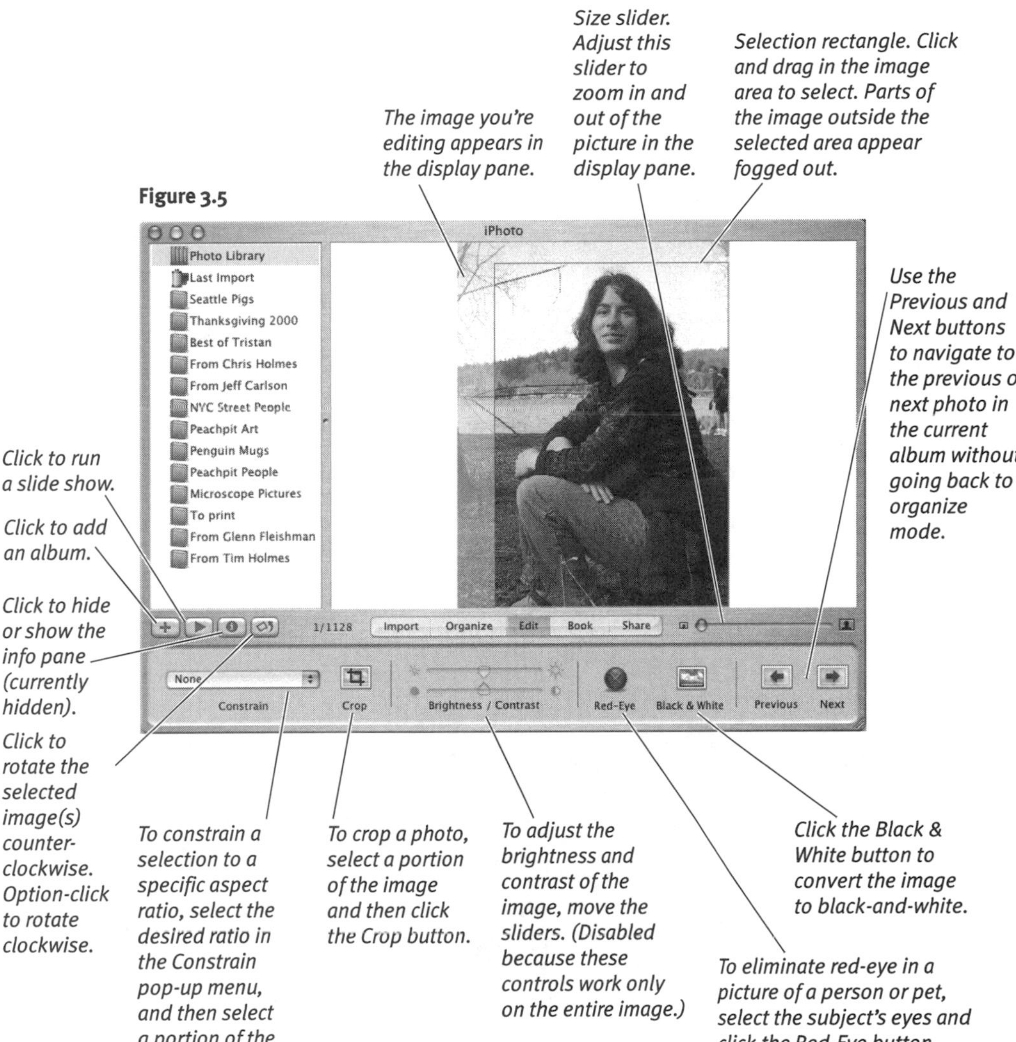

The image you're editing appears in the display pane.
Size slider. Adjust this slider to zoom in and out of the picture in the display pane.
Selection rectangle. Click and drag in the image area to select. Parts of the image outside the selected area appear fogged out.
Use the Previous and Next buttons to navigate to the previous or next photo in the current album without going back to organize mode.
Click to run a slide show.
Click to add an album.
Click to hide or show the info pane (currently hidden).
Click to rotate the selected image(s) counter-clockwise. Option-click to rotate clockwise.
To constrain a selection to a specific aspect ratio, select the desired ratio in the Constrain pop-up menu, and then select a portion of the image.
To crop a photo, select a portion of the image and then click the Crop button.
To adjust the brightness and contrast of the image, move the sliders. (Disabled because these controls work only on the entire image.)
Click the Black & White button to convert the image to black-and-white.
To eliminate red-eye in a picture of a person or pet, select the subject's eyes and click the Red-Eye button.
iPhoto
Photo Library
Last Import
Seattle Pigs
Thanksgiving 2000
Best of Tristan
From Chris Holmes
From Jeff Carlson
NYC Street People
Peachpit Art
Penguin Mugs
Peachpit People
Microscope Pictures
To print
From Glenn Fleishman
From Tim Holmes
1/1128
Import
Organize
Edit
Book
Share
None
Constrain
Crop
Brightness / Contrast
Red-Eye
Black & White
Previous
Next

Edit Tools Overview (Separate Window)

The tools available when you edit a photo in a separate window are slightly different from those available when editing in the display pane (**Figure 3.6**).

✔ Tip

- The image editing window doesn't remember its size, so you may need to resize or zoom the window every time you use it.

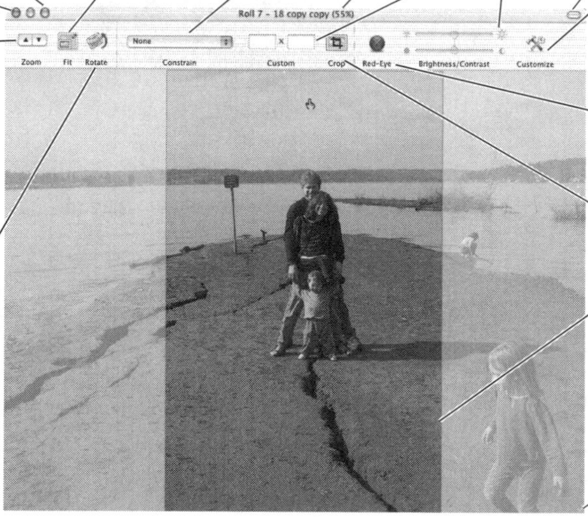

To adjust the brightness and contrast of the image, move the sliders. (Disabled because these controls work only on the entire image.)

Click the close button to close the window when you're done editing.

Click the zoom button to zoom the window, and the photo with it, to the largest possible size.

Click the Fit button to resize the image to match the window size. Note that clicking the Zoom buttons after clicking Fit starts zooming at the size the picture was before you clicked Fit.

To constrain a selection to a specific aspect ratio, select the desired ratio in the Constrain pop-up menu, press Return, and then select a portion of the image.

The title bar of the window shows you the title of the photo and the zoom percentage.

To constrain the selection to a custom aspect ratio (like 2 x 8), enter the desired numbers here.

Click to hide or show the toolbar.

Click the Customize button to show a sheet that lets you pick different tools for the toolbar.

Zoom buttons. Click these to zoom in and out of the image without resizing the window. Be careful when clicking multiple times or you could zoom in farther than you intend.

Click to rotate the current image counter-clockwise. Option-click to rotate clockwise.

To eliminate red-eye in a subject's eyes, select the subject's eyes and click the Red-Eye button.

To crop a photo, select a portion of the image and click the Crop button.

Selection rectangle. Click and drag in the image area to select. Parts of the image outside the selected area appear fogged out.

Resize handle. Click and drag to resize the window and the photo proportionally.

Figure 3.6

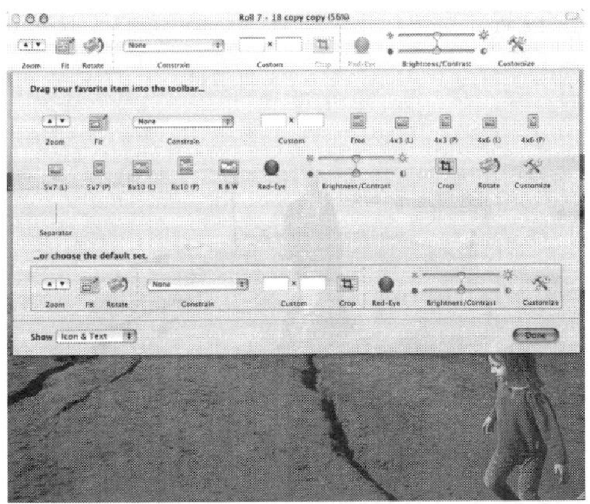

Figure 3.7 To customize the image editing window's toolbar, click the Customize button, and then drag items on to or off of the toolbar. Click Done to save your changes.

Customizing the Toolbar

iPhoto lets you customize the set and arrangement of tools in the image editing toolbar.

To customize the toolbar:

1. With the image editing window open, click the Toolbar button in the extreme upper right of the window to display the toolbar.
2. Either click the Customize button or, from the Window menu, choose Customize Edit Toolbar to reveal the Customize Toolbar sheet (**Figure 3.7**).
3. Drag items to or from the toolbar to customize to your liking.
4. Click Done to save your changes.

Toolbar customization options:

- To add an item to the toolbar, drag it from the sheet into the desired location.
- To remove an item from the toolbar, drag it off the toolbar (where it disappears with a satisfying poof).
- To move an item on the toolbar, drag it to the new location (other items move out of the way as you drag).
- To revert to the default set of tools, drag the default set to the toolbar, where it will replace whatever is up there.
- To change whether the tools display as icons, text, or icons and text, choose the desired option from the Show pop-up menu.

What Are All Those Tools?

Not all the tools you can add are either familiar or explained on the previous page, but in fact these seemingly unfamiliar tools don't offer any new functionality. Those with aspect ratios for names are shortcuts for choices available in the Constrain pop-up menu. Free is as well; it corresponds with None in the Constrain menu. Separators are purely cosmetic; they help you group similar items on your custom toolbar.

Using the Toolbar

Although most aspects of using the toolbar are obvious (click the buttons!), there are a few facts about it that you might not discover on your own.

To use the toolbar:

- To activate a toolbar button, click it. Be careful with the Zoom buttons, since they zoom several steps for each click and on slower Macs, it's easy to click too many times.
- To enter a custom aspect ratio in the Custom fields, type the desired numbers and press Return before dragging to select a portion of the photo.
- When tools are cut off due to the window being too narrow, click the chevron that appears to access them via a menu (**Figure 3.8** and **Figure 3.9**).
- Control-click a toolbar button to display a contextual menu that lets you remove the tool from the toolbar, change how toolbar buttons display, customize the toolbar, reset the toolbar to the default tools, and hide the toolbar (**Figure 3.10**).

✔ Tips

- Add the tools you want to use the most to the left side of the toolbar, since with small windows, the ones on the right will be cut off.
- You can use the space occupied by the Customize button for something more useful. Instead, choose Customize Toolbar from the Window menu or Control-click the toolbar for a pop-up menu that provides a Customize Toolbar command.

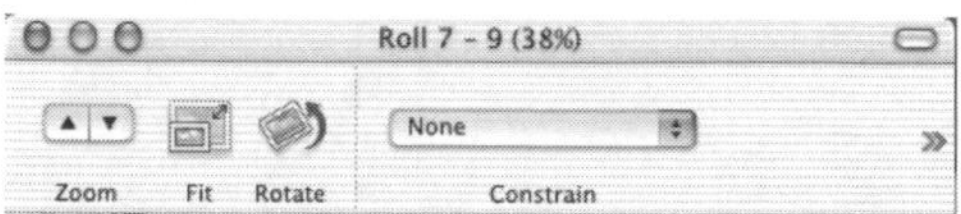
Roll 7 - 9 (38%)
None
Zoom
Fit
Rotate
Constrain

Figure 3.8 When the window is too small to display all the tools, a chevron appears on the right side.

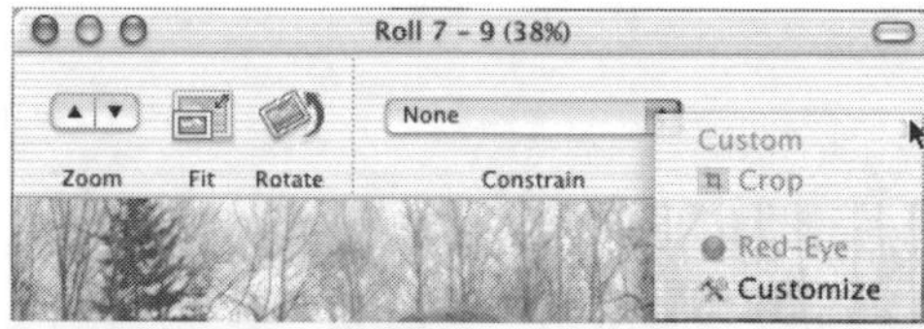
Roll 7 - 9 (38%)
None
Zoom
Fit
Rotate
Constrain
Custom
Crop
Red-Eye
Customize

Figure 3.9 Click the chevron to display a pop-up menu containing choices corresponding to the tools that didn't fit on the toolbar.

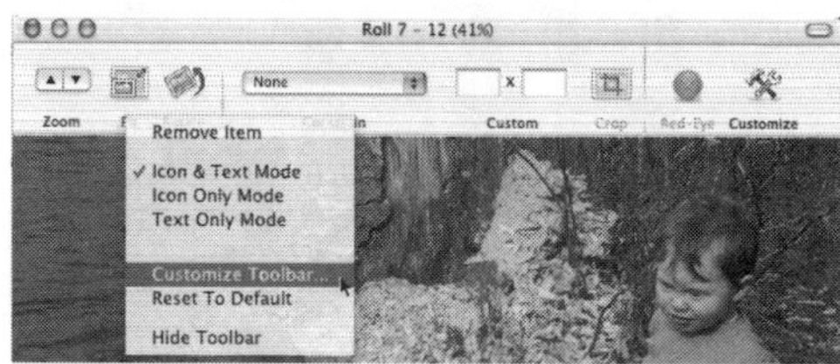
Roll 7 - 12 (41%)
Zoom
Custom
Customize
Remove Item
✓ Icon & Text Mode
Icon Only Mode
Text Only Mode
Customize Toolbar...
Reset To Default
Hide Toolbar

Figure 3.10 Control-click an item on the toolbar to access a contextual menu that lets you remove the item and modify the toolbar in various ways.

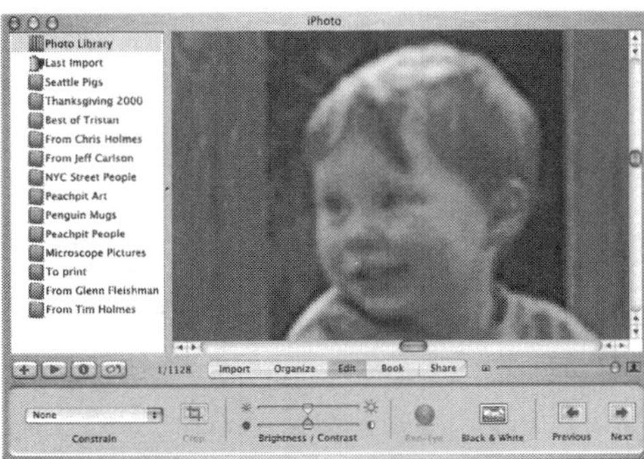
iPhoto
Photo Library
Last Import
Seattle Pigs
Thanksgiving 2000
Best of Tristan
From Chris Holmes
From Jeff Carlson
NYC Street People
Peachpit Art
Penguin Mugs
Peachpit People
Microscope Pictures
To print
From Glenn Fleishman
From Tim Holmes

Figure 3.11 To zoom in on a photo, drag the size slider to the right. Here I've zoomed all the way in, which is why the image looks so pixelated.

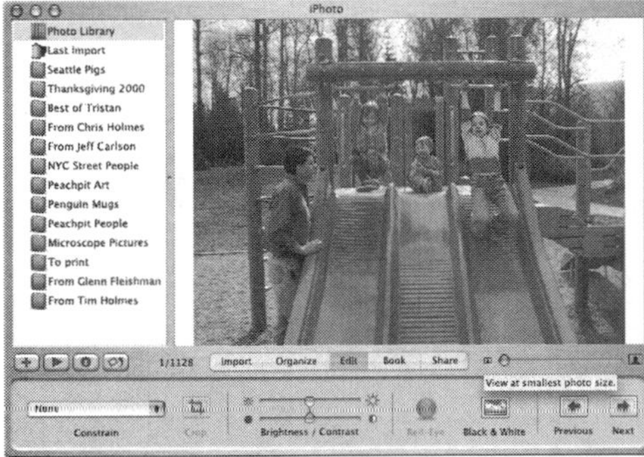
iPhoto
Photo Library
Last Import
Seattle Pigs
Thanksgiving 2000
Best of Tristan
From Chris Holmes
From Jeff Carlson
NYC Street People
Peachpit Art
Penguin Mugs
Peachpit People
Microscope Pictures
To print
From Glenn Fleishman
From Tim Holmes
View at smallest photo size.

Figure 3.12 To zoom back out, drag the slider to the left. Here I've zoomed back out to the size that matches the display pane's size.

Click to fit the image to the window.
Zoom percentage.
Zoom in.
Zoom out.

Figure 3.13 Click the zoom buttons in the toolbar to zoom in and out in the image editing window. Click Fit to make the image fit in the window if there's extra white space after zooming out.

Zooming Photos

It can be helpful to zoom in and out while editing, particularly when selecting eyes for red-eye reduction.

To zoom in the display pane:

◆ With an image showing in the display pane in edit mode, drag the size slider to the right to zoom in (**Figure 3.11**). To zoom out, drag the slider to the left (**Figure 3.12**).

To zoom in the image editing window:

◆ When the photo fills the image editing window exactly, drag the resize handle to resize the window and the photo. The window resizes proportionally. This approach limits zooming to the maximum and minimum window sizes.

◆ Click the left zoom button in the image editing window's toolbar to zoom in. Click the right zoom button to zoom out (**Figure 3.13**).

✔ Tips

- If the image doesn't fill the image editing window after zooming, click the Fit button to make it fit. If there's still white space along the edges of the photo, resize the window to eliminate the borders.
- Use the vertical and horizontal scroll bars to scroll the desired portion of the image into view.
- To scroll more quickly, hold down Cmd and drag the image.
- iPhoto can zoom in to 400 percent, and out to 5 percent.
- Each click of iPhoto's zoom buttons makes the image roughly a third larger or smaller than the previous size.

Duplicating Photos

iPhoto lets you duplicate photos, which turns out to be an important feature for a variety of reasons.

Reasons to duplicate photos:

- If you want a photo to appear twice in a book (as you might if you want it to be the cover image and to show up inside as well), you must duplicate that photo.
- If you want to crop a photo in different ways, or if you want to print the same photo in color and black-and-white, you'll need to duplicate the photo first.
- Although iPhoto lets you undo the last action by choosing Undo from the Edit menu, and you can throw away all changes by choosing Revert to Original from the File menu, Revert to Original doesn't always work with external applications unless you force iPhoto to start tracking changes by making a small edit. So if you're editing a particularly precious photo, you might want to work on a duplicate for safety's sake.

To duplicate a photo:

- In any mode, select a photo and choose Duplicate from the File menu (Cmd D).

  iPhoto switches to import mode, duplicates the photo by importing it, and switches back to the mode you were in.

✔ Tips

- The duplicate image shows up next to the original in the Photo Library, and iPhoto does not create a new film roll.
- The Last Import album shows the duplicated photo.
- If an album is selected when you duplicate the photo, the duplicate is added to the end of that album too.

Rotate buttons.

Figure 3.14 Here I'm showing a "before" photo that needs rotating in the display pane and in its own window purely so you can see both Rotate buttons.

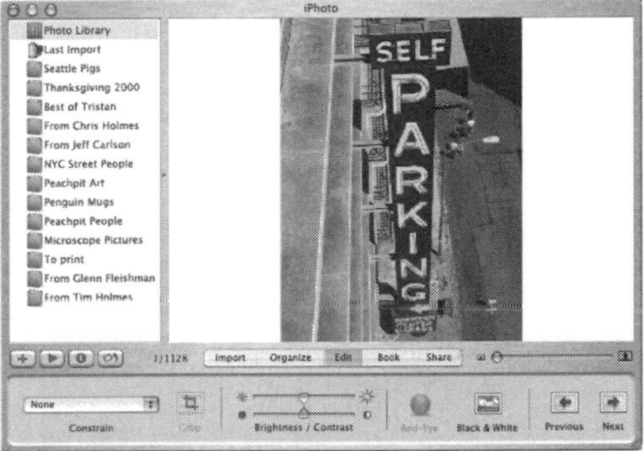

Figure 3.15 Here's the "after" picture that resulted from clicking the Rotate button.

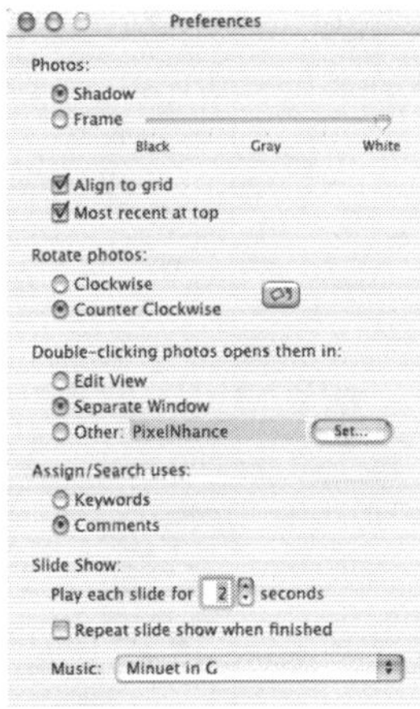

Figure 3.16 In the Preferences window, select which direction you want iPhoto to rotate photos by default.

Rotating Photos

With digital photos, if you've turned the camera to switch from landscape view (horizontal) to portrait view (vertical), you'll have to rotate the image in iPhoto to view it right side up. Rotating is such a common function that iPhoto provides a Rotate button that's available at all times.

To rotate photos:

- In any mode, to rotate one or more photos counter-clockwise, select them and click the Rotate button under the album pane (**Figure 3.14**). To rotate them clockwise, hold down Option and click the Rotate button.
- In any mode, select one or more photos and choose Counter Clockwise from the Edit menu's Rotate menu (Cmd R). To rotate in the other direction, choose Clockwise from the same menu (Cmd Shift R).
- In the image editing window's toolbar, to rotate the photo counter-clockwise, click the Rotate button (**Figure 3.15**). To rotate the photo clockwise, hold down Option when clicking the Rotate button.

✔ Tips

- You can change the direction used by the Rotate buttons in iPhoto's Preferences window; Option-clicking always reverses the default direction (**Figure 3.16**).
- It's usually easiest to rotate photos in batches in organize mode. Shrink the thumbnail size so you can see a number of photos at once, Cmd-click the ones that need rotating counter-clockwise, and click the Rotate button. Repeat with any images that need clockwise rotation, holding down Option when you click the Rotate button.

Making Photos Black-and-White

iPhoto
Photo Library
Last Import
Seattle Pigs
Thanksgiving 2000
Best of Tristan
From Chris Holmes
From Jeff Carlson
NYC Street People
Peachpit Art
Penguin Mugs
Peachpit People
Progress
Convert to Black And White
Cancel
1/1128
Import
Organize
Edit
Book
Share
None
Constrain
Brightness / Contrast
Black & White
Previous
Next

Figure 3.17 To convert a photo to black-and-white, switch to edit mode and click the Black & White button. Here I'm converting a picture of an old barn to make the bleached wood look more like bones, and to emphasize the starkness of the leafless trees against the sky.

Although almost all cameras take photos in color by default, some photos are improved by conversion to black-and-white. That's often true of portraits of people, since switching to black-and-white smoothes out skin coloration blemishes. Some landscapes also benefit tremendously from conversion to black-and-white, since eliminating color from the image helps the viewer focus on the composition and lighting. Think Ansel Adams.

To make a photo black-and-white:

- In edit mode, click the Black & White button in the edit pane or the image editing window's toolbar.

  iPhoto displays a progress dialog while it converts the image, and then displays it in black-and-white (**Figure 3.17**).

✔ Tips

- If you convert a photo to black-and-white and decide you don't like it, choose Undo from the Edit menu (Cmd Z).
- If you're not sure if you like the black-and-white version of a photo, choose Undo from the Edit menu to switch to color (Cmd Z), then choose Redo from the Edit menu to switch back to black-and-white quickly (Cmd Shift Z). Using the keyboard shortcuts, it's easy to flip back and forth quickly.
- Another way to compare color and black-and-white versions of the same photo is to duplicate the photo, convert one copy to black-and-white, and then look at them side-by-side in organize mode.

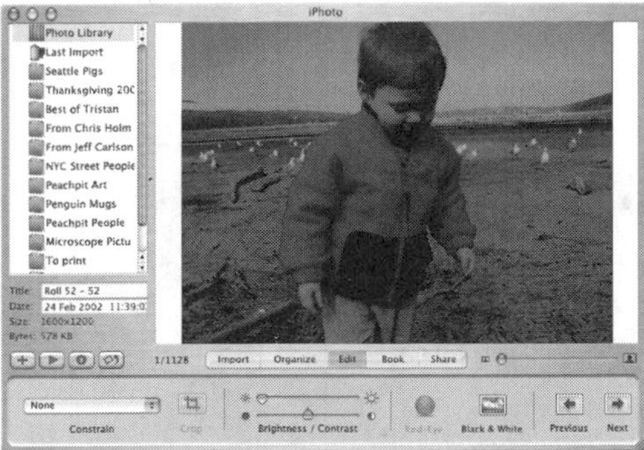
iPhoto
Photo Library
Last Import
Seattle Pigs
Best of Tristan
From Chris Holm
From Jeff Carlson
Peachpit Art
Penguin Mugs
Peachpit People
To print
Import
Organize
Edit
Book
Share
None
Constrain
Brightness / Contrast
Black & White
Previous
Next

Figure 3.18 Note how I've reduced the brightness all the way in this image, causing it to seem very dark.

iPhoto
Photo Library
Last Import
Seattle Pigs
Best of Tristan
From Chris Holm
From Jeff Carlson
Peachpit Art
Penguin Mugs
Peachpit People
To print
Import
Organize
Edit
Book
Share
None
Constrain
Brightness / Contrast
Black & White
Previous
Next

Figure 3.19 In this image, I've reduced the contrast all the way, making it seem as though fog on the camera lens obscured the picture.

Adjusting Brightness and Contrast

New in iPhoto 1.1.1 are controls for adjusting the brightness and contrast of a photo. Adjusting the brightness of the photo makes the entire image lighter or darker, whereas adjusting the contrast changes the degree of difference between light and dark areas of the image.

To adjust the brightness:

- In edit mode, drag the top slider left to decrease or right to increase the brightness of the image (**Figure 3.18**).

To adjust the brightness:

- In edit mode, drag the bottom slider left to decrease or right to increase the contrast of the image (**Figure 3.19**).

✔ Tips

- My examples are intentionally extreme; in most cases you will want to tweak brightness and contrast only slightly.
- If you make a change to the image's brightness or contrast, switch modes, and switch back to edit mode, you'll notice that the brightness and contrast sliders are in their middle position again. This means two things. First, in the unlikely event that you want to increase or decrease brightness or contrast more than the sliders allow, a second pass offers more leeway. Second, if you don't like the brightness or contrast changes you've made, you should choose Revert to Original from the File menu to fix the mistake rather than trying to readjust the sliders.

Understanding Aspect Ratios

iPhoto makes it easy to select and crop a portion of a photo using a specific aspect ratio, but why is this important? It matters because aspect ratios differ between traditional and digital photos.

First off, what is an aspect ratio? It's the ratio between the width of the image and its height, generally expressed with both numbers, as in the line from Arlo Guthrie's song "Alice's Restaurant Massacree" about "Twenty-seven *eight-by-ten* color glossy photographs with circles and arrows and a paragraph on the back of each one."

The aspect ratio of 35mm film is 4 x 6 (using iPhoto's terminology rather than the least common denominator of 2 x 3) because the negative measures 24mm by 36mm. Thus, traditional photographs are usually printed at sizes like 4" x 6", 5" x 7", or 8" x 10", all of which are close enough to that 4 x 6 aspect ratio so photos scale well. When there's a mismatch between the aspect ratio of the original negative and the final print, either the image must be shrunk proportionally to fit (producing unsightly borders) or some portion of the image must be cropped. (The alternative is resizing the image disproportionally, which makes people look like they're reflected in a fun-house mirror.)

The equivalent of film in digital photography is the CCD (charge-coupled device), which is essentially a grid of many light-sensitive elements that gain a charge when exposed to light. Through much digital wizardry, the camera translates those charges into the individual dots (called pixels) that, put together, make up the image. Zoom in on a picture all the way, and you can actually see these pixels. So if your digital camera, like many others, uses a CCD that can capture a

Roll 4 - 15 (39%)
4 x 6
4
6
Zoom
Fit
Rotate
Constrain
Custom
Crop
Red-Eye

Figure 3.20 This is a 4 x 3 image with a 4 x 6 landscape selection. A bit of the bottom of the image would be lost, which is fine.

Roll 4 - 15 (39%)
5 x 7
5
7
Zoom
Fit
Rotate
Constrain
Custom
Crop
Red-Eye

Figure 3.21 This is a 4 x 3 image with a 5 x 7 landscape selection. Very little of the bottom of the image would be lost to cropping.

Roll 4 - 15 (39%)
8 x 10
8
10
Zoom
Fit
Rotate
Constrain
Custom
Crop
Red-Eye

Figure 3.22 This is a 4 x 3 image with an 8 x 10 landscape selection. Losing the right side of the image would be problematic.

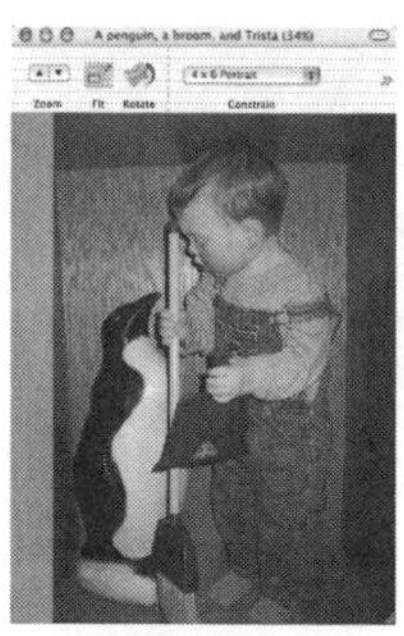

Figure 3.23 This is a 4 x 3 portrait image with a 4 x 6 portrait selection. A bit on the left would be lost, which is fine (a better crop would take some from the left, the right, and the top).

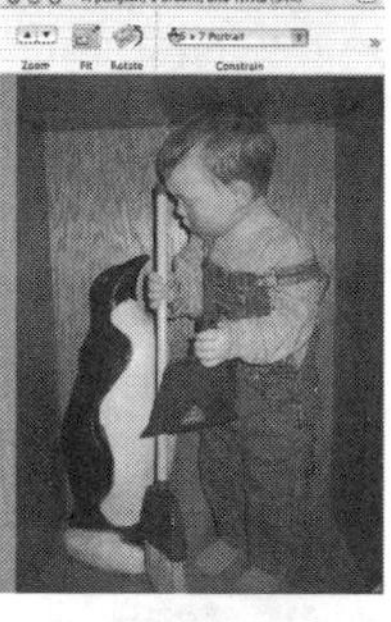

Figure 3.24 This is a 4 x 3 portrait image with a 5 x 7 portrait selection. A very small amount on the left would be lost, which is fine.

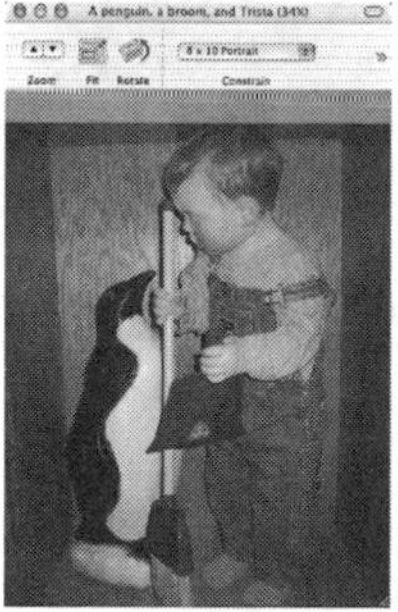

Figure 3.25 This is a 4 x 3 portrait image with an 8 x 10 portrait selection. As with the landscape image on the previous page, the aspect ratios match badly for this image, since the selection cuts off the top of Tristan's head.

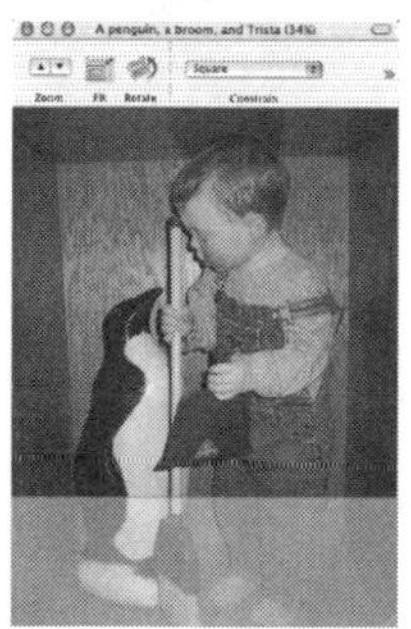

Figure 3.26 This is a 4 x 3 portrait image with square selection. As you can tell, the square selection is a lousy choice for this image.

picture composed of 1600 pixels wide by 1200 pixels high, basic math shows that your photos will have a 4 x 3 aspect ratio.

Why did digital camera manufacturers choose a 4 x 3 aspect ratio when 4 x 6 is the 35mm film standard? It matches the aspect ratios of almost all computer monitors. Whether your monitor runs at a resolution of 640 x 480, 800 x 600, or 1024 x 768, simple division reveals that they're all a 4 x 3 aspect ratio. Displaying a photo at full screen size without cropping thus requires a 4 x 3 aspect ratio. (And why do computer monitors use a 4 x 3 aspect ratio? Because that's the aspect ratio used by televisions.)

Hopefully the choices in iPhoto's Constrain pop-up menu make more sense now. If you're starting from a photo with a 4 x 3 aspect ratio, and you want a 20" x 30" print (a 4 x 6 aspect ratio), there's no way to print that photo without borders or cropping because of the mismatch in aspect ratios. The same applies to the other standard print sizes—they don't match the 4 x 3 aspect ratio of most digital photos. Rather than suffering borders or automatic cropping, it's better to crop the image yourself so you can be sure the important parts are retained. **Figures 3.20** through **3.26** show how cropping a 4 x 3 image at the other common aspect ratios works for two sample images (results will vary by image).

The 4 x 3 aspect ratio plays an important role in output too, since iPhoto's book designs all assume images in the 4 x 3 aspect ratio so you don't have to do as much cropping. The books vary the final image size depending on the page design, but as long as the aspect ratio of your images remains 4 x 3, the layout will work as Apple intended. You can use different aspect ratios in a book, of course, but the layout may not work as well.

Selecting Portions of Photos

iPhoto's remaining editing tools—cropping and reducing red-eye—require that you select a portion of the picture first.

To select part of a photo:

- In edit mode, drag to create a selection rectangle in the image (you see a crosshair cursor while doing this). iPhoto fogs the photo outside your selection rectangle to help you focus on the selection (**Figure 3.27**).
- To move your selection rectangle around, drag it (your cursor should be a hand). You may need to move a selection rectangle to force it up against the edges of a picture, since it's hard to start selecting right at the edge.
- To resize a selection rectangle, drag the rectangle's edge to resize (you'll have an arrow cursor at this point).
- To constrain the selection rectangle to specific proportions, choose an aspect ratio from the Constrain pop-up menu, or click a Constrain button in the image editing window's toolbar. If you haven't created a selection rectangle, it will be constrained when you do; if you have one already, iPhoto resizes it (**Figure 3.28**). To remove a constraint, choose None from the Constrain menu or click the Free button in the image editing toolbar.
- To constrain the selection rectangle to custom proportions, edit the image in its own window, enter the desired aspect ratio in the Custom fields in the toolbar, and press Return to set the size.
- To deselect everything and start over, click in the fogged area or switch to another photo.

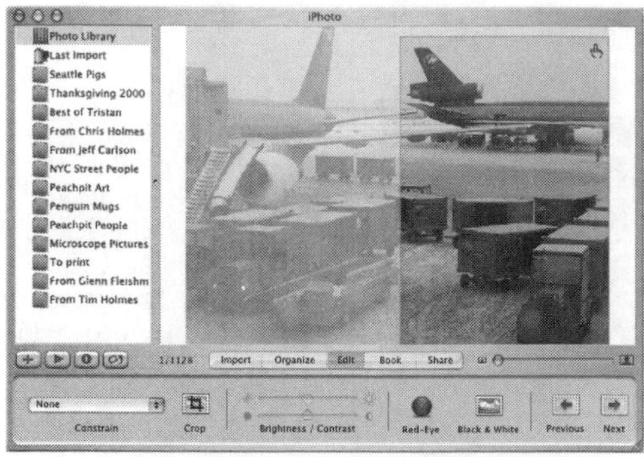
iPhoto
Photo Library
Last Import
Seattle Pigs
Thanksgiving 2000
Best of Tristan
From Chris Holmes
From Jeff Carlson
NYC Street People
Peachpit Art
Penguin Mugs
Peachpit People
Microscope Pictures
To print
From Glenn Fleishm
From Tim Holmes
1/1128
Import
Organize
Edit
Book
Share
None
Constrain
Crop
Brightness / Contrast
Red-Eye
Black & White
Previous
Next

Figure 3.27 To select a portion of a photo, drag to create a selection rectangle. Move it by dragging it; resize it by dragging an edge. Here I've created a selection rectangle with no specific proportion.

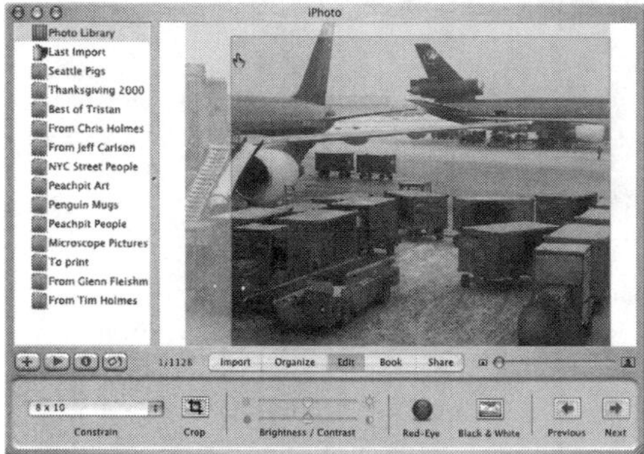
iPhoto
Photo Library
Last Import
Seattle Pigs
Thanksgiving 2000
Best of Tristan
From Chris Holmes
From Jeff Carlson
NYC Street People
Peachpit Art
Penguin Mugs
Peachpit People
Microscope Pictures
To print
From Glenn Fleishm
From Tim Holmes
1/1128
Import
Organize
Edit
Book
Share
8 x 10
Constrain
Crop
Brightness / Contrast
Red-Eye
Black & White
Previous
Next

Figure 3.28 To constrain an image to specific proportions, choose an aspect ratio from the Constrain menu. You can then move and resize the selection rectangle while maintaining the selected aspect ratio.

Roll 43 - 5 (101%)
8 x 10
8
x 10
Zoom
Fit
Rotate
Constrain
Custom
Crop
Red-Eye

Figure 3.29 To crop an image, select the desired portion and then click the Crop button. Here I've cropped out all the irrelevant background. Since my free-form selection was close to an 8 x 10 aspect ratio, I switched to that before clicking Crop.

Roll 43 - 5 (129%)
8 x 10
8
x 10
Zoom
Fit
Rotate
Constrain
Custom
Crop

Figure 3.30 As you can see, cropping this image improved it immensely.

Adjust Shooting Style

When taking pictures, you generally want to fill the frame with the scene, but if you plan to order prints of all your photos, you might want to include a little extra space on the edges to allow for cropping to a print aspect ratio.

Cropping Photos

If you're planning on printing a photo or displaying it on your Desktop, you'll want to crop it using an appropriate aspect ratio. Even if you don't plan to print a photo, cropping extraneous detail often improves an image a great deal.

To crop a photo:

1. Select the desired portion of the image.
2. Click the Crop button in the edit pane or the image editing window's toolbar.

   iPhoto deletes the fogged area of the picture, leaving just what you had selected (**Figure 3.29** and **Figure 3.30**).

✔ Tips

- If you want to compare the original photo with the cropped version right after cropping, choose Undo from the Edit menu to switch back to the original (Cmd Z), and then choose Redo from the Edit menu to see the cropped photo again (Cmd Shift Z). It's easy to flip back and forth using the keyboard shortcuts.
- If your selection rectangle is very close to one of the standard aspect ratios, it's best to use the standard aspect ratio in case you want to print the image later.
- Bear in mind that when you crop a photo, you remove pixels from it. So if you crop a 1600 x 1200 pixel photo (1,920,000 pixels) down to 1200 x 900 (1,080,000 pixels), you've removed almost half the image. Thus, if you print the original and the cropped version at the same size, the original will be of a much higher quality. Heavy cropping is one major reason why iPhoto shows a low resolution warning icon on a photo when you design a book or order prints.

Reducing Red-Eye

Perhaps the most annoying thing that can go wrong in a photograph is red-eye, a demonic red glow to subjects' eyes that plagues flash photography. Luckily, iPhoto makes reducing the effect of red-eye easy, although the approach it takes isn't always perfect.

To reduce red-eye in a photo:

1. Drag a selection rectangle that includes just the subject's eyes (**Figure 3.31**).
2. Click the Red-Eye button in the edit pane or the image editing window's toolbar.

   iPhoto converts the red shades in the selected areas to dark gray.

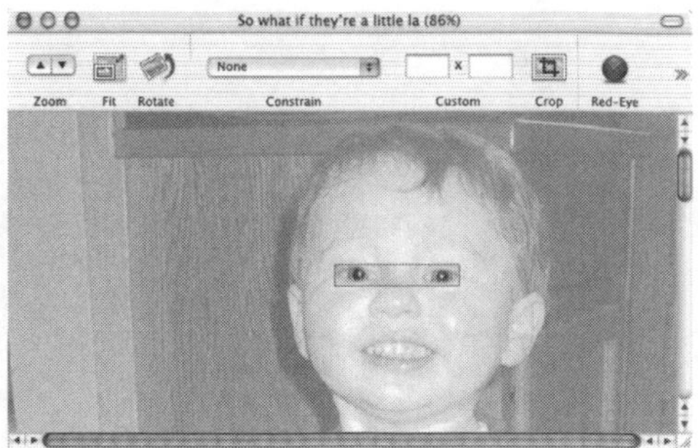
So what if they're a little la (86%)
None
Zoom
Fit
Rotate
Constrain
Custom
Crop
Red-Eye

Figure 3.31 To reduce the effect of red-eye in a photo, drag a selection rectangle around the subject's eyes, and then click the Red-Eye button.

✔ Tips

- It can be easier to select the subject's eyes accurately if you zoom in first, as I've done in **Figure 3.31**.
- If you're not happy with the results, try working with one eye at at time rather than both at once.
- Unfortunately, iPhoto's approach to reducing red-eye tends to make people look as though they have black eyes. That's better than glowing red eyes, but it's not ideal if the subject's eyes are a light blue or gray. You can achieve better results in a full-fledged image editing program, but that requires a fair amount of skill.
- The Red-Eye tool looks only for specific shades of red, as you can see if you select an entire image and click Red-Eye.

What is Red-Eye?

Red-eye is a phenomenon that occurs in photographs when light from the camera's flash reflects off the blood vessels in the retina of the subject's eyes. It's worse when the flash is close to the lens, with young children, with blue or gray eyes (which reflect more light than darker eyes), and in dim settings.

There are ways to prevent or reduce red-eye from occurring in the first place.

- Try to cause the subject's pupils to contract by increasing the room light, asking the person to look at a bright light right before taking the picture, or using a red-eye reduction feature in your camera (which pulses the flash before taking the picture).
- Have the subject look slightly away from the camera lens rather than directly toward it.
- If your camera supports an external flash unit, use it to increase the distance between the flash and the camera lens.

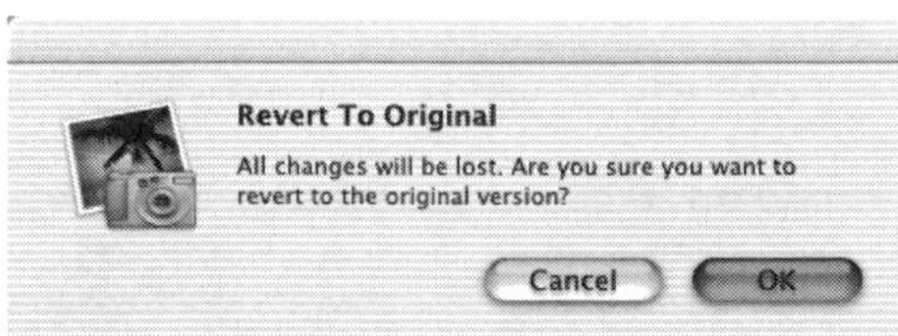
Revert To Original
All changes will be lost. Are you sure you want to revert to the original version?
Cancel
OK

Figure 3.32 To revert to the original version of an image after making a number of edits, select it and choose Revert to Original from the File menu. iPhoto warns you that you'll lose all your changes.

Recover Original

It turns out that Revert to Original isn't doing anything particularly hard. When you edit a photo, iPhoto makes a copy of the original in a folder called Originals that lives in the same directory as the image. As long as this happens, you can recover an original image no matter what might have gone wrong.

1. Drag the desired image onto the Show Image File AppleScript script to locate its file in the Finder. (The script is at `www.apple.com/applescript/iphoto/`.)
2. Note the name of the file you've found. Then open the Originals folder and Option-drag the file of the same name from the Originals folder to the Desktop to make a copy of it.
3. Launch iPhoto, and drag the newly copied file from the Desktop into iPhoto to import it again.

Undoing Changes

We all make mistakes, and that's certain to happen on occasion when you're working with your digital photos too. Luckily, since the photos are digital, your changes aren't necessarily irrevocable.

To undo changes to a photo:

- Immediately after you've performed an action, to undo just that action, choose Undo from the Edit menu (Cmd Z).
- To remove all changes from a photo, select it and choose Revert to Original from the File menu. iPhoto warns you that you'll lose all changes to the photo (**Figure 3.32**).

✔ Tips

- iPhoto 1.0 had some problems with the Revert to Original command, but in the testing I've done so far with iPhoto 1.1.1, it seems that Apple has addressed those problems. I haven't been able to create a situation where Revert to Original wasn't available when it should be. That said, the only guaranteed way to be able to revert to an original image is if you have a backup.
- iPhoto modifies the Undo command in the Edit menu to reflect your last action, so it may say Undo Crop Photo, for instance.
- Anything you can undo via the Undo command, you can Redo via the Redo command in the Edit menu. As with Undo, iPhoto makes the Redo command specific to the action that will be done again, so it might read Redo Crop Photo.
- Revert to Original works even if you edit a photo in another program—iPhoto starts tracking the original image as soon as you double-click the photo.

Editing in Another Program

In case you hadn't noticed, iPhoto's editing tools are quite minimal. They're all many people will need or be able to understand, but for other common changes to photos, you'll have to turn to another program. Luckily, Apple took this possibility into account.

To edit a photo in another program:

1. From the iPhoto application menu, choose Preferences (Cmd Y) to open the Preferences window.
2. Under "Double-clicking photos opens them in," select Other (**Figure 3.33**).
3. Click the Set button, and choose a program in the open dialog.
4. Close the Preferences window.
5. Double-click a photo.

   iPhoto launches your selected editing program and opens the image you double-clicked in that program.
6. Make your desired changes, and when you're done, save and close the photo.
7. Switch back to iPhoto.

✔ Tips

- iPhoto 1.0 didn't always update an image's thumbnail after you edited it in another program; that's been solved in iPhoto 1.1.1.
- Revert to Original works even on photos edited in another program.

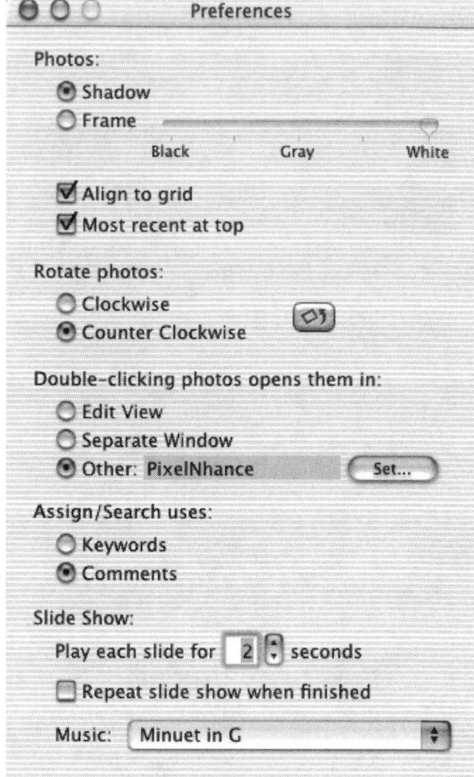
Preferences
Photos:
Shadow
Frame
Black
Gray
White
Align to grid
Most recent at top
Rotate photos:
Clockwise
Counter Clockwise
Double-clicking photos opens them in:
Edit View
Separate Window
Other: PixelNhance
Set...
Assign/Search uses:
Keywords
Comments
Slide Show:
Play each slide for 2 seconds
Repeat slide show when finished
Music: Minuet in G

Figure 3.33 To configure iPhoto to use another program for editing photos, choose Preferences from the iPhoto application menu, select Other from the "Double-clicking photos opens them in" section, click the Set button, select the desired application, and when you're done, close the Preferences window.

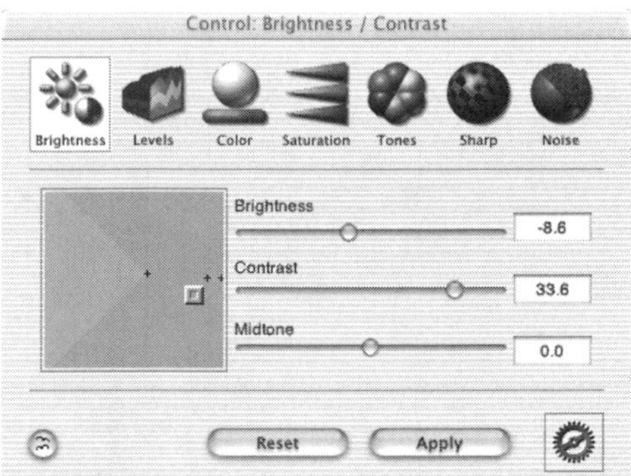
Control: Brightness / Contrast
Brightness
Levels
Color
Saturation
Tones
Sharp
Noise
Brightness
-8.6
Contrast
33.6
Midtone
0.0
Reset
Apply

Figure 3.34 PixelNhance provides a number of tools for editing your photos—click a tool at the the top of the window, and then use the controls to modify the image in its own window (see the next screenshot).

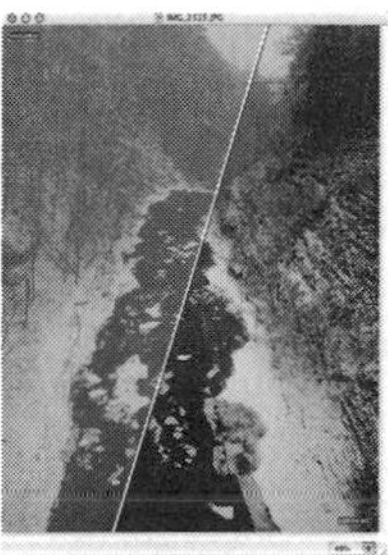

Figure 3.35 PixelNhance's image window displays the photo, with a movable bar separating how the image looked originally from how the changes you make will affect it. Here I've increased the contrast of a wintry scene to make it darker and more vibrant.

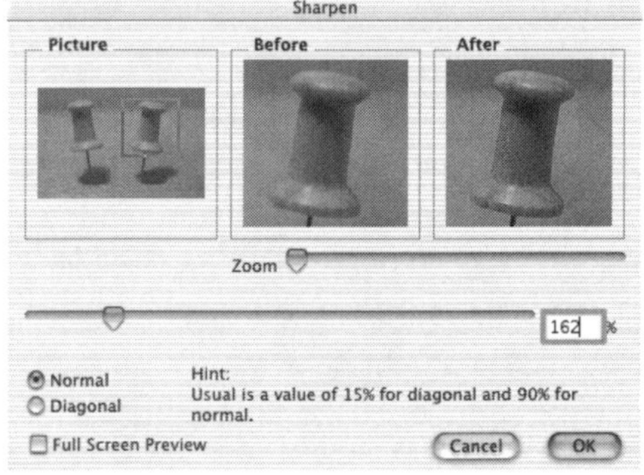
Sharpen
Picture
Before
After
Zoom
162 %
Normal
Diagonal
Hint:
Usual is a value of 15% for diagonal and 90% for normal.
Full Screen Preview
Cancel
OK

Figure 3.36 Via a relatively technical interface, GraphicConverter offers a vast number of features, such as the Sharpen tool shown above. Here I've used it to increase the sharpness of a photo of hand-turned thumbtacks to bring out the wood grain.

Recommended Image Editing Programs

You can use any image editing program with iPhoto, even older ones that run only in Mac OS X's Classic layer. However, a few Mac OS X-native applications are particularly appropriate for use with iPhoto.

PixelNhance

Caffeinesoft's free PixelNhance is an essential addition to iPhoto's simple editing tools. It helps you modify the brightness and contrast of your photos, adjust the levels of different colors, increase or decrease the sharpness, reduce the amount of visual noise in the image, and more (**Figure 3.34**).

What sets PixelNhance apart from other image editors is its ultra-easy interface. A movable bar separates two sections of the photo; one section shows how it looked originally, the other displays a preview of how your changes will affect the image (**Figure 3.35**). PixelNhance currently ships with all new Macs, or you can download a copy from `www.caffeinesoft.com`.

GraphicConverter

Lemke Software's $30 GraphicConverter is one of the most popular Mac shareware applications. Although its claim to fame is conversion of graphic files between a vast number of formats, it also offers extensive image editing features. You can sharpen images, adjust color levels, change brightness and contrast, modify image resolution, and mirror images, among many other features. GraphicConverter's more technical interface isn't as straightforward as PixelNhance's, but its power is undeniable (**Figure 3.36**). GraphicConverter currently ships with all new Macs, or you can download a copy from `www.lemkesoft.com`.

Creating Books

If I had to pick one feature that sets iPhoto apart from the crowd, I'd choose the way iPhoto creates custom photo albums that can be professionally printed and bound. Numerous programs can help you edit and organize photos. But when it first appeared, iPhoto instantly became the undisputed champion of sharing pictures in attractive ways, largely because of the customized photo albums iPhoto calls "books."

The beauty of the books, apart from their linen covers and quality printing on heavy, glossy paper, is that they help bridge the gap between the analog and digital worlds. Those of us who have grown up with computers are happy sharing our photos via slide show, a digital camera hooked to a TV, or on a Web page. But many people are still more comfortable with prints ensconced in acetate in a traditional photo album. Forget all the advantages of the digital world; for these people, the images somehow aren't real unless they're in a book. It's the "That's nice, dear" syndrome.

By the time you're done with this chapter and the next one (which covers ordering the books you create), you won't have to worry about your digital photo collection being a second-class citizen when it comes to being displayed in a "real" book.

Switching Modes while Creating Books

To switch into book mode, click the Book button while one of your albums is selected in the album list. That's both predictable and easy, but book mode is unusual in that you'll want to switch back and forth with other modes—mostly organize and edit—while working in book mode.

To enter book mode:

- Select an album (other than Photo Library or Last Import), and click the Book button under the display pane (**Figure 4.1**).

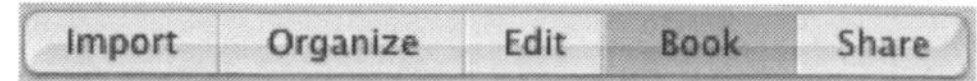
Import
Organize
Edit
Book
Share

Figure 4.1 To switch into book mode, click the Book button under the display pane.

Reasons to switch out of and back into book mode:

- To rearrange photos so they appear in the desired order in your book, switch to organize mode by clicking the Organize button, drag pictures into the right order, and then switch back by clicking the Book button.
- To crop a photo, eliminate red-eye, or adjust its brightness or contrast, double-click the photo to switch into edit mode. Alternatively, click it to select it, and then click the Edit button. When you're done, switch back into book mode by clicking the Book button.

✔ Tips

- You can rearrange photos by dragging pages of the book around, but it's easier to make changes in organize mode with the thumbnails at a small size.
- When you're in book mode, clicking another album name lets you work on a book for that other album without switching modes. Each album remembers its own book settings.

Book Tools Overview

Here's a quick reference to the tools available to you in book mode (**Figure 4.2**).

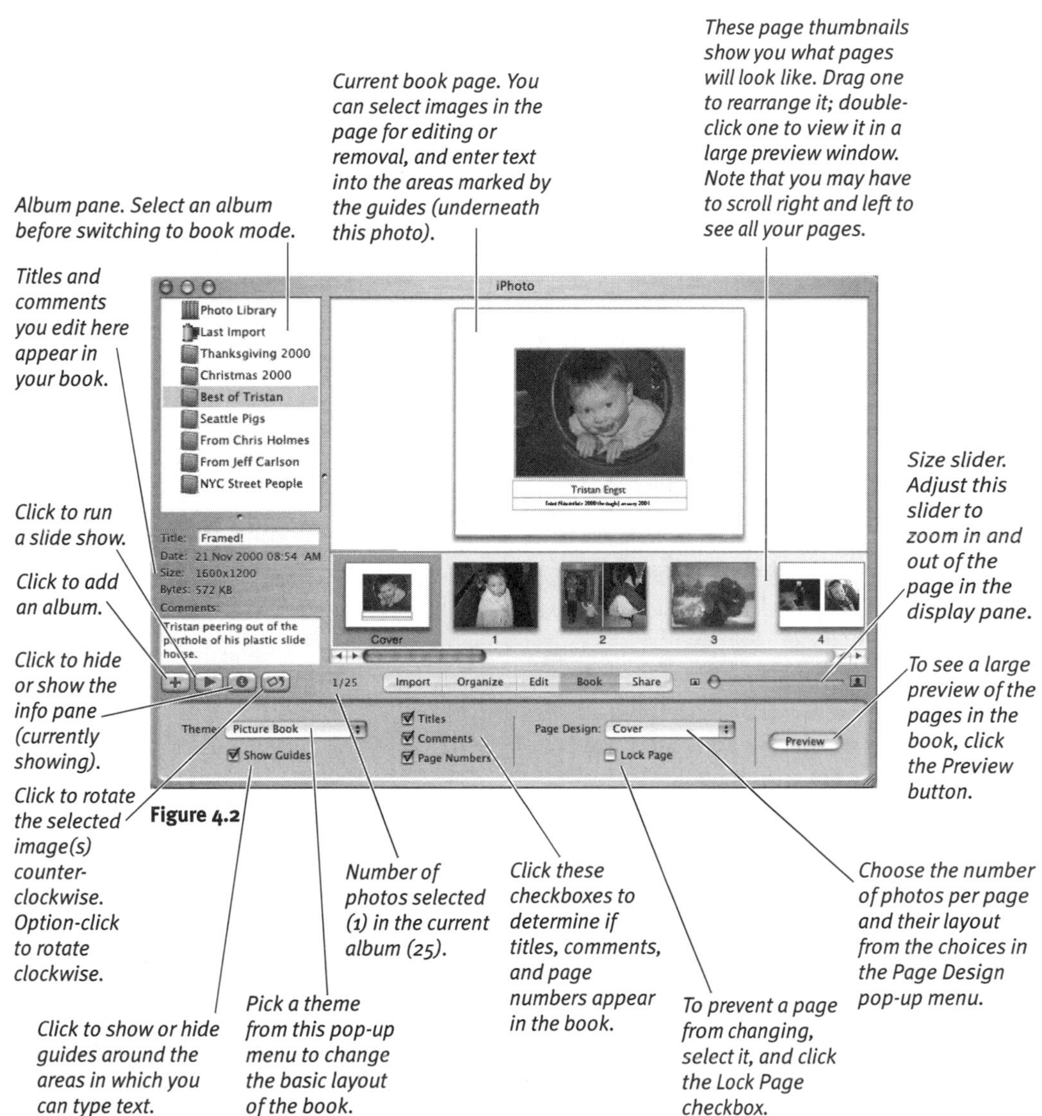

Album pane. Select an album before switching to book mode.
Current book page. You can select images in the page for editing or removal, and enter text into the areas marked by the guides (underneath this photo).
These page thumbnails show you what pages will look like. Drag one to rearrange it; double-click one to view it in a large preview window. Note that you may have to scroll right and left to see all your pages.
Titles and comments you edit here appear in your book.
Click to run a slide show.
Click to add an album.
Click to hide or show the info pane (currently showing).
Click to rotate the selected image(s) counter-clockwise. Option-click to rotate clockwise.
Size slider. Adjust this slider to zoom in and out of the page in the display pane.
To see a large preview of the pages in the book, click the Preview button.
Number of photos selected (1) in the current album (25).
Click these checkboxes to determine if titles, comments, and page numbers appear in the book.
Choose the number of photos per page and their layout from the choices in the Page Design pop-up menu.
To prevent a page from changing, select it, and click the Lock Page checkbox.
Pick a theme from this pop-up menu to change the basic layout of the book.
Click to show or hide guides around the areas in which you can type text.
iPhoto
Photo Library
Last Import
Thanksgiving 2000
Christmas 2000
Best of Tristan
Seattle Pigs
From Chris Holmes
From Jeff Carlson
NYC Street People
Title: Framed!
Date: 21 Nov 2000 08:54 AM
Size: 1600x1200
Bytes: 572 KB
Comments:
Tristan peering out of the porthole of his plastic slide house.
Tristan Engst
Cover
1
2
3
4
1/25
Import
Organize
Edit
Book
Share
Theme: Picture Book
Show Guides
Titles
Comments
Page Numbers
Page Design: Cover
Lock Page
Preview

Figure 4.2

Creating Books

Even though books end up looking highly professional, they're still easy to create. Here we'll skim over the process of making a book; subsequent pages go into the details.

To prepare a book:

1. Make an album containing the photos you want in your book (see "Creating Albums" and "Adding Photos to Albums" in Chapter 2, "Organizing Photos").
2. Click the album name to switch to it.
3. Click the Book button under the display pane to switch to book mode.
4. Pick a theme from the Theme pop-up menu in the book pane. Each theme offers different layout options.
5. Decide if you want titles, comments, and page numbers to show in your book. Not all themes display them regardless of how you set the checkboxes.
6. For each page of the book, choose the design from the Page Design pop-up menu. To keep a page from changing, click the Lock Page checkbox.
7. Click Preview at any time to see your book in its own window at a larger size. You can also print a draft book; choose Print from the File menu (Cmd P).
8. When you're done, click the Share button, click Order Book in the share pane, and order your book. For details about this process, see "Ordering Books" in Chapter 5, "Sharing Photos."

✔ Tips

- Your book must contain between 10 and 50 pages (if you have fewer pages, you'll get blanks in the printed copy).
- Remember that books cost $3 per page.

Stick with Color Photos

Although I haven't seen this personally, Apple is warning that black-and-white photos print poorly in books. Until Apple resolves this issue, which is related to the printing process used for books, stick with color images in your books.

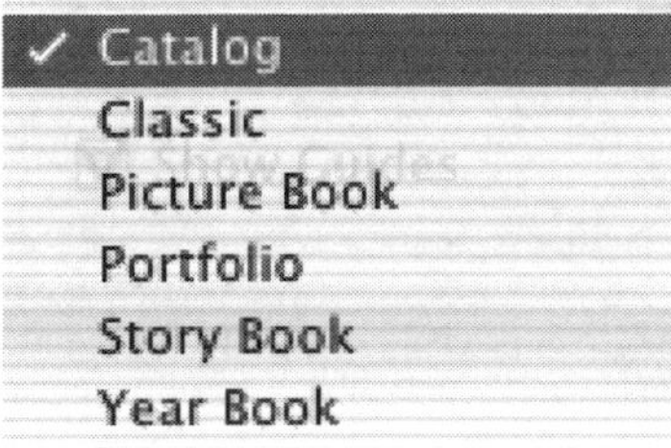
✓ Catalog
Classic
Picture Book
Portfolio
Story Book
Year Book

Figure 4.3 To switch between book designs, choose a theme from the Theme pop-up menu in the book pane.

25 photos
Import
Organize
Theme: Catalog
Show Guides
Titles
Comments
Page Numbers

Figure 4.4 To control whether or not titles, comments, and page numbers appear in your book, click the appropriate checkboxes in the book pane.

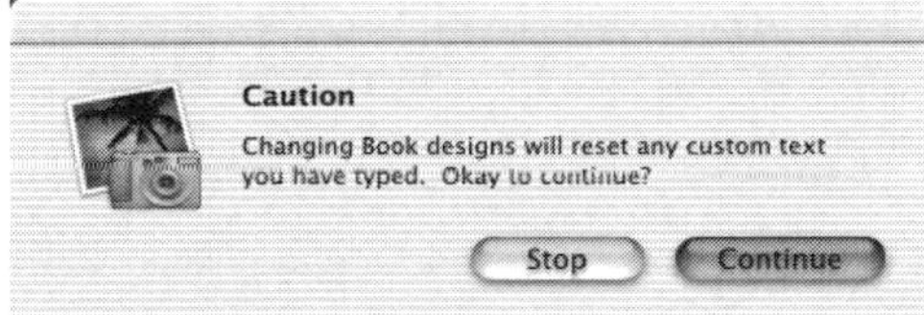
Caution
Changing Book designs will reset any custom text you have typed. Okay to continue?
Stop
Continue

Figure 4.5 iPhoto warns you if you try to switch themes after entering custom text.

Designing Books

The first thing to do after selecting an album and switching into book mode is to pick a theme for your book and set the book-wide options that affect all pages.

To design your book:

1. From the Theme pop-up menu, choose one of the six themes built into iPhoto (**Figure 4.3**).

   iPhoto switches to the new theme.

2. Click the Titles, Comments, and Page Numbers checkboxes to determine whether or not those items will appear in your book (**Figure 4.4**).

   iPhoto adds or removes those items from the current book design.

✔ Tips

- The Picture Book theme contains no text other than the book title on the cover page, so selecting the Titles and Comments checkboxes has no effect.
- If you enter custom text (any text other than titles or comments) in one theme, you'll lose it if you switch themes (**Figure 4.5**).

Designing Pages

Once you've chosen which theme you want and set the other options that affect the entire book, it's time to turn your attention to the individual pages in your book. The first page must always be the cover design, and it will appear on the cover of your book. You control the layout on all other pages.

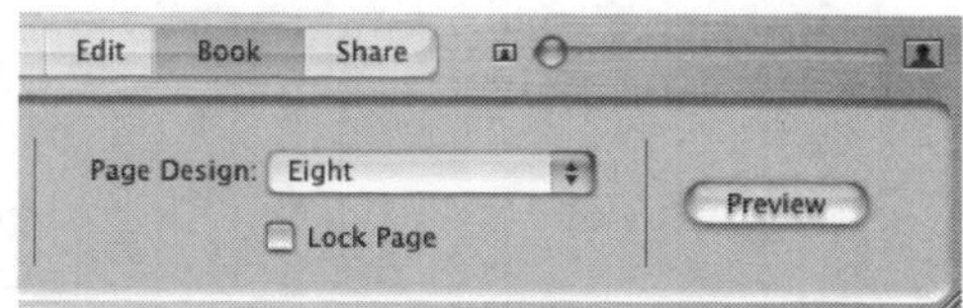
Edit
Book
Share
Page Design:
Eight
Lock Page
Preview

Figure 4.6 To switch page designs, select a page and choose a design from the Page Design pop-up menu.

To set a page design:

1. Select a page thumbnail by clicking it.
2. From the Page Design pop-up menu, choose a design (**Figure 4.6**).

   iPhoto changes the design of the selected page, reflowing photos as necessary.

✔ Tips

- Each book theme offers different page designs, so spend some time looking at the page designs in each theme to get a feel for which ones you like best and which ones are most appropriate for your purposes.
- After the cover page, which is required, the other page designs are entirely optional. You could use all of them or only a single one—it's up to you.
- The more photos in a page design, the smaller they appear on the page.
- The page designs all assume an aspect ratio of 4:3, so if you use a non-standard cropping ratio, photos may not line up as you expect (see "Cropping Photos" in Chapter 3, "Editing Photos"). A different page design might help, or you may have to crop the image again with a 4:3 aspect ratio or revert to the original.
- If you want your cover image to appear inside the book as well, you'll have to duplicate the photo (see "Duplicating Photos" in Chapter 3, "Editing Photos").

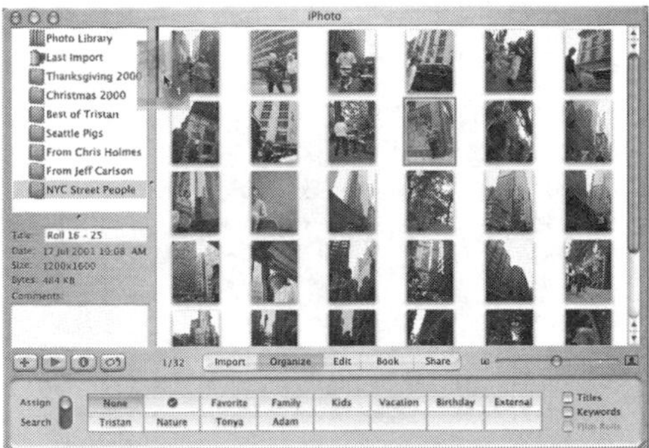
iPhoto
Photo Library
Last Import
Christmas 2000
Best of Tristan
Seattle Pigs
From Chris Holmes
From Jeff Carlson
NYC Street People
Import
Organize
Edit
Book
Share

Figure 4.7 Drag your desired cover photo into the top-left position so it's the first image in the album.

Cover
1
2
4
Import
Organize
Edit
Book
Share

Figure 4.8 To move an entire page, drag it to the desired location. iPhoto rearranges the photos in the album in organize mode automatically.

Cover
1
2
3
4
Import
Organize
Edit
Book
Share
Titles
Comments
Page Numbers
Page Design: Two
Lock Page
Preview

Figure 4.9 To prevent a page from being affected by photos sliding around to accommodate other pages, select the page and click the Lock Page checkbox. A small lock icon appears underneath the page to indicate that it's locked.

Arranging Photos on Pages

As you design pages, you'll need to arrange photos so they appear in the right order.

To arrange photos on pages:

1. Make sure that your desired cover photo is the first (top left) image in the album in organize mode. If not, drag it into the top-left position (**Figure 4.7**).
2. Switch to book mode and select the second page. Choose a page design for it; all themes have an optional Introduction design with plenty of room for text.
3. Click the next page thumbnail and choose a design. Choosing a design with more spots for photos pulls them from the pages to the right; choosing a design with fewer photo spots pushes the photos to the pages on the right.
4. To move a single image so it appears in a different spot, switch to organize mode, and drag the image to the desired location. Switch back to book mode.
5. To move a page containing multiple photos, drag it to the desired location. The other pages hop out of the way as you drag (**Figure 4.8**). iPhoto rearranges the photos in organize mode for you.
6. Repeat steps 3 through 5 for the remaining pages.

✔ Tips

- Work left to right because the pictures to the right move around based on the page designs you pick.
- Once you get a page looking just right, click the Lock Page checkbox to prevent it from being affected by photos flowing onto or off of other pages (**Figure 4.9**).

Dealing with Low Resolution Warning Icons

One problem that crops up any time you print a digital photo is quality, or rather, your inability to predict the quality of the result. Numerous variables can play a part in reducing the quality of a printed image, but iPhoto tries to help prevent one of the most common—printing an image at a size larger than is appropriate for the image's resolution. Whenever you have an image that's too low resolution for the proposed size in a book, iPhoto attaches a triangular warning icon to the photo to alert you to the problem (**Figure 4.10**).

iPhoto
Cover
1
2
3
4
Import
Organize
Edit
Book
Share

Figure 4.10 When a page design calls for a photo to be printed larger than its resolution allows (for good quality), iPhoto places a warning icon next to the offending image (all three on the page above).

To deal with a low resolution warning icon:

- Choose a different page design so the photo with the warning icon shrinks to a size small enough that the icon disappears.
- Move the image to a different location on the current page or another page where it will appear at the necessary smaller size (**Figure 4.11**).
- Cropping a photo makes it more likely that the image won't be large enough to print properly. To remove cropping, switch back to organize mode, select the image, and from the File menu, choose Revert to Original. Be warned that this will remove all of your changes, not just the cropping. Try again after cropping the image less heavily.
- If you run into this problem regularly, make sure you're taking pictures at the highest resolution offered by your camera.

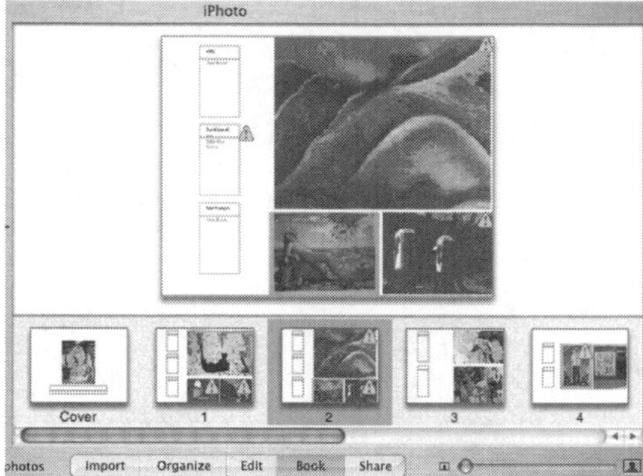
iPhoto
Cover
1
2
3
4
Import
Organize
Edit
Book
Share

Figure 4.11 To make the warning icon disappear, move the offending image to another location where the printed size better matches the resolution of the image. Note how the mermaid picture no longer has the warning icon now that it's set to print smaller.

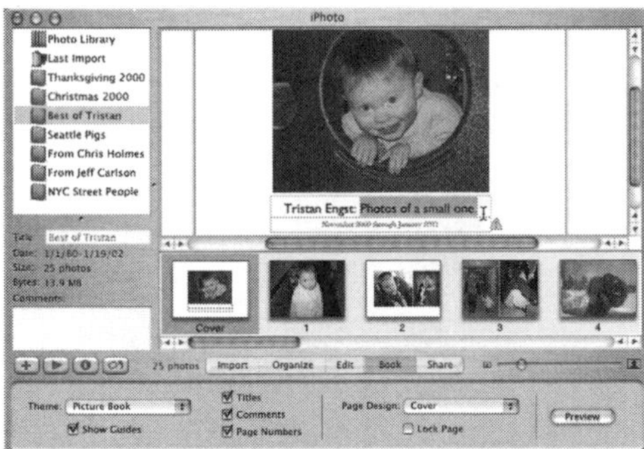
iPhoto
Photo Library
Last Import
Thanksgiving 2000
Christmas 2000
Best of Tristan
Seattle Pigs
From Chris Holmes
From Jeff Carlson
NYC Street People
Tristan Engst: Photos of a small one
Cover
Import
Organize
Edit
Book
Share
Theme: Picture Book
Show Guides
Titles
Comments
Page Numbers
Page Design: Cover
Lock Page
Preview

Figure 4.12 To edit or enter text, click in a text box and enter new text or edit the existing text. If there is too much text in the text box, a warning icon appears to alert you when you click out of the box. No scroll bars will appear; you must edit the extra text blindly.

Entering and Editing Text

Once you have all your pages laid out right, you can enter or edit the text that appears with the photos in most layouts.

To enter or edit text:

- Click a text box indicated by the guide lines and either enter new text or edit the existing text (**Figure 4.12**).
- You can use all the standard editing techniques and commands that you've become accustomed to as a Mac user—things like Cut, Copy, and Paste, not to mention double- and triple-clicking.
- You can check the spelling of your text. See "Checking Spelling" in this chapter.

✔ Tips

- Leave individual text boxes empty to hide them. Deselect the Titles and Comments checkboxes to hide all title and caption text boxes. Photos don't take over the empty space; it just prints blank.
- iPhoto picks up existing album names, titles, and comments for books; changes you make to titles and comments in the book appear in other modes as well.
- If you find the guide lines too obtrusive, deselect the Show Guides checkbox to turn them off. It can be difficult to locate text boxes without the guides, but they still show in the page thumbnails.
- iPhoto tries to simplify editing by zooming in on the page in the display pane so the text displays larger. When you click outside the text box, iPhoto zooms out. This feature isn't entirely reliable; sometimes you have to use the size slider to zoom manually. Editing can be easier in the preview window; click the Preview button to open it.

Text Warning Icons

If you see a small, yellow, triangular warning icon next to a text box while designing pages (**Figure 4.12** on this page and **Figure 4.10** and **Figure 4.11** on the previous page all show examples), it's because the text doesn't fit in the box. The font size is predetermined by the theme, but you can switch to a different font that takes up less space or edit the text to solve the problem.

iPhoto can generate these warning icons spuriously when you're zoomed all the way out; if they go away when you zoom in, everything should still print fine.

Typing Text "Correctly"

You're going to crop your photos perfectly and arrange them just so...are you then going to write text that looks downright trashy? Follow a few simple rules to make sure your text looks as good as your pictures and iPhoto layouts (if you don't believe me, look at the example captions to the right). For details, snag a copy of Robin Williams's classic book *The Mac is not a typewriter.*

Rules for classy looking text:

- Put only one space after periods, commas, question marks, parentheses, or any other punctuation.
- Use true quotation marks (" ") instead of double hash marks (" "). To get them, type Option [and Option Shift [.
- Use true apostrophes (' ') instead of hash marks (' '). To get them, type Option [and Option Shift [.
- Punctuation goes inside quotes.
- Instead of double hyphens (--), use an em dash (—) by typing Option Shift -.
- If you want to put a copyright symbol (©) in your book instead of (c), get it by typing Option G.
- To make a list, use bullets (•) rather than asterisks (*). To type a bullet, press Option 8.
- In text boxes that have relatively long lines of text, edit to prevent the last line from containing only a single word.
- Avoid underlining text if possible. Unfortunately, iPhoto can't italicize a single word, which is the usual approach.
- Use uppercase sparingly, and only in titles. Uppercase text is hard to read.

The Wrong Way

Here it's a cold afternoon in March. Mary is gazing out over the GRAND CANYON at sunset--check out the sweater Grandma Bunny actually knitted
for her. The other folks in this picture are:

* My friend Samuel from work.

* Mary's cousin JoAnn.

* JoAnn's husband, who goes by "Chuck".

Copyright (c) 2002 Joe Schmoe

The Right Way

Here it's a cold afternoon in March. Mary is gazing out over the Grand Canyon at sunset—check out the sweater Grandma Bunny actually knitted for her. The other folks in this picture are:

• My friend Samuel from work.

• Mary's cousin JoAnn.

• JoAnn's husband, who goes by "Chuck."

Copyright © 2002 Joe Schmoe

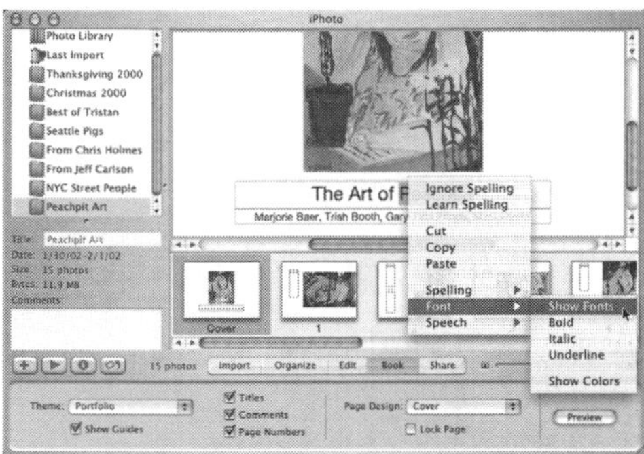
iPhoto
Photo Library
Last Import
Thanksgiving 2000
Christmas 2000
Best of Tristan
Seattle Pigs
From Chris Holmes
From Jeff Carlson
NYC Street People
Peachpit Art
The Art of
Ignore Spelling
Learn Spelling
Cut
Copy
Paste
Spelling
Font
Speech
Show Fonts
Bold
Italic
Underline
Show Colors
Import
Organize
Edit
Book
Share
Titles
Comments
Page Numbers
Show Guides
Lock Page
Preview

Figure 4.13 To change fonts and styles, first Control-click a text box, and from the hierarchical Font menu, choose Show Fonts.

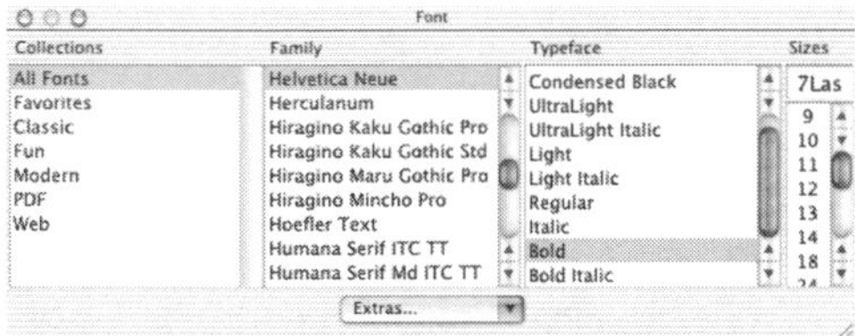
Font
Collections
Family
Typeface
Sizes
All Fonts
Favorites
Classic
Fun
Modern
PDF
Web
Helvetica Neue
Herculanum
Hiragino Kaku Gothic Pro
Hiragino Kaku Gothic Std
Hiragino Maru Gothic Pro
Hiragino Mincho Pro
Hoefler Text
Humana Serif ITC TT
Humana Serif Md ITC TT
Condensed Black
UltraLight
UltraLight Italic
Light
Light Italic
Regular
Italic
Bold
Bold Italic
Extras...

Figure 4.14 Then, from the Font panel, click a collection in the Collections column if you want to narrow the selection of fonts, click a font in the Family column, and choose a style from the Typeface column. Ignore the Sizes column—you can't change sizes in iPhoto.

Forcing a Refresh

Sometimes a font or style change will affect the current caption text box, for instance, but won't seem to affect all the others on the page. To force iPhoto to refresh the display, switch to another page thumbnail and then switch back.

Changing Fonts and Styles

iPhoto doesn't let you modify font size to increase the likelihood that your text will fit in the provided text boxes. But you can change the font and style of text boxes.

To change fonts and styles (I):

1. From the Edit menu's Font menu, choose Show Fonts (Cmd T), or Control-click a text box and from the hierarchical Font menu, choose Show Fonts (**Figure 4.13**).

   iPhoto opens the Font panel (**Figure 4.14**).

2. Click a text box (not necessary if you chose Show Fonts from the contextual menu), from the Family column, choose a font, and, if there are multiple choices in the Typeface column, choose a style.

   iPhoto changes the text of the current text box and all others like it (such as all titles or all comments).

To change fonts and styles (II):

1. Select text that has a font and style that you want to copy for another text box, and from the Edit menu's Font menu, choose Copy Font (Cmd 3).

2. Select all the text (Cmd A) in the text box which you want to take on the font and style used in the first text box, and from the Edit menu's Font menu, choose Paste Font (Cmd 4).

   iPhoto copies the font and style settings to the second text box and others like it.

✔ Tip

- This second method is a fast way to make different types of text boxes use the same font and style, which is always a safe design choice.

Changing Styles

iPhoto also provides several ways to change just the style of text.

To change styles (I):

- Click a text box, and from the Edit menu's hierarchical Fonts menu, choose Bold or Italic.

  iPhoto changes all the text in that text box and all others like it (such as all titles or all comments) to the selected style.

To change styles (II):

- Control-click either a text box or selected text within the box, and choose Bold, Italic, or Underline from the contextual Font menu.

  For Bold and Italic, iPhoto changes all the text in that text box and all others like it (such as all titles or all comments) to the selected style. With Underline, iPhoto underlines just the selected text in the text box.

✔ Tips

- Bold and Italic are dimmed in the menus if the current font has no Bold or Italic typeface. Check the Font panel to verify.
- Unfortunately, iPhoto does not provide keyboard shortcuts for styles.

Wacky Style Behavior

When it comes to fonts and styles, iPhoto 1.0 and 1.1.1 exhibit some odd behavior that I hope Apple will fix or clarify in a future version of the program.

- Bold and Italic are available from both the Edit menu's Fonts menu and the contextual Fonts menu, but Underline exists only in the contextual menu.
- Bold and Italic apply to the entire text box, but Underline applies only to text that you have selected in one text box.
- If a font has Bold and Italic styles, but no Bold Italic combination, you can switch from Bold to Italic using the menus, but not from Italic to Bold without first turning off Italic. It's a bug, not a feature.
- When you paste a font using the Paste Font command, the pasted font will initially appear in the size of the original, but iPhoto resets it to the default font size when you click out of the text box.

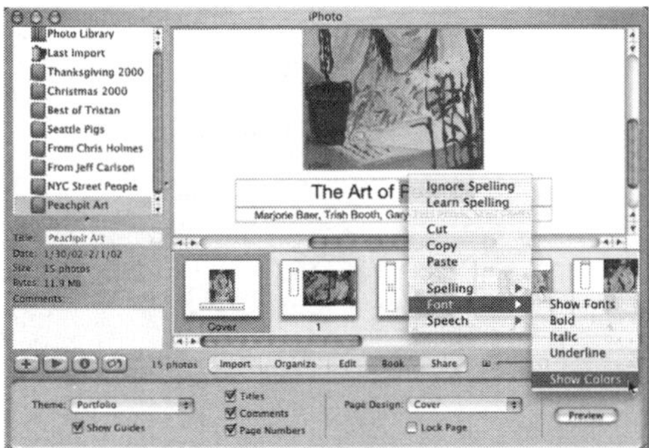
Photo Library
Last Import
Thanksgiving 2000
Christmas 2000
Best of Tristan
Seattle Pigs
From Chris Holmes
From Jeff Carlson
NYC Street People
Peachpit Art
The Art of
Ignore Spelling
Learn Spelling
Cut
Copy
Paste
Spelling
Font
Speech
Show Fonts
Bold
Italic
Underline
Show Colors

Figure 4.15 To open the Colors panel, Control-click a text box, and from the hierarchical Font menu, choose Show Colors.

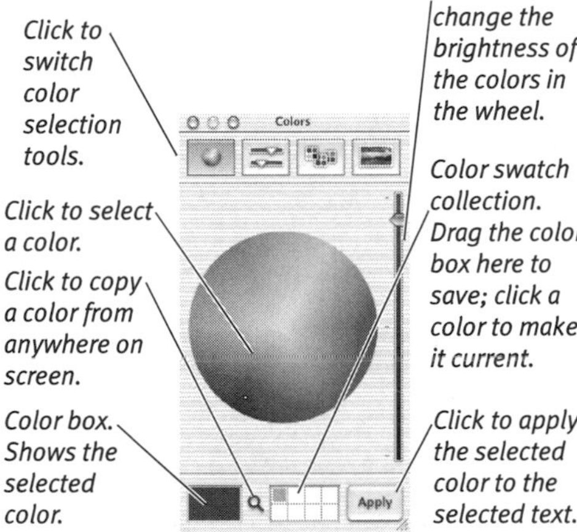
Click to switch color selection tools.
Click to select a color.
Click to copy a color from anywhere on screen.
Color box. Shows the selected color.
Click to change the brightness of the colors in the wheel.
Color swatch collection. Drag the color box here to save; click a color to make it current.
Click to apply the selected color to the selected text.
Colors
Apply

Figure 4.16 Click a color in the color wheel to put it in the color box, and then click the Apply button to apply it to the selected text.

Changing Text Color

Although it's not obvious, you can change the color of text. Unfortunately, a bug in iPhoto 1.0 and 1.1.1 prevents these changes from sticking, so don't bother trying to use these instructions until Apple fixes the bug.

To change colors:

1. To open the Colors panel, Control-click a text box and choose Show Colors from the Font menu (**Figure 4.15**).

   or

   From the Extras pop-up menu in the Font panel, choose Color.

   iPhoto opens the Colors panel (**Figure 4.16**).
2. Select the text to which you want to apply a color, click a color in the color wheel, and click the Apply button.

   iPhoto changes the color of the text.

✔ Tips

- The Colors panel offers four different color selection tools. Unless you understand the others, stick with the color wheel.
- To copy a color from elsewhere on the screen to the color box, click the magnifying glass icon, and then click a color anywhere on the screen.
- Drag the color box to one of the cells of the color swatch collection to save it for repeated use. Clicking one of the color swatches selects it, and clicking Apply applies it to the selected text.
- Use color carefully and sparingly—it's far too easy to make a book garish by applying too much color. You don't want your text to compete with your photos.
- Copying fonts also copies colors.

Checking Spelling

You won't be typing much in iPhoto, but since its editing environment is fairly crude, typos are likely. The last thing you want in a beautifully designed book of great photos is a glaring typo, so I recommend you check the spelling of your titles and captions using iPhoto's spelling checker.

To check spelling (I):

1. To open the Spelling panel, Control-click a text box and from the Spelling menu, choose Spelling (**Figure 4.17**).

   or

   Click a text box, and from the Edit menu's Spelling menu, choose Spelling (Cmd :).

   iPhoto opens the Spelling panel (**Figure 4.18**).
2. Click the Find Next button to select the first misspelled word.
3. To replace the misspelled word with one of iPhoto's guesses, double-click the guess, or click the word, and then click the Correct button. You can also edit the misspelled word or type a new one in the Spelling panel before clicking Correct.

   To ignore the misspelled word for only this spell checking session, click Ignore.

   To add the word to your system-wide Mac OS X dictionary, click Learn.

To check spelling (II):

1. Click a text box, and from the Edit menu's Spelling menu, choose Spelling (Cmd ;).

   iPhoto underlines the next misspelled word.
2. Control-click the word and choose a replacement word, Ignore Spelling, or Learn Spelling from the pop-up menu.

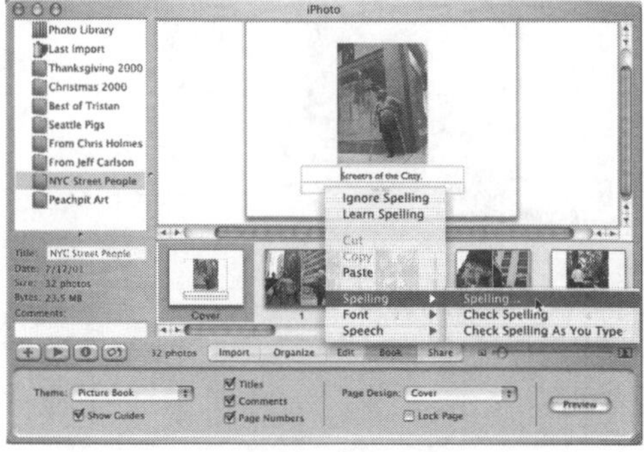
Ignore Spelling
Learn Spelling
Paste
Spelling
Font
Speech
Check Spelling
Check Spelling As You Type

Figure 4.17 To open the Spelling panel, Control-click a text box and from the Spelling menu, choose Spelling.

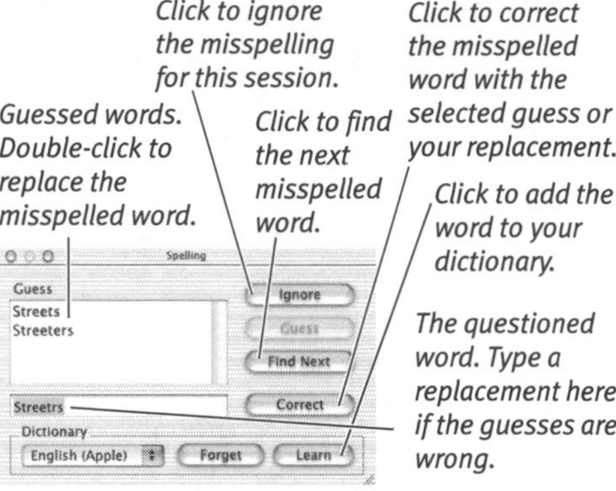
Click to ignore the misspelling for this session.
Click to correct the misspelled word with the selected guess or your replacement.
Guessed words. Double-click to replace the misspelled word.
Click to find the next misspelled word.
Click to add the word to your dictionary.
The questioned word. Type a replacement here if the guesses are wrong.
Spelling
Guess
Streets
Streeters
Ignore
Guess
Find Next
Correct
Streetrs
Dictionary
English (Apple)
Forget
Learn

Figure 4.18 Use the controls in the Spelling panel to replace misspelled words, ignore them for this session, or add them to your user dictionary so they won't be flagged as misspelled ever again.

The Best Strategy for Checking Spelling

iPhoto's implementation of Mac OS X's spelling tools is crude at best. Since you can check only one text box at a time, and iPhoto won't move from one to the next, the easiest approach to checking an entire book is to click in a text box, use the keyboard shortcut for Check Spelling, and then use the contextual menu to correct, ignore, or learn the word.

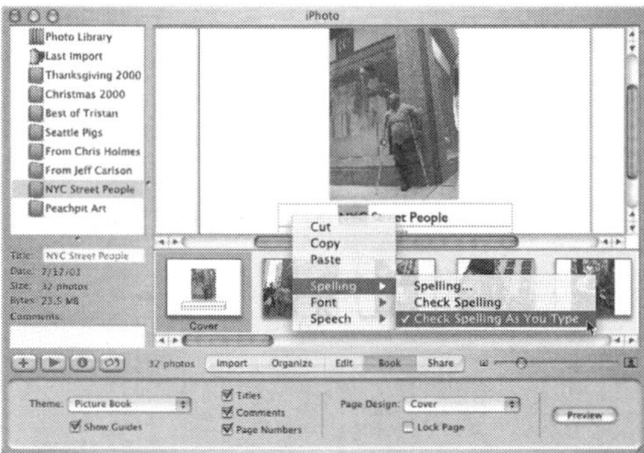
iPhoto
Photo Library
Last Import
Thanksgiving 2000
Christmas 2000
Best of Tristan
Seattle Pigs
From Chris Holmes
From Jeff Carlson
NYC Street People
Peachpit Art
Cut
Copy
Paste
Spelling
Font
Speech
Spelling...
Check Spelling
Check Spelling As You Type
Import
Organize
Edit
Book
Share
Preview

Figure 4.19 To make iPhoto mark misspelled words as you type, Control-click a text box and choose Check Spelling As You Type from the Spelling menu.

Streest of the Coty.

Figure 4.20 Note how iPhoto has underlined the misspelled words that I've typed. If we were in Oz rather than in a black-and-white book, the underlines would be red too, as they are on my screen.

iPhoto
Photo Library
Last Import
Thanksgiving 2000
Christmas 2000
Best of Tristan
Seattle Pigs
From Chris Holmes
From Jeff Carlson
NYC Street People
Peachpit Art
Streets
Streeters
Ignore Spelling
Learn Spelling
Cut
Copy
Paste
Spelling
Font
Speech
Preview

Figure 4.21 To replace a misspelled word with one of iPhoto's guesses, Control-click the word and choose a guess from the contextual menu that appears. You can also ignore the misspelling for the session or add the word to your dictionary.

Checking Spelling As You Type

Although you don't do much typing in iPhoto, you can have the program check your spelling automatically while you type.

To check spelling as you type:

1. Control-click a text box and from the Spelling menu, choose Check Spelling As You Type (**Figure 4.19**).

   or

   Click a text box, and from the Edit menu's Spelling menu, choose Check Spelling As You Type.

2. Type your text.

   iPhoto displays a red line underneath any words that aren't in the system-wide Mac OS X spelling dictionary (**Figure 4.20**).

3. Control-click a word with a red underline to display a contextual menu that enables you to replace the word with one of iPhoto's guesses, ignore the misspelling for this spell checking session, or have iPhoto learn the spelling by adding it to your system-wide Mac OS X dictionary (**Figure 4.21**).

✔ Tips

- Unfortunately, iPhoto keeps the Check Spelling As You Type setting active only for the currently selected text box, which changes when you switch to another page. In short, it's useless unless you're typing a large chunk of text on a book's Introduction page.
- Since iPhoto ends a spell checking session when you switch pages, Ignore Spelling is useless—if you check that text box again later, iPhoto will have forgotten that you ignored the word.

Previewing Books

You'll certainly want to preview what you've done before having your book printed at $3 per page.

To preview a book:

- Either double-click a page thumbnail or click the Preview button on the right side of the book pane (**Figure 4.22**).

  iPhoto opens a new window that shows only the contents of the current book page, along with controls for moving between pages and a checkbox that shows or hides the outlines of text boxes (**Figure 4.23**).

✔ Tips

- You can enter and edit text in the preview window just as though you were working in the display pane. Working in the preview window may prove easier than using the display pane.
- Turn off the guides by deselecting the Show Guides checkbox for a better representation of what your page will look like.
- You can leave the preview window open behind the main iPhoto window and it will change as you switch pages. If it doesn't reflect a change you've made, switch pages to force an update.

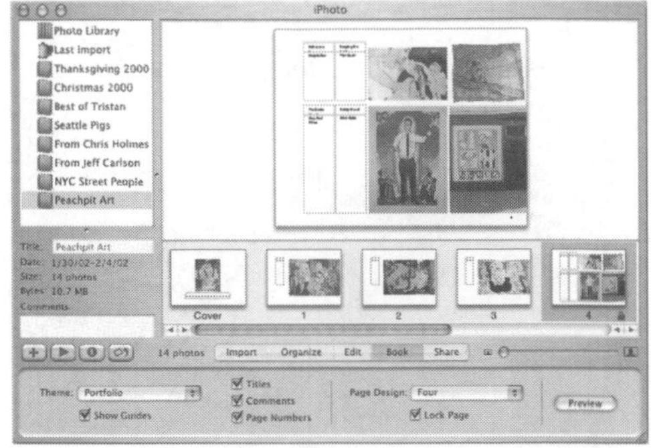
iPhoto
Photo Library
Last Import
Thanksgiving 2000
Christmas 2000
Best of Tristan
Seattle Pigs
From Chris Holmes
From Jeff Carlson
NYC Street People
Peachpit Art
Cover
Import
Organize
Edit
Book
Share
Theme:
Portfolio
Show Guides
Titles
Comments
Page Numbers
Page Design:
Four
Lock Page
Preview

Figure 4.22 To preview a book, either double-click a page thumbnail or click the Preview button in the book pane.

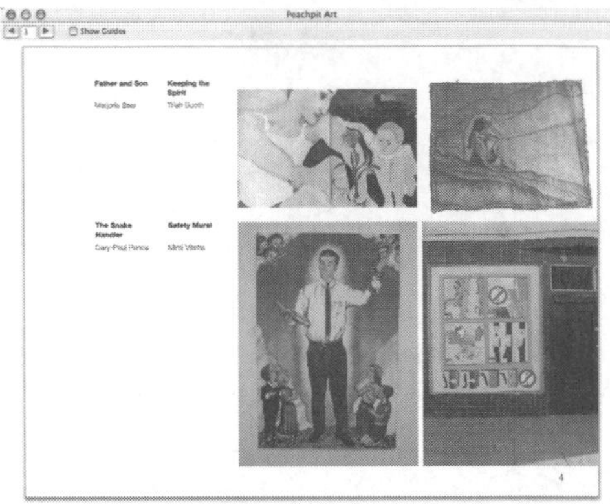
Peachpit Art
Show Guides
Father and Son
Keeping the Spirit
The Snake Handler
Safety Mural

Figure 4.23 The preview window shows exactly what your pages will look like. Click the arrows at the top to switch pages, or enter a page number and press Return or Tab to go to a specific page. Click the Show Guides checkbox to see the text box outlines.

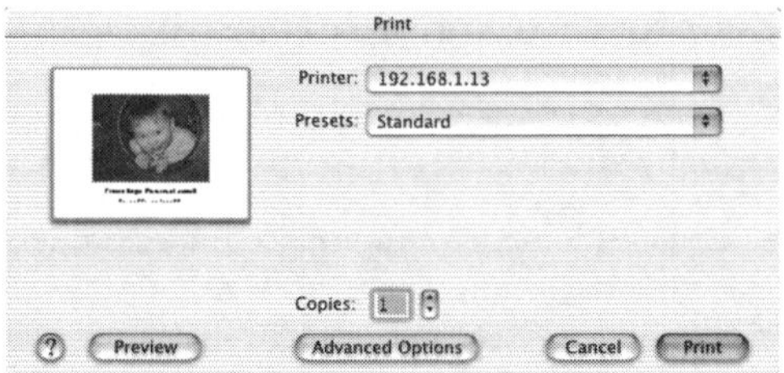
Print
Printer: 192.168.1.13
Presets: Standard
Copies: 1
Preview
Advanced Options
Cancel
Print

Figure 4.24 To print a book on your own printer, make sure you're in book mode, then choose Print from the File menu to open the Print dialog. For additional options, such as a custom page range, click the Advanced Options button.

Printing Books on Your Own Printer

iPhoto makes it easy to preview a book on screen, and it's equally as easy to print a book on your own printer. Printing on your own printer is not only a good way to see what your book will look like on paper, it's also a great way to print multiple photos on a page with more control over text and size than you get when printing using iPhoto's normal printing options.

To print a book on your own printer:

1. Making sure you're in book mode, choose Print from the File menu (Cmd P).
   iPhoto displays the standard Print dialog (**Figure 4.24**).
2. For additional options, click Advanced Options, choose the options you want, and click the Print button.

✔ Tips

- To print only one or two of the pages in your book, click Advanced Options and enter the appropriate page numbers in the Print dialog's Pages fields. Be sure to add one to the page number iPhoto displays underneath the page thumbnails, since it doesn't count the cover page, but your printer will.
- Remember that you can also click the Preview button in the Print dialog to generate a PDF instead of printing. I like to do this before printing to double-check that I entered the correct page numbers. You can even save the PDF from Apple's Preview application for sending to a friend.

Ordering Books

For instructions on how to order books from Apple, read "Ordering Books" in Chapter 5, "Sharing Photos."

Catalog Book Example and Ideas

The obvious use for iPhoto's Catalog theme is for a catalog listing products with names and descriptions. The grid-like layout works well for giving each item an equal amount of space with plenty of room for text. Catalogs are often throwaway items, so it might make sense to print catalogs on your own printer rather than paying $3 per page, although getting one copy printed by Apple could make a good historical record of your sales. Along with the cover and introduction pages, you can have one, four, and eight photo layouts (**Figure 4.25**).

Here I've used the Catalog theme for my prized collection of penguin mugs, which are definitely not for sale!

Ideas for the Catalog theme:

- Photos of expensive pieces for sale at a fancy auction.
- Object identification images for a teacher trying to familiarize a class with similar objects, such as bark and leaves from different types of trees.
- Photos showing houses sold by a real estate agent for prospective clients.
- Pictures of your possessions for a home inventory (print on your own printer).

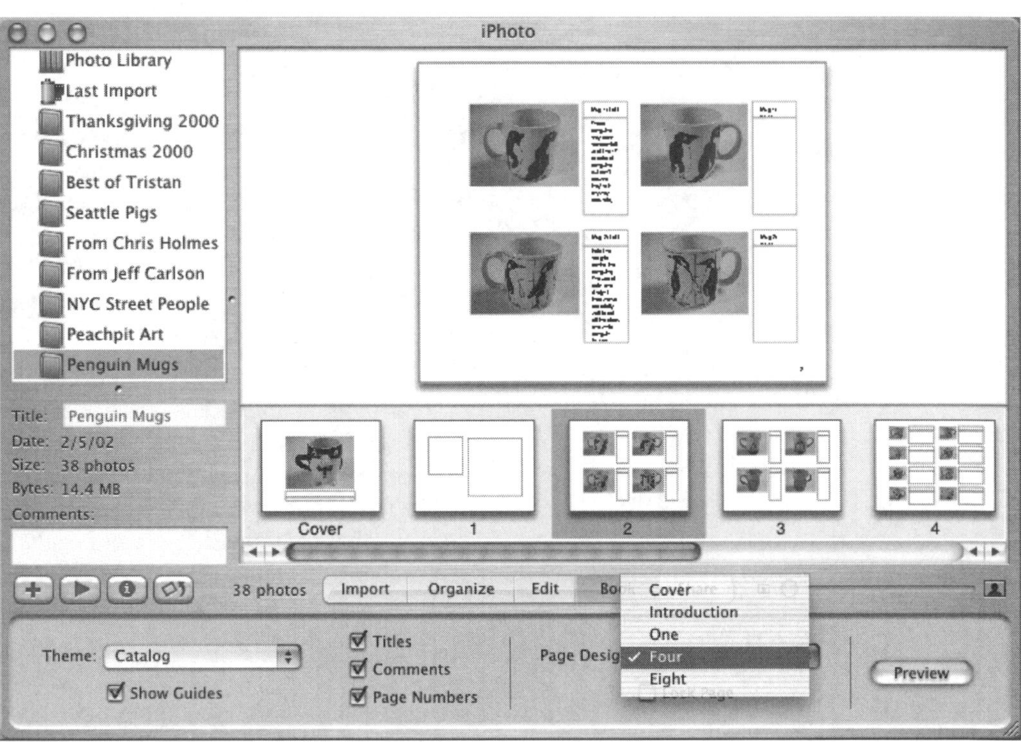
iPhoto
Photo Library
Last Import
Thanksgiving 2000
Christmas 2000
Best of Tristan
Seattle Pigs
From Chris Holmes
From Jeff Carlson
NYC Street People
Peachpit Art
Penguin Mugs
Title: Penguin Mugs
Date: 2/5/02
Size: 38 photos
Bytes: 14.4 MB
Comments:
Cover
1
2
3
4
38 photos
Import
Organize
Edit
Cover
Introduction
One
Four
Eight
Theme: Catalog
Show Guides
Titles
Comments
Page Numbers
Page Desig
Preview

Figure 4.25 Catalog theme example.

Classic Book Example and Ideas

With the Classic theme, iPhoto attempts to mimic traditional photo albums, with a regular layout and both titles and captions underneath each picture. The Classic theme isn't exciting, but it's perfect for kid or trip photo collections where you need to add some commentary (which isn't possible in the Picture Book theme). Rearranging photos can result in more interesting layouts; play with it for a while. Page designs include the cover, an optional introduction page, and pages containing one, two, three, and four photos (**Figure 4.26**).

My example below shows the classic kid photo collection, with my own personal classic kid, Tristan.

Ideas for the Classic theme:

- Pictures of far-flung relatives so parents can help a small child learn what his or her family looks like. (We did this with Tristan, and it was a great success for helping him recognize relatives he saw infrequently.)
- Photos of appropriate people as a gift for a significant milestone, like a retirement party or 50th wedding anniversary.

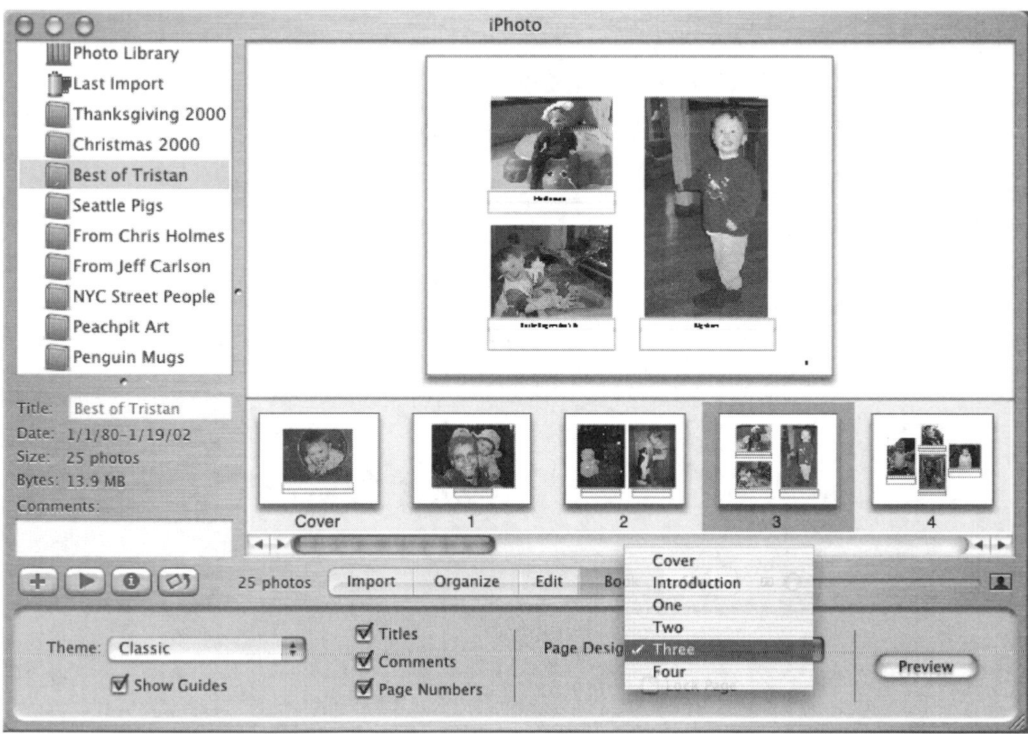
iPhoto
Photo Library
Last Import
Thanksgiving 2000
Christmas 2000
Best of Tristan
Seattle Pigs
From Chris Holmes
From Jeff Carlson
NYC Street People
Peachpit Art
Penguin Mugs
Title: Best of Tristan
Date: 1/1/80-1/19/02
Size: 25 photos
Bytes: 13.9 MB
Comments:
Cover
1
2
3
4
25 photos
Import
Organize
Edit
Cover
Introduction
One
Two
Three
Four
Theme: Classic
Show Guides
Titles
Comments
Page Numbers
Page Desig
Preview

Figure 4.26 Classic theme example.

Picture Book Example and Ideas

iPhoto's Picture Book theme is ideal for books in which you don't want any text distracting the reader from the images. Plus, in the Picture Book theme, the photos use more of the page than in any other theme. You can choose from page designs containing one, two, three, and four image layouts along with the cover and introduction (**Figure 4.27**).

Here I've used it for my black-and-white pictures of people on the streets of New York City; I don't have anything particular to say about individual images, and the faces and poses speak for themselves.

Ideas for the Picture Book theme:

- Art photos that aren't improved or explained by titles and captions.
- Photos of extremely familiar subjects (such as kid pictures) that don't need captions or that were taken so close together that the cover or introduction text is sufficient.
- Real estate photos of a house and property in different seasons and times of day. A classy iPhoto book would be an improvement on the photo albums that many real estate agents do now.

iPhoto
Photo Library
Last Import
Thanksgiving 2000
Christmas 2000
Best of Tristan
Seattle Pigs
From Chris Holmes
From Jeff Carlson
NYC Street People
Peachpit Art
Title: NYC Street People
Date: 7/17/01
Size: 32 photos
Bytes: 23.5 MB
Comments:
Cover
1
2
3
4
32 photos
Import
Organize
Edit
Cover
Introduction
One
Two
Three
Four
Theme: Picture Book
Show Guides
Titles
Comments
Page Numbers
Page Desig
Preview

Figure 4.27 Picture Book theme example.

Portfolio Book Example and Ideas

iPhoto's Portfolio theme is clearly aimed at anyone who needs a classy, hardcover portfolio of their work. Like the Picture Book theme, the Portfolio theme tries to show images at the largest sizes reasonable, but it also includes text boxes for titles and captions. Aside from the cover and introduction, page designs in the Portfolio theme include one, two, three, and four photo layouts (**Figure 4.28**).

Below is a Portfolio book showing off the original art created by four of the creative and talented people at Peachpit Press: Marjorie Baer, Trish Booth, Gary-Paul Prince, and Mimi Vitetta.

Ideas for the Portfolio theme:

- Photos of an artist's work that need titles and captions. Many artists use portfolios that aren't as classy as an iPhoto book, so it could be a nice step up.
- A collection of photos of the pieces from a specific gallery or museum show.
- Pictures of crafts to show additional work not present at a crafts fair booth.
- Digital photos of a small child's artwork, so you can remember it without keeping reams of paper in the attic for the rest of time.

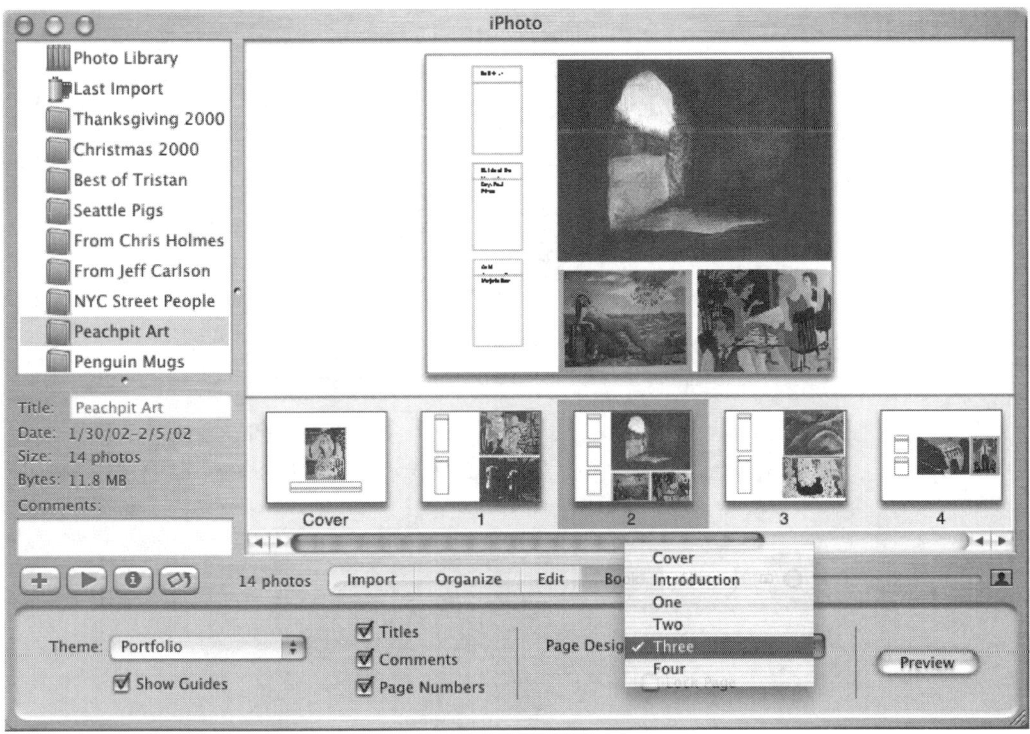
iPhoto
Photo Library
Last Import
Thanksgiving 2000
Christmas 2000
Best of Tristan
Seattle Pigs
From Chris Holmes
From Jeff Carlson
NYC Street People
Peachpit Art
Penguin Mugs
Title: Peachpit Art
Date: 1/30/02-2/5/02
Size: 14 photos
Bytes: 11.8 MB
Comments:
Cover
1
2
3
4
14 photos
Import
Organize
Edit
Cover
Introduction
One
Two
Three
Four
Theme: Portfolio
Show Guides
Titles
Comments
Page Numbers
Preview

Figure 4.28 Portfolio theme example.

Story Book Example and Ideas

Most of the other themes are quite formal, but not the Story Book theme. Photos appear at angles, overlap, and share a single text box per page. Photo placement can also change radically with different sized pictures. Be careful the overlap doesn't cover important parts of a photo—it's worth previewing books using this theme carefully. Available page designs include the cover and a unique introduction page that has photos on it, pages with one, two, or three images, and an ending page with a text box underneath the images (**Figure 4.29**).

Here I've used the Story Book theme for a chronological set of photos from our Thanksgiving trip in 2000.

Ideas for the Story Book theme:

- Pictures of a trip, complete with the story of what's happening in each set of pictures.
- Pictures of local attractions for guests at a bed & breakfast to use when planning excursions for the day. (Think of it as a high-class brochure.)
- Photos of a child's favorite objects acting out a simple story.
- Snapshots from a family reunion or other significant party, made available for guests as a party favor.

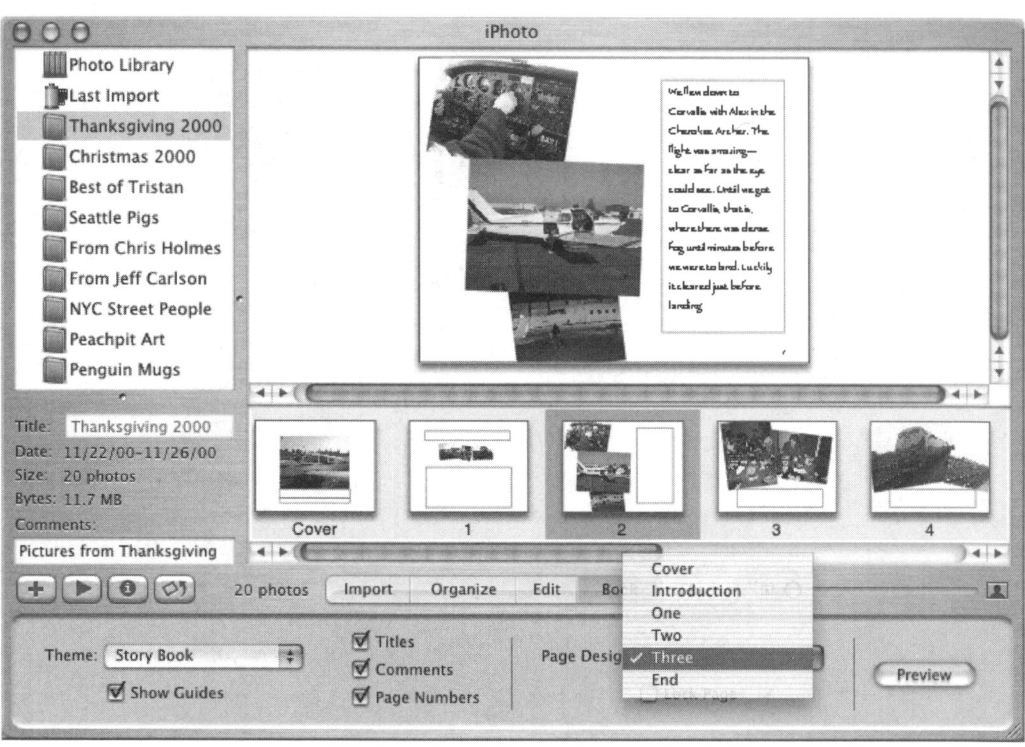
iPhoto
Photo Library
Last Import
Thanksgiving 2000
Christmas 2000
Best of Tristan
Seattle Pigs
From Chris Holmes
From Jeff Carlson
NYC Street People
Peachpit Art
Penguin Mugs
Title: Thanksgiving 2000
Date: 11/22/00-11/26/00
Size: 20 photos
Bytes: 11.7 MB
Comments:
Pictures from Thanksgiving
Cover
1
2
3
4
20 photos
Import
Organize
Edit
Cover
Introduction
One
Two
Three
End
Theme: Story Book
Show Guides
Titles
Comments
Page Numbers
Page Desig
Preview

Figure 4.29 Story Book theme example.

Year Book Example and Ideas

Like the Catalog theme, the Year Book theme offers a highly regularized grid-like layout. In fact, the four-photo page design is almost identical between the two themes. But the Year Book theme goes on to offer page designs that include many more images on a page. Aside from cover and introduction pages, you can design pages that have one, two, four, six, eight, twelve, eighteen, twenty, and even thirty-two photos on a page. The traditional yearbook, with names and descriptions, is the obvious use for this theme (**Figure 4.30**).

The mug shots collected here are of some of the fine folks at Peachpit Press.

Ideas for the Year Book theme:

- Photos of the members of a sports team, day care, scout troop, music class, or any other group that might want a record of the faces of its participants, either for the organizer of the group (such as a day care provider wanting to remember the kids each year) or the members (such as folks who want to remember a championship team).
- Annual photos of everyone in a family, so everyone in the family can keep up with how their relatives change over the years.

iPhoto
Photo Library
Last Import
Thanksgiving 2000
Christmas 2000
Best of Tristan
Seattle Pigs
From Chris Holmes
From Jeff Carlson
NYC Street People
Peachpit Art
Penguin Mugs
Peachpit People
The People of Peachpit
Title: Peachpit People
Date: 06 Feb 2002
Size: 24 photos
Bytes: 28.5 MB
Cover
1
4
Cover
Introduction
One
Two
Four
Six
Eight
Twelve
Eighteen
Twenty
Thirty Two
24 photos
Import
Organize
Edit
Theme: Year Book
Show Guides
Titles
Comments
Page Numbers
Preview

Figure 4.30 Year Book theme example.

5

Sharing Photos

I can imagine an avant-garde photo exhibit where all the frames are empty, because the artist is making a statement about his reluctance to transfer art from the hidden world of the camera to the open light of day. Luckily, I'm sure no one reading this book would suffer from such intellectual foolishness. We take pictures to look at them, and to share them with our family, friends, colleagues, and customers.

iPhoto shines when it comes to sharing photos. It lets you print photos on your own printer, run custom slide shows accompanied by music, email photos to friends, order higher quality prints than you may be able to coax out of your printer, order the books we created in the last chapter, publish photos on Apple's free Web-based iTools HomePage service, create custom screen savers, export pictures to individual files, create Web pages for posting on your own Web site, and even generate QuickTime movie slide shows that you can share with anyone.

For the most part, Apple has done a good job of implementing these features, although I'll help you avoid some pitfalls and use some other programs and plug-ins that extend iPhoto's flexibility and power.

Entering Share Mode

Share mode isn't particularly special—it merely provides access to buttons that start the process of sharing photos in different ways. In fact, other than those buttons in the share pane, the rest of the iPhoto window looks and acts as though it were still in the mode it was in before you clicked the Share button.

To enter share mode:

- At any time, click the Share button under the display pane (**Figure 5.1**).

✔ Tips

- You can run a slide show without switching into share mode. Just select an album or some individual photos, and then click the triangular slide show button under the album pane.
- Some of share mode's functions are accessible from the File menu even when you're in other modes (**Figure 5.2**). You can print photos at any time by selecting one or more photos (or an entire album) and choosing Print from the File menu (Cmd P)—it's the same as clicking the Print button in the share pane. Also, choosing Export from the File menu (Cmd E) is another way to display the Export Images dialog.
- One function that would seem to be appropriate to share mode is almost entirely hidden in book mode. You can print copies of books on your own printer, but the only way to do so is to choose Print from the File menu (Cmd P) when you're in book mode.

Import
Organize
Edit
Book
Share

Figure 5.1 To switch into share mode, click the Share button under the display pane.

File
New Album ⌘N
Import...
Export... ⌘E
Show Info ⌘I
Duplicate ⌘D
Revert to Original
Page Setup... ⇧⌘P
Print... ⌘P

Figure 5.2 To access printing and exporting features without switching into share mode, choose Print or Export from the File menu.

Share Tools Overview

Most of what you do in share mode takes place in windows and dialogs that appear when you click the buttons in the share pane (**Figure 5.3**). The rest of the window acts as though you were still in whatever mode you were in before clicking Share.

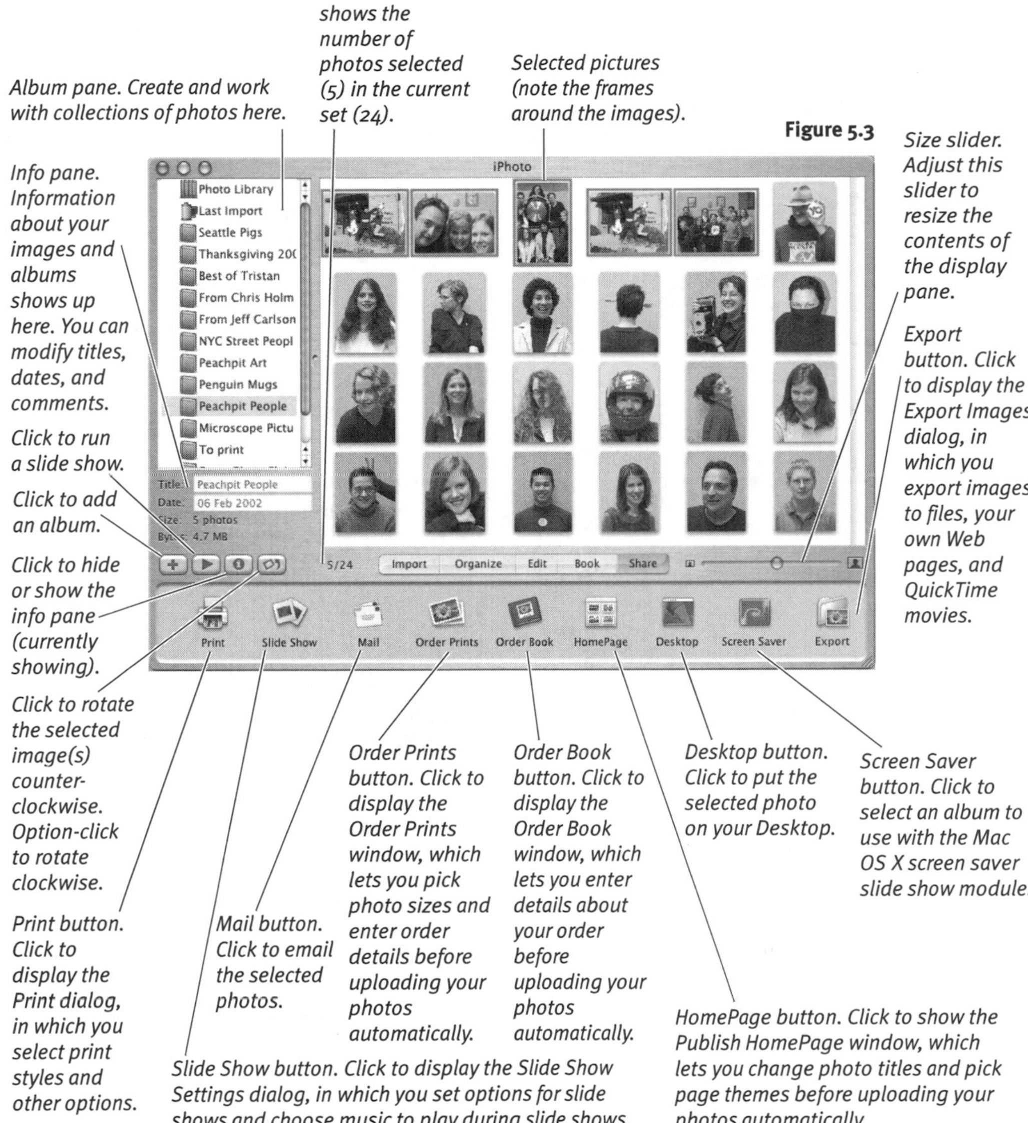
Album pane. Create and work with collections of photos here.
This indicator shows the number of photos selected (5) in the current set (24).
Selected pictures (note the frames around the images).
Size slider. Adjust this slider to resize the contents of the display pane.
Export button. Click to display the Export Images dialog, in which you export images to files, your own Web pages, and QuickTime movies.
Info pane. Information about your images and albums shows up here. You can modify titles, dates, and comments.
Click to run a slide show.
Click to add an album.
Click to hide or show the info pane (currently showing).
Click to rotate the selected image(s) counter-clockwise. Option-click to rotate clockwise.
Print button. Click to display the Print dialog, in which you select print styles and other options.
Mail button. Click to email the selected photos.
Order Prints button. Click to display the Order Prints window, which lets you pick photo sizes and enter order details before uploading your photos automatically.
Order Book button. Click to display the Order Book window, which lets you enter details about your order before uploading your photos automatically.
Desktop button. Click to put the selected photo on your Desktop.
Screen Saver button. Click to select an album to use with the Mac OS X screen saver slide show module.
HomePage button. Click to show the Publish HomePage window, which lets you change photo titles and pick page themes before uploading your photos automatically.
Slide Show button. Click to display the Slide Show Settings dialog, in which you set options for slide shows and choose music to play during slide shows.
iPhoto
Photo Library
Last Import
Seattle Pigs
Best of Tristan
From Chris Holm
From Jeff Carlson
Peachpit Art
Penguin Mugs
Peachpit People
To print
Title: Peachpit People
Date: 06 Feb 2002
5 photos
4.7 MB
5/24
Import
Organize
Edit
Book
Share
Print
Slide Show
Mail
Order Prints
Order Book
HomePage
Desktop
Screen Saver
Export

Figure 5.3

Share Tools Overview

Printing Photos

Many people prefer to print their own photos on inexpensive color inkjet printers rather than waiting for online orders. Printers may not offer the same level of quality as Kodak's Ofoto processing service, but it's hard to beat the instant gratification.

To print photos:

1. In organize mode, select one or more photos to print.
2. Either choose Print from the File menu (Cmd P), or click the Share button and then the Print button in the share pane.

   iPhoto displays the Print dialog (**Figure 5.4**).
3. From the Presets pop-up menu, choose appropriate settings (the contents are printer-specific). If you don't like the presets, you can access all available settings by clicking Advanced Options.
4. From the Style menu, choose the desired style: contact sheet, full page, greeting card, or standard prints.
5. Set the options for the style you selected.
6. Enter the number of copies to print.
7. Click the Print button.

   iPhoto sends your photos to the printer.

✔ Tips

- In book mode, choosing Print from the File menu lets you print book pages that mix photo sizes on a single page.
- If you see a yellow warning icon in the Print dialog, see "Dealing with Warning Icons" in Chapter 6, "Troubleshooting."
- Photos print at their aspect ratios; iPhoto shrinks images proportionally to make them fit, thus increasing the border size.

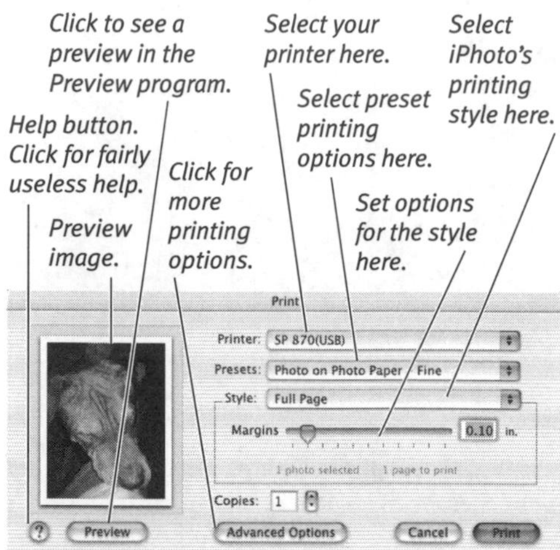
Click to see a preview in the Preview program.
Select your printer here.
Select iPhoto's printing style here.
Select preset printing options here.
Help button. Click for fairly useless help.
Click for more printing options.
Set options for the style here.
Preview image.
Print
Printer:
SP 870(USB)
Presets:
Photo on Photo Paper / Fine
Style:
Full Page
Margins
0.10
in.
Copies:
1
Preview
Advanced Options
Cancel
Print

Figure 5.4 To print photos, select one or more, choose Print from the File menu to display the Print dialog, select your desired options, and click the Print button.

Adding a Printer

If you've never printed from Mac OS X before, follow these steps to add a printer.

1. In the Print dialog, choose Edit Printer List from the Printer pop-up menu to display the Printer List window.
2. Click the Add Printer button to show the printer selection sheet.
3. Choose a printer connection method from the pop-up menu at the top of the sheet.
4. In the area below the pop-up menu, enter printer details or select a printer.
5. Click the Add button to dismiss the sheet.
6. Close the Printer List window.

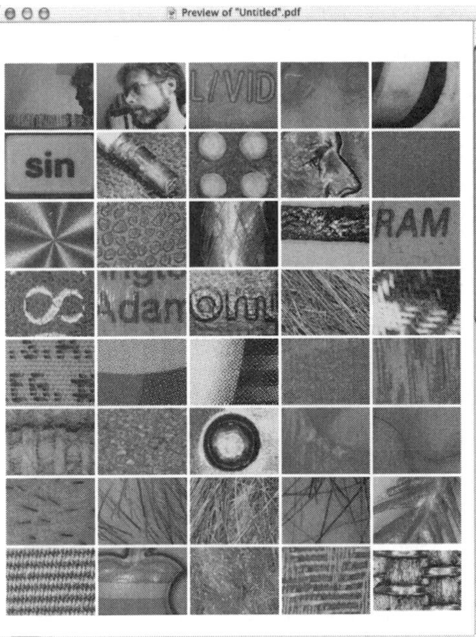

Figure 5.5 To preview a printout in Apple's Preview application (shown above), click Preview in the Print dialog.

Test, Test, Test

Between your printer's driver options, iPhoto's printing capabilities, and Mac OS X's settings in the Page Setup dialog and the ColorSync preferences panel, it may take you several tries to determine the best combination of settings. Some you may be able to try in economy mode on cheap paper, but in the end, you simply may have to expend some ink on a few sheets of expensive photo paper (I certainly did while writing this chapter!). To reduce the waste (and cost), keep good notes about what you did for subsequent printing sessions.

Previewing Prints

Ink and paper for color inkjet printers are expensive, particularly glossy photo paper. If you're unsure about what's going to print, it's easy to preview the output before committing it to expensive paper.

To preview prints:

1. In organize mode, select one or more photos to print.
2. Either choose Print from the File menu (Cmd P), or click the Share button and then the Print button in the share pane to display the Print dialog.
3. Pick a style and set desired options.
4. Click the Preview button.

   iPhoto "prints" the selected photos to a temporary PDF document called "Untitled" and opens it in Apple's Preview application (**Figure 5.5**).
5. Scroll to see multiple pages, and when you're done, close the window.

✔ Tips

- It's especially important to preview prints when printing contact sheets, since the small preview in iPhoto's Print dialog sometimes shows more photos per page than will actually print.
- You can save the temporary document in the Preview application if you want a PDF version.
- Previewing in this fashion won't help you determine if your photos will fit within the margins of your printer. Also, any printer-specific changes you make (such as requiring black ink on a color printer) won't be reflected in the preview. See if your printer has an economy or draft mode you can use to test those features.

Printing Contact Sheets

The first printing style iPhoto offers is the Contact Sheet style, which prints multiple images per sheet of paper (**Figure 5.6**).

Print
Printer: SP 870(USB)
Presets: Photo on Plain Paper
Style: Contact Sheet
Across
3
Save paper
52 photos selected 4 pages to print
Copies: 1
Preview
Advanced Options
Cancel
Print

Figure 5.6 iPhoto's Contact Sheet style prints multiple images per sheet of paper.

Uses for contact sheets

- Contact sheets are traditionally used to look at a number of photos at once. You can do that in iPhoto's display pane, of course, but there may still be uses for a printed contact sheet. For instance, you could show one to relatives who don't have a computer, let them choose some photos, and order prints for them.
- You can buy special paper for stickers or decals, so printing a contact sheet could be an easy way to make custom stickers. You don't have enough control in iPhoto to print on perforated sticker stock, so you'll have to cut out the stickers.

✔ Tips

- If you select only one photo and print a contact sheet, iPhoto replicates the image to as many spots on the page as are available.
- The maximum number of photos to print across the page is eight.
- If you care about how many thumbnails print per piece of paper, preview the print job first, since the small preview in the Print dialog isn't always accurate.
- For more white space between photos, deselect the Save paper checkbox.
- If you want titles or comments printed as well, print pages from the Catalog book theme instead of a contact sheet.
- If you see a yellow warning icon in the Print dialog, increase the number of photos per page (which prints the photos at a smaller size).

Print
Printer: SP 870(USB)
Presets: Photo on Plain Paper
Style: Full Page
Margins 0.00 in.
Copies: 1
Preview
Advanced Options
Cancel
Print

Figure 5.7 iPhoto's Full Page style prints a single photo at the largest size that will fit on a piece of paper.

Printing Full-Page Photos

iPhoto's second printing style simply prints each selected photo at the largest size that will fit on a piece of paper (**Figure 5.7**).

Use for full-page prints:

- Anything you want to print as large as possible but don't mind if it doesn't match standard aspect ratios.

✔ Tips

- If a photo's aspect ratio does not match that of your paper, iPhoto shrinks the photo proportionally to make it fit. That has the potentially undesirable effect of increasing the white borders.
- Assuming your printer has the same margin on every side of the paper (not always true), you can enter the paper size into the Custom fields in the image editing window's toolbar before cropping to ensure that iPhoto doesn't shrink the image to fit on the page.
- Don't assume iPhoto can print to your printer's minimum margins. My Epson Stylus Photo 870 claims it has minimum margins of 3mm, but the closest I can get to the edge is 5mm, and the other three sides have 7mm margins. Test a few full-page prints first to make sure you understand what will come out.
- Don't bother entering your printer's minimum margins to get the smallest possible margins; any number (including 0.00) lower than the printer's minimum margins results in a printout that uses as much of the paper as possible within the printer's actual margins.
- If you see a yellow warning icon in the Print dialog, try increasing your margins. Also see "Dealing with Warning Icons" in Chapter 6, "Troubleshooting."

Printing Greeting Cards

iPhoto's third printing style offers two options for printing folded greeting cards (**Figure 5.8**).

Print
Printer: SP 870(USB)
Presets: Photo on Plain Paper
Style: Greeting Card
Style: Single-fold Double-fold
Copies: 1
Preview
Advanced Options
Cancel
Print

Figure 5.8 iPhoto's Greeting Card style lets you choose between single-fold and double-fold greeting cards, but unfortunately doesn't let you enter text.

Uses for greeting cards:

- Print your own holiday cards rather than buying pre-printed ones.
- Make custom birthday cards for friends and family.
- Print invitations to a party.

✔ Tips

- You can choose between single-fold and double-fold greeting cards. Single-fold greeting cards print the photo on half the paper; double-fold greeting cards print the photo on one-quarter of the paper.
- Cropping a photo to an aspect ratio of 8 x 5 increases the size of the photo for a single-fold greeting card. However, cropping to 5.5 x 4.25 for a double-fold greeting card doesn't make a noticeable difference because it's too close to the original aspect ratio of 4 x 3.
- There's no way to prevent photos from printing right at the folded edges.
- iPhoto doesn't let you enter text inside the greeting cards. Doing so is tricky to do correctly, particularly for double-fold cards (for which the text needs to be upside down). If you want to print a lot of greeting cards, buy a copy of Nova Development's $59.95 Print Explosion, which is designed to create greeting cards, along with a wide variety of other printed materials. Find them on the Web at `www.novadevelopment.com`.
- You can buy special paper for greeting cards that's pre-scored for easier and more attractive folding.

Greeting Card Alternatives

Most online photo processors enable you to print customized greeting cards from your photos, and in fact, Kodak's Ofoto service, which is what Apple uses for ordering prints online, also offers this feature. Until iPhoto supports it internally, however, you'll have to upload prints to an online service manually and customize your greeting card on the Web.

To find the file associated with a photo you want to use, either drop the photo onto Apple's Show In Finder AppleScript script to find its location or drag the photo to the Desktop to make a copy that you can delete after uploading. You can download the script from `www.apple.com/applescript/iphoto/`.

Or, of course, you could just write your message by hand inside cards printed from iPhoto!

Print
Printer: SP 870(USB)
Presets: Photo on Plain Paper
Style: Standard Prints
Size: 4x6 5x7 8x10
One photo per page
Copies: 1
Preview
Advanced Options
Cancel
Print

Figure 5.9 iPhoto's Standard Prints style enables you to print photos at traditional sizes so they fit in standard frames and photo albums.

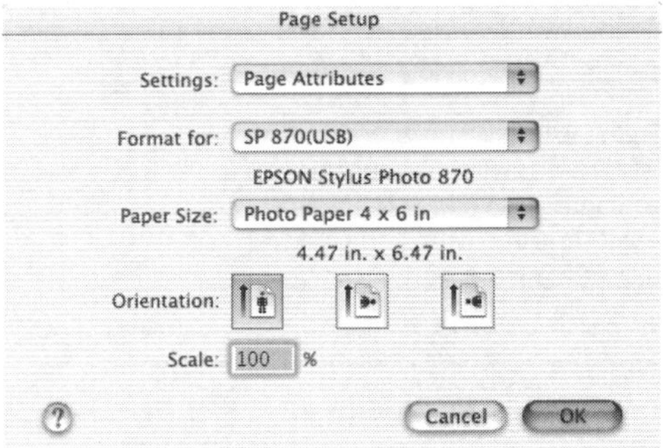
Page Setup
Settings: Page Attributes
Format for: SP 870(USB)
EPSON Stylus Photo 870
Paper Size: Photo Paper 4 x 6 in
4.47 in. x 6.47 in.
Orientation:
Scale: 100 %
Cancel
OK

Figure 5.10 To print on unusual paper sizes, you must first select the appropriate paper size in the Page Setup dialog, accessible by choosing Page Setup from the File menu.

Portraits & Prints

For greater printing flexibility, check out the $19.95 Portraits & Prints program, available at `www.econtechnologies.com`. To import images into Portraits & Prints, drag them onto the Portraits & Prints window from iPhoto. Then you can print your photos using a variety of templates (another $9.95 tool lets you create your own templates), including putting two 4" x 6" or 5" x 7" prints, four 4" x 5" prints, or eight wallet-sized prints on a page. Other templates arrange different sized prints on the same page, much like Apple's book designs. It's pretty neat.

Printing Standard Prints

iPhoto's fourth and final printing style prints photos in three standard sizes: 4" x 6", 5" x 7", and 8" x 10" (**Figure 5.9**).

Uses for standard prints:

- Print photos for inclusion in traditional photo albums that accept only standard size prints.
- Frame your pictures using standard frame sizes.

✔ Tips

- It's important to crop photos to the appropriate aspect ratio before printing, because otherwise iPhoto shrinks the images proportionally to fit, increasing the white borders.
- If you are printing more than one 4" x 6" or 5" x 7" image, deselect the "One photo per page" checkbox to print two per page, thus saving paper.
- You can buy photo paper in sheets of 4" x 6" paper that work with specific brands of printers. However, to print on paper of unusual sizes, you must change the paper size in the Page Setup dialog (**Figure 5.10**). Open it by choosing Page Setup from the File menu (Cmd Shift P) and select the desired paper size.
- If you see a yellow warning icon in the Print dialog, check to see if you get the warning icon in the Full Page style. If not, it's probably spurious; otherwise pick a smaller print size. See "Dealing with Warning Icons" in Chapter 6, "Troubleshooting."

Setting up Slide Shows

A slide show is the easiest way to display your photos while at your computer.

To configure slide shows:

1. From the File menu, choose Preferences (Cmd Y).

   iPhoto opens the Preferences window (**Figure 5.11**).

   or

   Click the Share button, and then click the Slide Show button in the share pane.

   iPhoto opens the Slide Show Settings dialog, which offers the same controls as the Preferences window (**Figure 5.12**).

2. Enter the length of time you want each photo to remain on the screen.

3. Select the "Repeat slide show" checkbox if you want your slide show to loop until you stop it manually.

4. From the Music pop-up menu, select a song (or None) to play while the slide show runs. You can also edit the menu.

To edit the Music menu:

- To add an MP3 song to the Music menu, choose Other and select the desired song in the open file dialog that appears.

- To remove a song, choose Edit List from the Music menu, and in the sheet that appears, select the unwanted song and click Delete (**Figure 5.13**).

✔ Tips

- There's no way to chain songs together or select a folder of songs. The selected song repeats until the slide show finishes.

- iPhoto lets you select only files with .mp3 filename extensions. Isn't Unix great!?

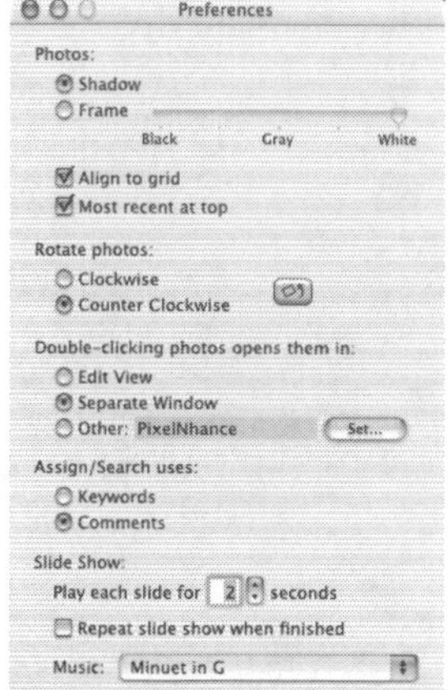
Preferences
Photos:
Shadow
Frame
Black
Gray
White
Align to grid
Most recent at top
Rotate photos:
Clockwise
Counter Clockwise
Double-clicking photos opens them in:
Edit View
Separate Window
Other: PixelNhance
Set...
Assign/Search uses:
Keywords
Comments
Slide Show:
Play each slide for 2 seconds
Repeat slide show when finished
Music: Minuet in G

Figure 5.11 In iPhoto's Preferences window you can configure the slide duration, repetition, and what MP3 song plays during the slide show.

Slide Show Settings
Play each slide for 2 seconds
Repeat slide show
Music: Cool Water
Cancel
OK

Figure 5.12 Alternatively, click the Share button, and then click the Slide Show button to bring up the Slide Show Settings dialog, in which you can configure slide duration, repetition, and music.

Slide Show Settings
Cool Water
Minuet in G
Jesu, Joy Of Man's Desiring
Born In The U.S.A.
Delete
Done

Figure 5.13 To remove a song from the Music pop-up menu, choose Edit List, and in the sheet that appears, select the unwanted song and click Delete. Click Done to dismiss the sheet.

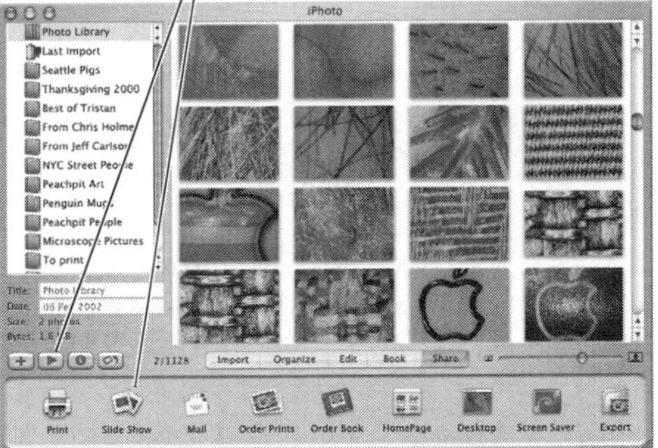
Click to run a slide show.

Figure 5.14 To run a slide show, click either the permanent slide show button under the album pane, or click Share, click the Slide Show button in the share pane to display the Slide Show Settings dialog, and click OK. The permanent button is easier unless you need to change some settings.

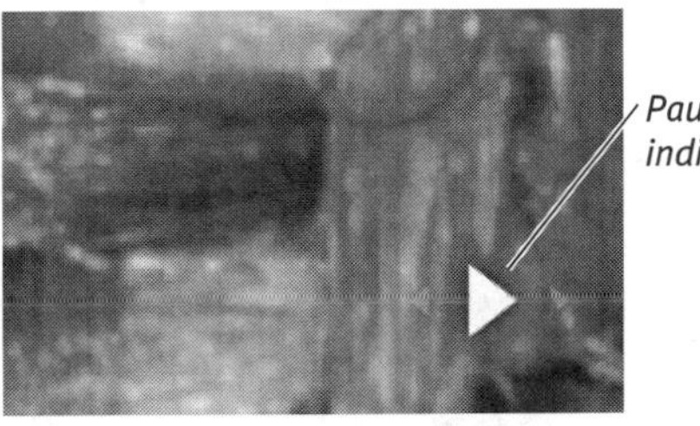
Pause/play indicator.

Figure 5.15 Note the indicators that iPhoto displays when you press Spacebar or one of the other keys to control the slide show.

Mac OS X's Screen Saver Slide Show

Mac OS X offers a built-in screen saver, accessible in the Screen Saver preferences panel in System Preferences. One of the modules is Slide Show, which cycles through images in a folder you select. Thanks to the Screen Saver button in the share pane, you can easily have Mac OS X's screen saver display a series of photos from an iPhoto album. See "Creating a Screen Saver" later in this chapter for more information.

Running Slide Shows

Configuring slide shows is easy, but running them is even easier.

To run a slide show:

1. Select the photos you want to appear in the slide show.
2. Click the slide show button that's always available under the album pane (**Figure 5.14**).

   or

   Click the Share button, click the Slide Show button, and then click OK in the Slide Show Settings dialog.

To control a slide show:

- To pause and restart the slide show, press Spacebar.

  iPhoto briefly displays a subtle pause/play indicator in the lower-right corner of the screen (**Figure 5.15**).
- To move back to the previous slide, press ← (the left arrow). This also pauses the slide show.
- To move on to the next slide, press → (the right arrow). This also pauses the slide show.
- Press ↑ (the up arrow) to speed the slide display time up by one second per slide; press Press ↓ (the down arrow) to slow it down by one second per slide.
- To stop the slide show, press any key (other than modifier keys or the other two arrow keys) or click the mouse.

✔ Tips

- If no photos are selected, iPhoto shows all the photos in the album.
- Slide shows start with the image in the upper-left position of the selection.

Emailing Photos

For many people, email is a preferred method of communication, and it works well for sending the occasional photo to a colleague, client, friend, or relative.

To send photos via email:

1. Select the photos you want to send.
2. In share mode, click the Mail button.
   iPhoto displays a dialog with options for your photos (**Figure 5.16**).
3. Choose the size you want the photos to appear at from the Size pop-up menu, and if you want titles and comments included in the message, check the appropriate checkboxes.
4. Click the Compose button.
   iPhoto resizes copies of the selected images, launches Apple's Mail program, creates a new message, and inserts the photos (**Figure 5.17**).

✔ Tips

- iPhoto lets you use only Apple's Mail. If you rely on a different email program, check out Simon Jacquier's free iPhoto Mailer Patcher (**Figure 5.18**). It's a free utility that modifies iPhoto to work with Eudora, Entourage, Mailsmith, PowerMail, and QuickMail. It's at: `http://homepage.mac.com/jacksim/software/imp.html`.
- If you send too many photos, or don't shrink their size, your message may be too large to be delivered.
- You can't change too much about the layout of your photos, but don't worry about it, because your recipient's email program will probably display the images differently anyway.

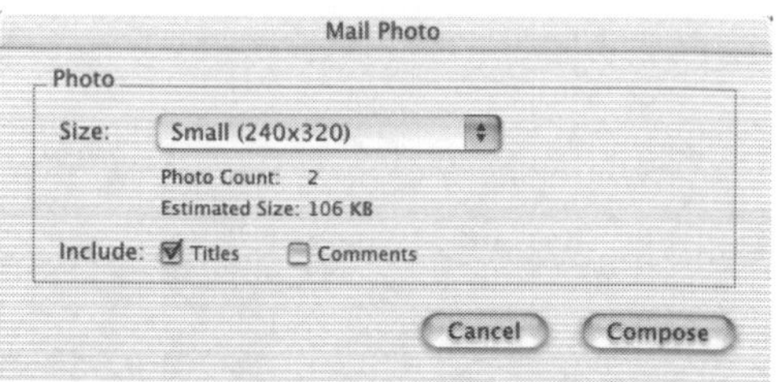
Mail Photo
Photo
Size: Small (240x320)
Photo Count: 2
Estimated Size: 106 KB
Include: Titles Comments
Cancel
Compose

Figure 5.16 Make sure to set a reasonable size for your photos before sending them via email or they'll take too long to transfer for you and your recipient.

2 great iPhotos
Send Attach Address Fonts Colors Save As Draft
To: eel1@cornell.edu
Cc:
Subject: 2 great iPhotos
Hi Mom,
cheers... -Adam
Tonya Fez
Adam Fez

Figure 5.17 Here's what the message looks like in Mail. You don't get much control over the layout, but don't worry, since there's no way of telling what it will look like on the receiving end anyway.

iPhoto Mailer Patcher
iPhoto 1.1.1 has not been patched yet.
Click on Patch to patch iPhoto 1.1.1.
Make iPhoto send mail with: Eudora
Ready to patch
Quit
Restore
Patch

Figure 5.18 iPhoto Mailer Patcher lets you modify iPhoto to send photos with other email programs.

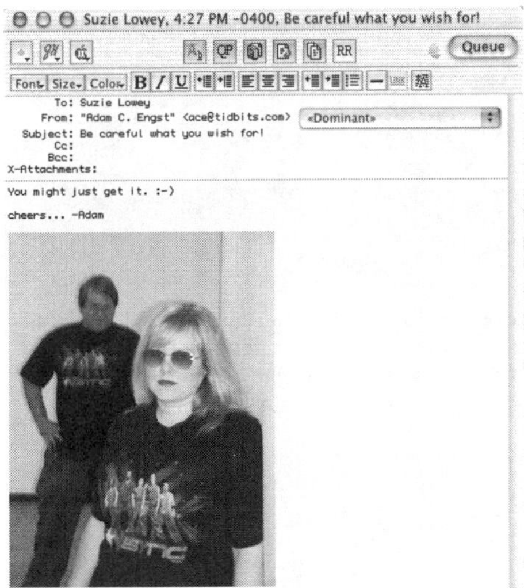
Suzie Lowey, 4:27 PM -0400, Be careful what you wish for!
Queue
To: Suzie Lowey
From: "Adam C. Engst" <ace@tidbits.com>
«Dominant»
Subject: Be careful what you wish for!
Cc:
Bcc:
X-Attachments:
You might just get it. :-)
cheers... -Adam

Figure 5.19 To send a photo via email, drag it from iPhoto into an outgoing message window, as I've done here with Eudora.

Mail iPhoto Images

Figure 5.20 Alternatively, drag a photo from iPhoto onto the Mail iPhoto Images AppleScript script icon in the Finder.

Apple - iCards
Store
iTools
iCards
QuickTime
Support
Mac OS X
Create Your Own
This font is Comic Sans
This font is Copperplate
This font is Brush Script
This font is Arial
This font is Marker Felt
Want to ride the rails with me?

Figure 5.21 A final way to send a photo via email is to use the iCards tool on Apple's iTools Web site.

Other Ways of Emailing Photos

Although I recommend that you use iPhoto's built-in support for sending photos via email, there are several alternative methods left over from iPhoto 1.0. In some situations, one of them might work better for you.

To send photos via email:

- Drag one or more photos from iPhoto into a message window of your favorite email program (**Figure 5.19**).
- Drag one or more photos onto the Mail iPhoto Images AppleScript script available from Apple's Web site at `www.apple.com/applescript/iphoto/` (**Figure 5.20**).
- Using a Web browser, connect to iTools at `http://itools.mac.com/` and send an iCard using a photo that you've uploaded while creating a Web-based photo album using HomePage (**Figure 5.21**).

✔ Tips

- Dragging photos into new outgoing email messages works with at least Apple's Mail, Eudora, and Microsoft Entourage.
- When dragging photos into an email program, remember that you aren't compressing or resizing them, so they may take a long time to send and receive.
- Apple's Mail iPhoto Images script resizes images to reduce transfer time. Double-click it to set its preferences.

Setting up an Apple ID

Before you can order prints or books, you must have an Apple ID with 1-Click ordering enabled. If you haven't previously set up an Apple ID to order from the Apple Store, you can create one within iPhoto.

To set up an Apple ID:

1. Click the Share button, make sure you're connected to the Internet, and click the Order Print button to display the Order Prints window.
2. Click the Enable 1-Click Ordering button (if it doesn't show, click the Edit 1-Click Settings button instead—either works).

   iPhoto displays the sign-in dialog (**Figure 5.22**).
3. Click the Create New Apple ID button.

   iPhoto displays the first of several dialogs that collect the data necessary to create an Apple ID (**Figure 5.23**). The first asks for your email address and password, the second collects billing information, and the third garners shipping information.
4. Enter the necessary information, clicking the Continue button to move through the process until you're done.

   Apple sends email confirmation at the end of the process.

✔ Tips

- Remember that your Apple ID is always your email address.
- Choose a password that can't easily be guessed. Otherwise miscreants could go in, change your shipping settings, order prints or books with your credit card, and switch back without you realizing.
- If you have trouble with your Apple ID, visit `http://myinfo.apple.com` and confirm or re-enter your settings.

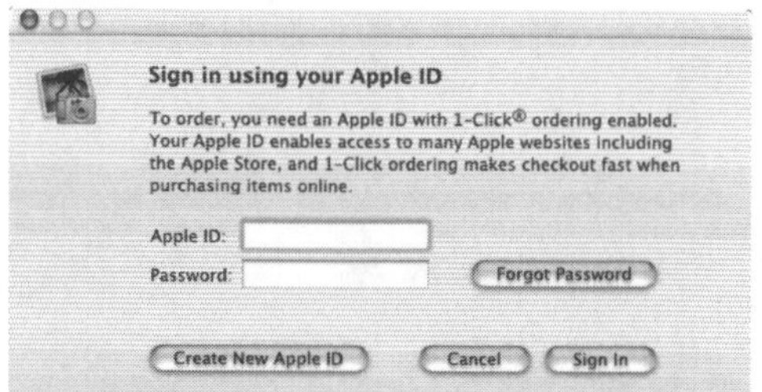
Sign in using your Apple ID
To order, you need an Apple ID with 1-Click® ordering enabled. Your Apple ID enables access to many Apple websites including the Apple Store, and 1-Click ordering makes checkout fast when purchasing items online.
Apple ID:
Password:
Forgot Password
Create New Apple ID
Cancel
Sign In

Figure 5.22 To create a new Apple ID, click the Edit 1-Click Settings or Enable 1-Click Ordering button in the Order Prints window to bring up the sign-in dialog. Then click the Create New Apple ID button.

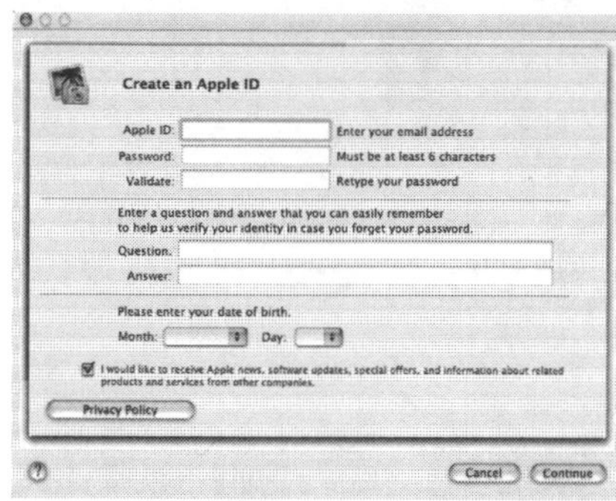
Create an Apple ID
Apple ID:
Enter your email address
Password:
Must be at least 6 characters
Validate:
Retype your password
Question:
Answer:
Please enter your date of birth.
Month:
Day:
Privacy Policy
Cancel
Continue

Figure 5.23 Enter your sign-in information, billing details, and shipping address in the dialogs that appear.

Strong Passwords

Apple requires that your password be at least six characters long, but you can make it stronger by ensuring that it contains numbers and punctuation along with uppercase and lowercase letters. One good strategy is to take a phrase you'll remember, like "Take me out to the ball game!" and use the first letter of each word, adding numbers where possible. The above phrase could be turned into this strong password: Tmo2tbg!

Whatever you do, do not use a proper name or a word that will appear in the dictionary—they're too easy to guess.

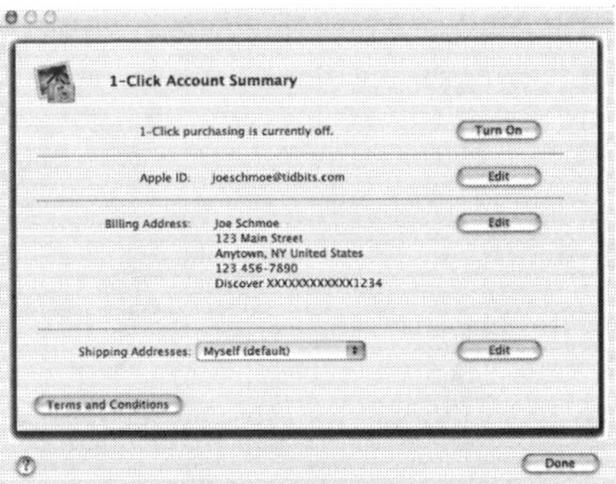
1-Click Account Summary
1-Click purchasing is currently off.
Turn On
Apple ID:
joeschmoe@tidbits.com
Edit
Billing Address:
Joe Schmoe
123 Main Street
Anytown, NY United States
123 456-7890
Discover XXXXXXXXXXXX1234
Edit
Shipping Addresses:
Myself (default)
Edit
Terms and Conditions
Done

Figure 5.24 To sign in, click either the Edit 1-Click Settings or Enable 1-Click Ordering button to display the sign-in dialog. Enter your email address and password, and click the Sign In button to display the 1-Click Account Summary dialog (shown above). Turn on 1-Click ordering if it's off, and then click the Done button.

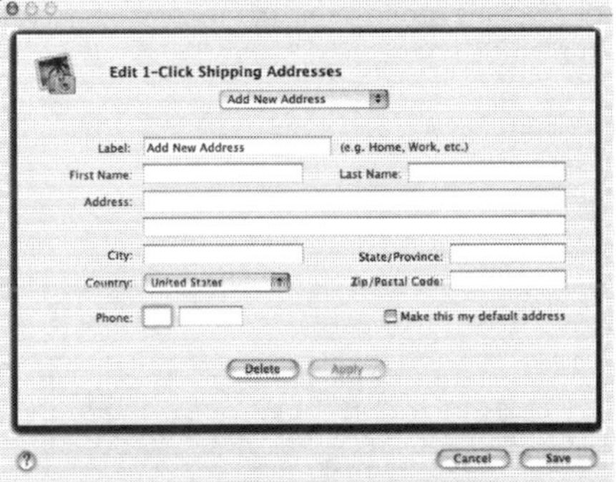
Edit 1-Click Shipping Addresses
Add New Address
Label:
Add New Address
(e.g. Home, Work, etc.)
First Name:
Last Name:
Address:
City:
State/Province:
Country:
United States
Zip/Postal Code:
Phone:
Make this my default address
Delete
Apply
Cancel
Save

Figure 5.25 To enter a new shipping address, choose Add New Address from the pop-up menu, and then enter the new address in the Edit 1-Click Shipping Addresses dialog.

Forgotten Passwords

If you've forgotten your password, enter your email address in the Apple ID field, click the Forgot Password button, and go through the necessary Web pages. Apple sends you an email message containing your password. The vagaries of Internet email mean that the message may not arrive immediately.

Using Your Apple ID

Once you have your Apple ID set up, you use it with Apple's print and book ordering services. It's also useful if you want to use some of Apple's online tech support services or order from the Apple Store. iPhoto generally remembers your Apple ID, but if not, you can always sign in.

To sign in using your Apple ID:

1. In either the Order Prints or Order Books window, click either the Edit 1-Click Settings button or the Enable 1-Click Ordering button to display the sign-in dialog.
2. Enter your email address and password, and then click the Sign In button.

   iPhoto displays the 1-Click Account Summary dialog (**Figure 5.24**).
3. If 1-Click purchasing is turned off, click the Turn On button.
4. Verify that everything else looks correct (if not, click the Edit button next to the incorrect data and make the necessary corrections), and then click the Done button.

✔ Tips

- You can switch between Apple IDs using the method above with two sets of email addresses and passwords. This is handy if multiple people want to order prints or books on separate accounts.
- You can add additional shipping addresses by choosing Add New Address from the pop-up menu in either the Order Prints or Order Book window and filling in the details in the dialog that appears (**Figure 5.25**). Switch between the addresses by choosing the desired one from the Ship To pop-up menu.

Preparing to Order Prints

You will want to spend some time preparing your photos for printing by cropping them to the appropriate aspect ratios. But what if you, like me, want to use the same photos for a book, which uses a 4 x 3 aspect ratio? Follow these steps for a solution.

To prepare photos for printing:

1. Make a new album, and add the photos that you want to order prints of.
2. Switch to the album, and edit each photo as you want it to appear in the book. Don't crop images yet!
3. In organize mode, select all the photos (Cmd A) and choose Duplicate from the File menu (Cmd D) to make copies of all of them (see "Duplicating Photos" in Chapter 3, "Editing Photos" for details).
4. Carefully go through and remove the copies from the album (they're the ones with "copy" appended to their titles, and remember that removing them here doesn't delete them from the Photo Library), by selecting them and pressing Delete. They appear at the end of the album, so they're easy to select.
5. Go through the images again in edit mode, this time cropping each to the desired aspect ratio. If cropping to the desired aspect ratio simply doesn't work for an image, crop to a different aspect ratio and print at that size, or crop as close to the desired aspect ratio as you can and be resigned to larger borders.
6. If you're printing photos in different sizes, manually group them by size in the album. That will make keeping track of them in the Order Prints window easier.
7. Now you're ready to order the prints!

What About the Other Photos?

The steps on this page involve preparing to order prints. The photos that you've removed from this album are the ones you'll want to use for building a book. Depending on what you've already done, consider copying all the images to another album (from which you'll design the book) after step 3. You'll have to repeat the laborious process of removing the photos you plan to print, but that's probably easier than selecting them all in the Photo Library again. I realize this all sounds fairly awkward, but there's no good way around the problem of wanting to use the same photos for prints and books in this version of iPhoto.

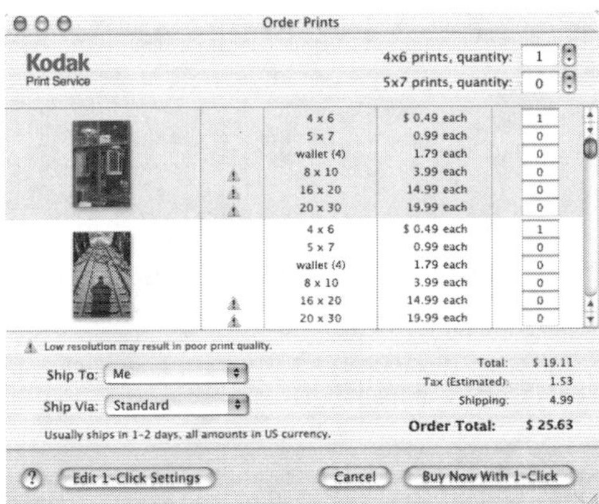
Order Prints
Kodak
Print Service
4x6 prints, quantity: 1
5x7 prints, quantity: 0
4 x 6 $ 0.49 each 1
5 x 7 0.99 each 0
wallet (4) 1.79 each 0
8 x 10 3.99 each 0
16 x 20 14.99 each 0
20 x 30 19.99 each 0
4 x 6 $ 0.49 each 1
5 x 7 0.99 each 0
wallet (4) 1.79 each 0
8 x 10 3.99 each 0
16 x 20 14.99 each 0
20 x 30 19.99 each 0
Low resolution may result in poor print quality.
Ship To: Me
Ship Via: Standard
Usually ships in 1-2 days, all amounts in US currency.
Total: $ 19.11
Tax (Estimated): 1.53
Shipping: 4.99
Order Total: $ 25.63
Edit 1-Click Settings
Cancel
Buy Now With 1-Click

Figure 5.26 To order prints, select one or more photos, click Share, click the Order Prints button, and in the Order Prints window, enter the number of prints of each photo that you want. When you're done, click the Buy Now With 1-Click button.

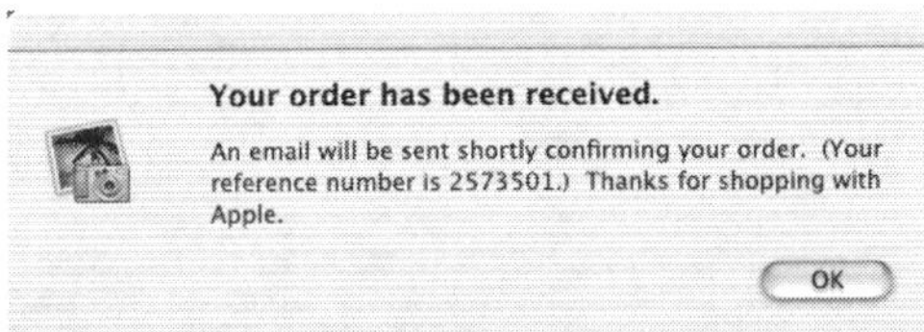
Your order has been received.
An email will be sent shortly confirming your order. (Your reference number is 2573501.) Thanks for shopping with Apple.
OK

Figure 5.27 After iPhoto finishes uploading all your photos to Kodak's Ofoto service, it tells you that it's done and will send a confirmation email message.

Shipping Details

Unfortunately, you can have prints delivered only to U.S. and Canadian addresses right now. Check Apple's iPhoto Web page at `www.apple.com/iphoto/` for any updates to this situation.

Shipping charges vary with the number of prints you order. For 1 to 20 prints, it costs $2.99. For 21 to 50 prints, it's $4.99. And if you order more than 50 prints, you'll pay $6.99 in shipping.

Ordering Prints

Once you've prepared your photos, it's time to order prints.

To order prints:

1. Making sure you're connected to the Internet, select one or more photos, click the Share button, and click Order Prints.

   iPhoto opens the Order Prints window (**Figure 5.26**).

2. For each picture, enter the number of each size print you'd like to order.

   iPhoto automatically updates the total cost as you add and subtract prints.

3. Choose the appropriate shipping address and method from the Ship To and Ship Via pop-up menus.

4. Check your order carefully to make sure you're getting the right number of each print, and confirm that each photo can print at the size you've selected.

5. Click the Buy Now With 1-Click button.

   iPhoto uploads your pictures, which could take a very long time over a slow Internet connection, and alerts you when it's done (**Figure 5.27**).

✔ Tips

- If nothing is selected when you click Order Prints, iPhoto includes all the photos in the current album.
- If you mostly want 4" x 6" or 5" x 7" prints, enter the number of each into the "4x6 prints, quantity" and "5x7 prints, quantity" fields. You can reset the numbers for individual prints later.
- If you see a yellow warning icon next to a size you want, see "Dealing with Warning Icons" in Chapter 6, "Troubleshooting."

Ordering Books

Once you've designed a book (see Chapter 4, "Creating Books"), ordering it is easy.

To order a book:

1. Select the album for which you want to order a book, and verify that each page looks right in the Preview window.
2. Click the Share button, and then, making sure that you're connected to the Internet, click the Order Book button.
   iPhoto assembles the book, warning you if some photos aren't high enough resolution to print well (**Figure 5.28**), if some text doesn't fit, or if your book contains fewer than 10 pages. iPhoto then opens the Order Book window (**Figure 5.29**).
3. Choose a color for the cover from the Cover Color pop-up menu.
4. Choose the appropriate shipping address and method from the Ship To and Ship Via pop-up menus.
5. Enter the number of books you want to order in the Quantity field.
   iPhoto automatically updates the total cost as you add and subtract books.
6. Click the Buy Now With 1-Click button.
   iPhoto uploads your pictures, which could take a very long time over a slow Internet connection, and alerts you when it's done.

✔ Tips

- Books cost $3 per page, with a 10-page minimum and a 50-page maximum.
- If you're warned about low resolution images, see "Dealing with Warning Icons" in Chapter 6, "Troubleshooting."

Low Quality Warning
One or more photos in your book may print at too low a quality based on the design you have chosen. Do you want to continue?
Stop
Continue

Figure 5.28 If some photos aren't of sufficient quality to print well, iPhoto warns you with this dialog. Similar dialogs warn you if not all of your text will fit in the book's text boxes or if you try to print a book containing fewer than 10 pages.

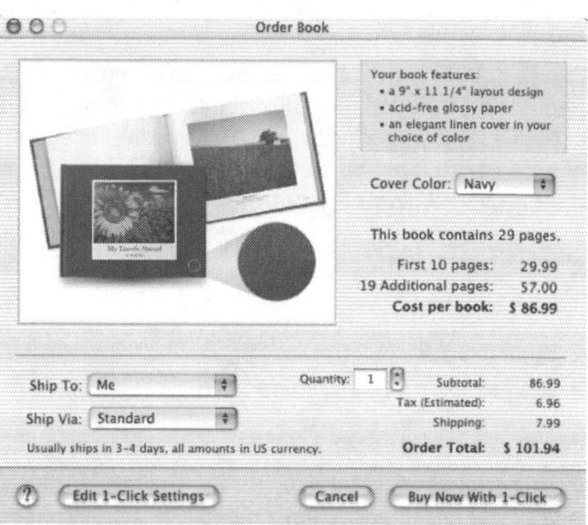
Order Book
Your book features:
• a 9" x 11 1/4" layout design
• acid-free glossy paper
• an elegant linen cover in your choice of color
Cover Color: Navy
This book contains 29 pages.
First 10 pages: 29.99
19 Additional pages: 57.00
Cost per book: $ 86.99
Ship To: Me
Ship Via: Standard
Quantity: 1
Subtotal: 86.99
Tax (Estimated): 6.96
Shipping: 7.99
Order Total: $ 101.94
Usually ships in 3-4 days, all amounts in US currency.
Edit 1-Click Settings
Cancel
Buy Now With 1-Click

Figure 5.29 To order a book, verify that it looks right in book mode, click the Share button, and click Order Book to open the Order Book window. Then choose a cover color from the Cover Color pop-up menu, choose the appropriate shipping address and method, enter the number of books you want to order, and click the Buy Now With 1-Click button.

Shipping Details

Unfortunately, you can have books delivered only to U.S. and Canadian addresses right now. Check Apple's iPhoto Web page at `www.apple.com/iphoto/` for any updates to this situation.

It costs $7.99 to ship a single book, but each additional book you have shipped to the same address adds only $1 more per book.

Book Observations

Since the relatively high cost of printing a book from iPhoto may cause some people to shy away from trying them, I thought I'd offer a few observations based on the books I've ordered.

The good stuff:

- The binding for the books is top-notch. It looks and feels completely professional.
- The paper is heavy stock, quite glossy, and acid-free, so it should last well (although it does show creases quickly).
- Turnaround time from placing the order to receiving a book is only about a week.
- The packaging for the book was very good, with the book inside a reusable plastic sleeve, everything packed snugly inside a cardboard box that protected the edges from being dinged, and all that inside a mailing box.

The bad stuff:

- The image quality of the photos in books isn't as good as prints you can order from within iPhoto or prints you can create with a relatively inexpensive, six-color inkjet printer like my Epson Stylus Photo 870. Overall, the quality is similar to that you'd see in a magazine, with the caveat that consumer-level digital cameras can't match the output quality of equipment used by professional photographers. Realistically, no one I've shown the book to has noticed this on their own.
- On one book I ordered, the cover photo was pasted on slightly crooked.
- Black-and-white photos don't print well because of the color printing process used for the books. Avoid using black-and-white photos in books.

Similar Book Service

It turns out that if people who can't use iPhoto want to order a book like those you can design in iPhoto, they can do so from a service called myPublisher. You can visit myPublisher's Web site at `www.mypublisher.com`. I don't know the relationship between Apple and myPublisher; it's possible myPublisher is printing the books for Apple, or Apple may have licensed the same technology that myPublisher uses.

The main advantages to building a book using iPhoto over building one using myPublisher's service are that you don't have to upload photos manually, the process is much easier in iPhoto, and Apple provides better-designed layouts and more fonts. The only advantage of ordering from myPublisher is that they also offer leather covers ($10), laminated book jackets ($5), and slipcases ($10).

Setting up an iTools Account

Before you can upload pictures to Apple's HomePage Web publishing tool so anyone on the Web can view your favorite photos, you need an iTools account. It's free and easy to set up.

To set up an iTools account:

1. Click the System Preferences icon in your Dock to open the System Preferences window, and in there, click the Internet icon to display the Internet preferences panel (**Figure 5.30**).
2. Make sure you're connected to the Internet and click the Sign Up button.

   iPhoto launches your default Web browser and takes you to the iTools signup page (**Figure 5.31**).
3. Enter your information in the fields provided. When you're done, click Continue at the bottom of the page.

   iPhoto displays a summary page, offers you the chance to send an iCard announcing the fact that you have a new email address (`yourusername@mac.com`—you don't have to use it), and takes you to the iTools home page.
4. Click System Preferences to return to the Internet preferences panel, and enter your new iTools member name and password.
5. Close the System Preferences window.

✔ Tip

- Since so many people have registered iTools accounts, you may need to choose a more awkward username than would be ideal. Try combining your first name and last name.

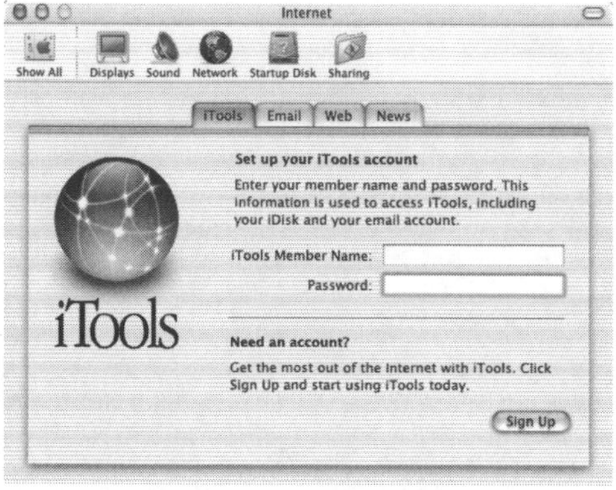
Internet
Show All
Displays
Sound
Network
Startup Disk
Sharing
iTools
Email
Web
News
Set up your iTools account
Enter your member name and password. This information is used to access iTools, including your iDisk and your email account.
iTools Member Name:
Password:
iTools
Need an account?
Get the most out of the Internet with iTools. Click Sign Up and start using iTools today.
Sign Up

Figure 5.30 To set up an iTools account, click System Preferences in the Dock to open the System Preferences window, click the Internet icon to show the Internet preferences panel, and click the Sign Up button, which takes you to an iTools signup page in your Web browser.

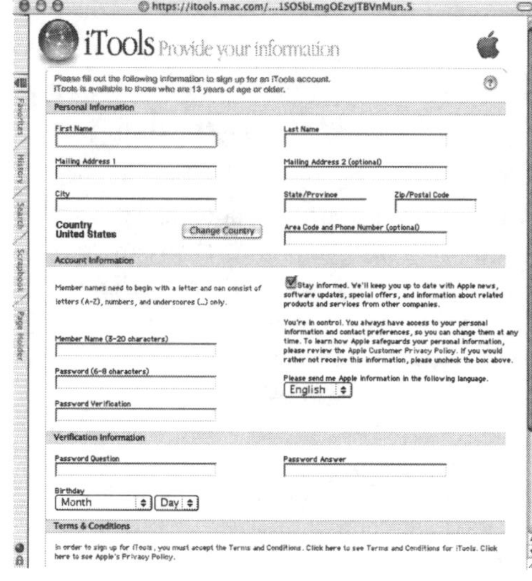
iTools Provide your information
Personal Information
First Name
Last Name
Mailing Address 1
Mailing Address 2 (optional)
City
State/Province
Zip/Postal Code
Country
United States
Change Country
Account Information
Member Name (3-20 characters)
Password (6-8 characters)
Password Verification
English
Verification Information
Password Question
Password Answer
Birthday
Month
Day
Terms & Conditions

Figure 5.31 Enter your information in the iTools signup page, and click the Continue button (it's just out of sight at the bottom of this screenshot) when you're done. A confirmation page will appear; copy the username and password from that page to the Internet preferences panel and you're done.

iTools
iPhoto for You
Free Prints Offer
Game Time
Get More Space

Figure 5.32 To use iTools, connect to the iTools Web page and click the links at the top of the window.

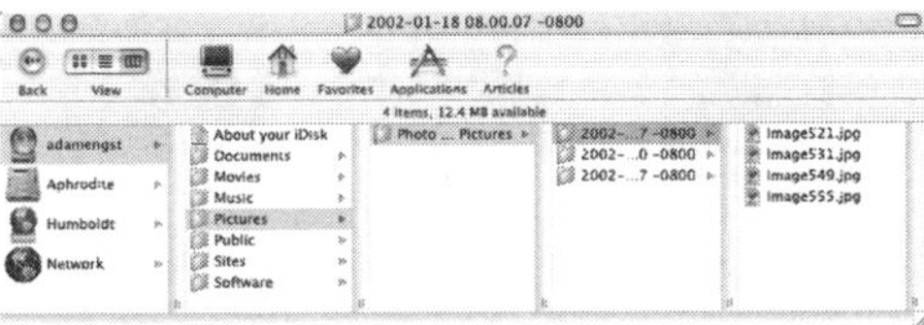
2002-01-18 08.00.07 -0800
Back
View
Computer
Home
Favorites
Applications
Articles
4 items, 12.4 MB available
adamengst
Aphrodite
Humboldt
Network
About your iDisk
Documents
Movies
Music
Pictures
Public
Sites
Software
Image521.jpg
Image531.jpg
Image549.jpg
Image555.jpg

Figure 5.33 To connect to your iDisk, choose iDisk from the Finder's Go menu. Any pictures you publish using HomePage from within iPhoto are stored in your Pictures folder.

iCards Create Your Own

Figure 5.34 Use the iCards tool to create personalized email greeting cards using your own photos or images Apple provides.

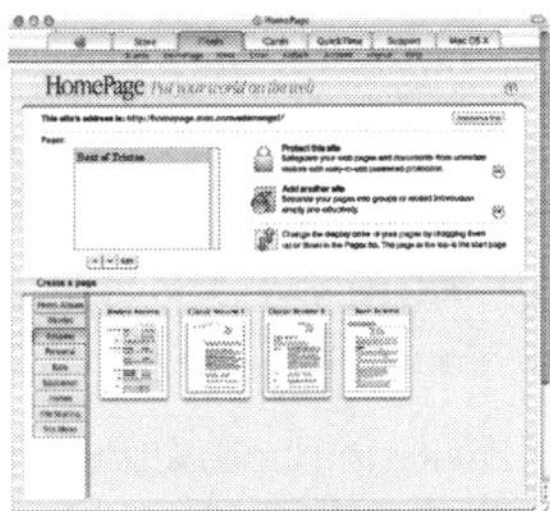
HomePage

Figure 5.35 Use the HomePage Web publishing tool to create and manage a number of different types of Web pages.

Mac.com
Email
Your prestigious Internet address.
Forward your mail
Auto Reply
Spread the word

Figure 5.36 You can check your Mac.com email directly, set it to forward, or create an auto-reply.

iTools Features

iTools provides a number of features, some of which integrate with iPhoto. Click the links in the iTools tab at the top of the iTools page at `http://itools.mac.com/` to configure and use each tool (**Figure 5.32**).

iDisk

Apple provides 20 MB of disk space on their servers for each iTools user, accessed like any other disk (choose iDisk from the Finder's Go menu). Predefined folders store documents, pictures, movies, public files, Web pages, and music. A Software folder contains software you can download (**Figure 5.33**).

When you publish a Web page of pictures using iPhoto and HomePage, the photos go in your Pictures folder, and the Web page itself goes in your Sites folder.

iCards

The iCards tool helps you use either the photos in your Pictures folder or images Apple provides to send email greeting cards (**Figure 5.34**).

HomePage

The HomePage Web publishing tool enables you to create different types of Web pages without learning any HTML (**Figure 5.35**). If you know how to create Web pages, you can upload them to your Sites folder to make them available to anyone on the Web at `http://homepage.mac.com/yourusername/`.

Email

You probably have an email address, but iTools provides you with another address—`yourusername@mac.com`. You can either retrieve mail from it directly or have it forward messages to another account (**Figure 5.36**).

Publishing Photos Using HomePage

It's almost trivially easy to create a Web-based photo album from within iPhoto.

To publish photos using HomePage:

1. Select an album or the individual photos you wish to publish.
2. Click the Share button, and then, making sure that you're connected to the Internet, click the HomePage button.

   iPhoto opens the Publish HomePage window, displaying a rough preview of how your page will appear (**Figure 5.37**).
3. Enter or edit titles for the page and the individual photos (iPhoto picks up album and photo titles automatically).
4. Pick a theme from the five at the bottom to change the font and frame style.
5. Select the desired iTools account from the Publish to pop-up menu.
6. Click the Publish button.

   iPhoto uploads your pictures, and, when it's done, shows a dialog that tells you the URL for your new page and offers to take you there (**Figure 5.38**).

Publish HomePage
Streets of the City, 2001
Pictures taken walking the streets of New York City one fine summer day.
The Gap
Opposites
Going somewhere
Black Man, White Man
Half-life
Audrey & Ann
Publish to: adamengst
Cancel
Publish

Figure 5.37 Preview your photos in the Publish HomePage window and click Publish when you're ready to upload them.

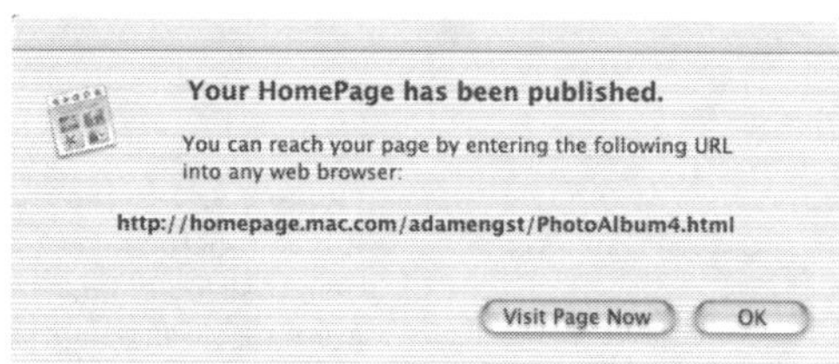
Your HomePage has been published.
You can reach your page by entering the following URL into any web browser:
http://homepage.mac.com/adamengst/PhotoAlbum4.html
Visit Page Now
OK

Figure 5.38 When iPhoto finishes uploading photos, it informs you of the URL and offers to take you there.

✔ Tips

- The photos appear in the same order as those in the album or your selection.
- iPhoto resizes images to reduce upload time and so they'll fit onscreen, but only if they're JPEG images—other formats will quickly eat up your 20 MB of space (you can buy more from Apple).
- Clicking Visit Page Now in the confirmation dialog loads the page in your Web browser, where you can easily copy the URL from the Address field.

✔ More Tips

- You can have up to 48 images in a HomePage photo album.
- Any changes you make to photo titles in the Publish HomePage window are reflected everywhere else, too.
- iPhoto's spell-checking tools work in the Publish HomePage window.
- You can't control line wrapping at all.
- To publish to your own Web site, see "Exporting to Web Pages" in this chapter.

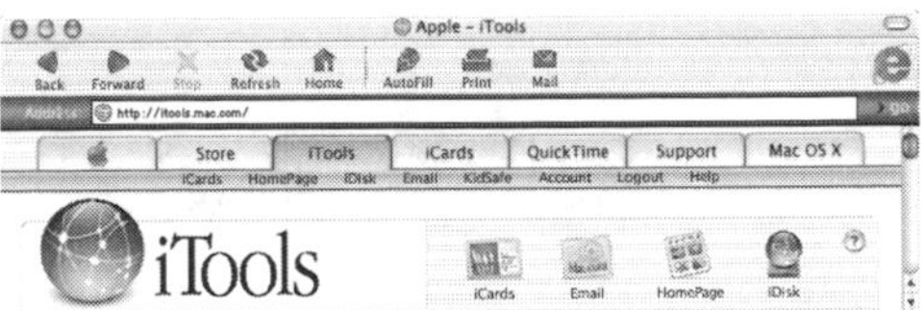
Apple - iTools
Back
Forward
Stop
Refresh
Home
AutoFill
Print
Mail
Store
iTools
iCards
QuickTime
Support
Mac OS X
iTools
iCards
Email
HomePage
iDisk

Figure 5.39 To make any changes to your HomePage iPhoto albums, first use your Web browser to connect to iTools at `http://itools.mac.com/` and then click the HomePage link at the top.

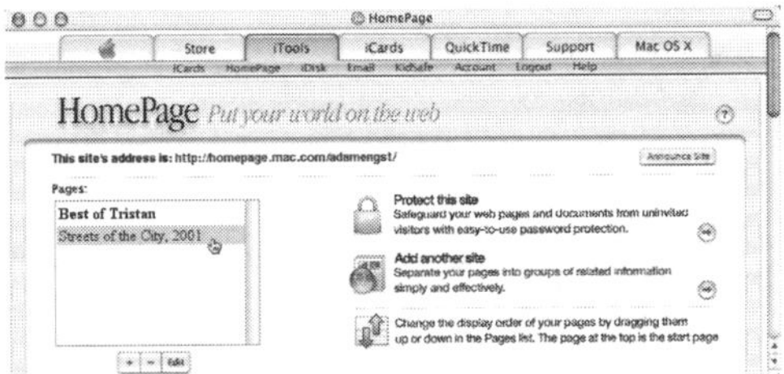
HomePage
Store
iTools
iCards
QuickTime
Support
Mac OS X
HomePage Put your world on the web
Pages:
Best of Tristan
Streets of the City, 2001
Protect this site
Add another site

Figure 5.40 To edit a photo album, select it in the Pages list, and click the Edit button. To delete an album, select it and click the – button.

HomePage
Store
iTools
iCards
QuickTime
Support
Mac OS X
HomePage Edit your page
Themes
Preview
Publish
Best of Tristan
Streets of the City, 2001
Pictures taken walking the streets of New York City one fine summer day.
Show
Show
Show
The Gap
Opposites
Going somewhere

Figure 5.41 To change text, edit the desired text box. To remove a picture from the album (but not from your iDisk), deselect the Show checkbox under the picture. To change the theme, click the Themes button at the top and select a theme. To save any of these changes, click the Publish button.

Managing HomePage Albums

You can only create Web-based albums from within iPhoto. Changing albums after the fact requires using the iTools Web site. It may be easiest to delete a bad album and upload a new one. For all of these tasks, first log in to iTools at `http://itools.mac.com/` and click the HomePage link (**Figure 5.39**).

To edit text:

- Select an album in the Pages list, click the Edit button (**Figure 5.40**), and in the "Edit your page" screen, change the text in the desired text boxes (**Figure 5.41**). Click Publish when you're done.

To remove photos:

- Select the album in the Pages list, click Edit, and in the "Edit your page" window, deselect the Show checkboxes under the photos you want to remove (they aren't deleted from your iDisk's Pictures folder). Click Publish when you're done.

To add photos:

- In the Finder, drag photos you want to add to the album into the album's folder in your iDisk's Pictures folder. Edit the page afterwards to make sure it looks right. Deleting and rebuilding the album may be easier.

To change the theme:

- Select an album in the Pages list, click the Edit button, and in the "Edit your page" window, click the Themes button, and click the desired theme. Click Publish when you're done.

To delete an album:

- Select an album in the Pages list, and click the [–] button.

Setting the Desktop Picture

In Mac OS X, you can display a picture on your Desktop, and with iPhoto, putting one of the photos you've taken on your Desktop is a matter of just clicking a button.

To set the Desktop picture:

◆ Select a photo, and in the share pane, click the Desktop button (**Figure 5.42**).

iPhoto immediately changes the picture on your Desktop (**Figure 5.43**).

Figure 5.42 Use the Desktop button to set the selected photo as your Desktop picture.

Figure 5.43 With a single click, you can put the photo you have selected in iPhoto on your Desktop.

✔ Tips

- If the picture is in landscape orientation (wider than it is tall), iPhoto scales the photo up or down to make it fit.
- If the photo is in portrait orientation (taller than it is wide), iPhoto takes a landscape chunk out of the middle to display on the Desktop. Stick with photos in landscape orientation, or crop the photo appropriately first.
- There's an item in the edit pane's Constrain pop-up menu to help you constrain photos to the size of your Mac's screen. This is helpful primarily for PowerBook G4s, because their wide screens don't match the 4x3 aspect ration of most normal monitors. If you have a normal monitor, there's little point in cropping pictures for your Desktop.
- If you have multiple monitors, I'm sorry, but iPhoto can put a picture on only the main monitor. To put a picture on the second monitor, you must use the Desktop preference pane in System Preferences.

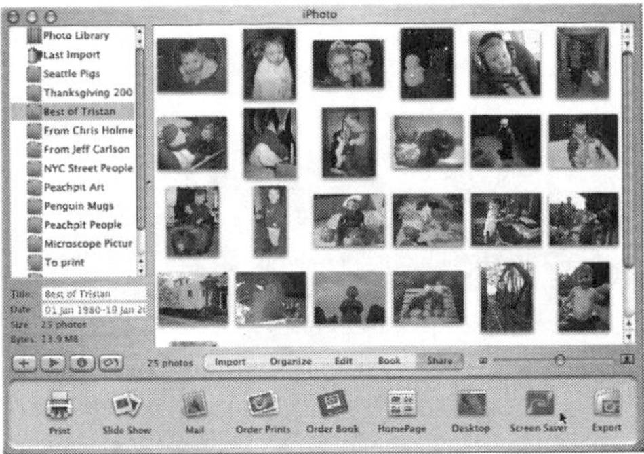
Figure 5.44 Click the Screen Saver button to select an album to use as your screen saver.

Screen Saver
This panel allows you to select an album to be used as your Screen Saver. Your preferences will be set to use the photos in that album.
Use: Best of Tristan
Album contains 25 photos.
Preferences...
Go to Screen Saver preferences.
Cancel
OK
Figure 5.45 In the Screen Saver dialog, choose an album to use for your screen saver and click OK. You can also click Preferences to open the Screen Saver preference pane in System Preferences.

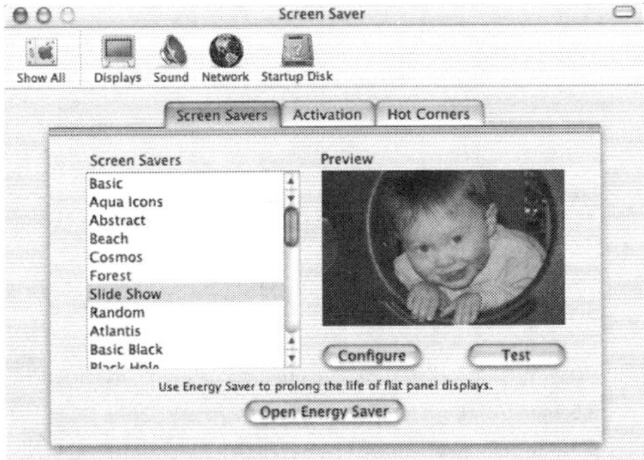
Screen Saver
Show All
Displays
Sound
Network
Startup Disk
Screen Savers
Activation
Hot Corners
Screen Savers
Preview
Basic
Aqua Icons
Abstract
Beach
Cosmos
Forest
Slide Show
Random
Atlantis
Basic Black
Configure
Test
Use Energy Saver to prolong the life of flat panel displays.
Open Energy Saver
Figure 5.46 In the Screen Saver preference pane of System Preferences, you can adjust settings for your screen saver, such as how much idle time is necessary for it to kick in, if you can activate it manually by putting your cursor in a corner, and so on.

Creating a Screen Saver

Mac OS X offers a built-in screen saver that can display photos in a sort of automated slide show. With iPhoto, you can use any of your albums as the photos for Mac OS X's screen saver.

To create a screen saver:

1. In the share pane, click the Screen Saver button (**Figure 5.44**).

   iPhoto displays the Screen Saver dialog (**Figure 5.45**).

2. Choose an album from the Use pop-up menu, and click OK.

   iPhoto tells Mac OS X's Slide Show screen saver to use the photos in that album. The next time your screen saver kicks in, you'll see it panning around in those photos.

✔ Tips

- To configure the screen saver settings, click the Preferences button in the Screen Saver dialog to open the Screen Saver preference panel in System Preferences (**Figure 5.46**).
- If you have an album selected when you click Screen Saver, iPhoto thoughtfully makes it the default choice in the Use pop-up menu.

Exporting Files

iPhoto's export capabilities are fairly limited, but they should suffice for most situations.

To export files:

1. Select one or more photos.
2. Either choose Export from the File menu (Cmd E) or click the Share button followed by the Export button in the share pane.

   iPhoto displays the Export Images dialog (**Figure 5.47**).
3. If it's not active, click the File Export tab.
4. Choose the format for the exported photos, select how you want them named, and select an image scale before clicking the Export button.
5. iPhoto displays a save dialog. Navigate to your desired folder and click OK to save your images.

✔ Tips

- iPhoto can export into only JPEG, TIFF, and PNG formats. For other formats, use a tool like GraphicConverter, available at `www.lemkesoft.com/us_index.html`.
- Only JPEG files can be scaled to a different size; if you save in TIFF or PNG format, you're stuck with the full image size.
- When iPhoto scales an image, it does so proportionally with the limits you set.
- If you export only a single image, iPhoto gives you a chance to rename the image manually before saving.

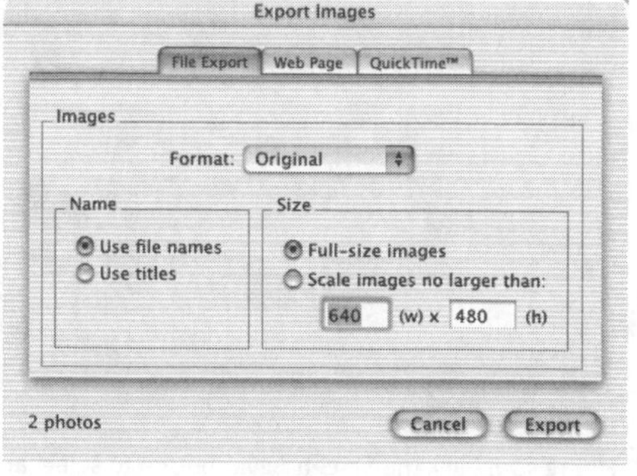
Export Images
File Export
Web Page
QuickTime™
Images
Format: Original
Name
Use file names
Use titles
Size
Full-size images
Scale images no larger than:
640 (w) x 480 (h)
2 photos
Cancel
Export

Figure 5.47 Use the File Export tab in the Export Images dialog to choose the format, name, and scale for your exported images.

Use GraphicConverter

If you want to do anything more than basic exporting of files, try the $30 shareware GraphicConverter, available at `www.lemkesoft.com/us_index.html`. GraphicConverter is far better at converting images between formats, resizing them, and performing many other useful tasks, a number of which can be used in batch mode on an entire collection of images.

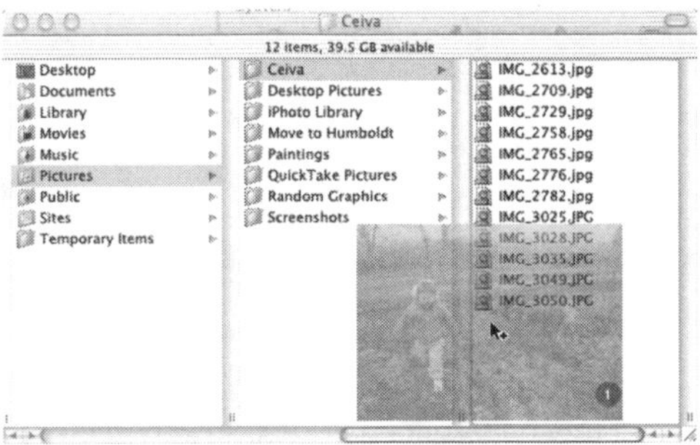

Ceiva
12 items, 39.5 GB available
Desktop
Documents
Library
Movies
Music
Pictures
Public
Sites
Temporary Items
Ceiva
Desktop Pictures
iPhoto Library
Move to Humboldt
Paintings
QuickTake Pictures
Random Graphics
Screenshots
IMG_2613.jpg
IMG_2709.jpg
IMG_2729.jpg
IMG_2758.jpg
IMG_2765.jpg
IMG_2776.jpg
IMG_2782.jpg
IMG_3025.JPG
IMG_3028.JPG
IMG_3035.JPG
IMG_3049.JPG
IMG_3050.JPG

Figure 5.48 For a quick export without any chance to reformat, rename, or resize the exported photos, just drag one or more to the Finder.

Exported Photos Not Rotated

If you want to export a photo you've edited only by rotating it, you'll notice the exported file isn't rotated if you use the drag-to-the-Finder method of exporting. This error happens because iPhoto rotates only the photo's thumbnail initially, rotating the actual photo only if necessary. You can work around this problem in two ways. First, use the Export button in the share pane instead of dragging to the Finder. Second, make another editing change to the photo, such as red-eye reduction, and then undo that change before dragging the photo to the Finder. Any editing change other than rotation forces iPhoto to modify the photo's file instead of just the thumbnail, which sets the rotation properly as well.

Exporting Files by Dragging

If you just want copies of a couple of photos and don't need to reformat or resize them, you can just drag the files to the Finder.

To export multiple files:

- Select one or more photos in import or organize mode and drag them to the desired location in the Finder (**Figure 5.48**).

  iPhoto saves the files where you dropped them.

✔ Tips

- If you hold down Command and Option while dragging a photo to the Finder, iPhoto makes an alias of the photo instead of copying it there.
- When you drag photos to export them, you aren't given the opportunity to change their scale or image format.

Exporting to Web Pages

Along with using Apple's HomePage Web publishing tool, iPhoto can export selected images to a set of Web pages you can upload to your own Web server or Web space at your Internet service provider.

To export photos to Web pages:

1. Select an album or the individual photos you wish to publish.
2. Either choose Export from the File menu (Cmd E) or click the Share button followed by the Export button in the share pane.

   iPhoto shows the Export Images dialog.
3. If it's not active, click the Web Page tab (**Figure 5.49**).
4. Enter the title for your Web page.
5. Enter the desired number of columns and rows of photo thumbnails.
6. If desired, select a background color or image.
7. Select the maximum width and height for the thumbnails and the full-size images.
8. Select the Show title checkbox if you want to include your photos' titles.
9. Click Export, navigate to the desired destination folder (it's best to create a new folder inside your user directory's Sites folder), and click OK.

   iPhoto exports the photos and builds the appropriate HTML files.
10. Switch to the Finder, open the folder in which you saved your Web page, and double-click the index.html file to open it in your Web browser and see the results (**Figure 5.50**).

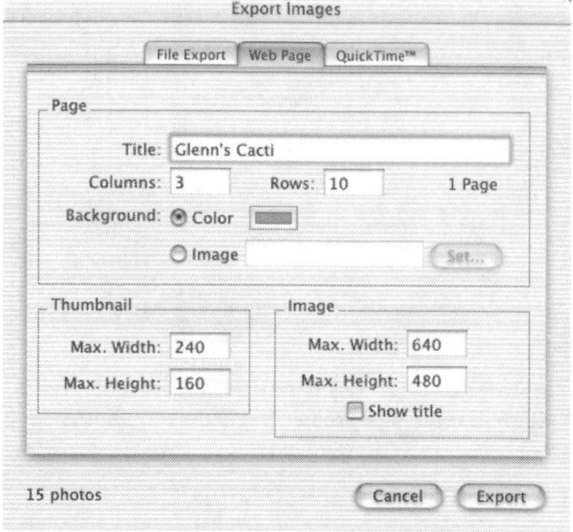
Export Images
File Export
Web Page
QuickTime™
Page
Title: Glenn's Cacti
Columns: 3
Rows: 10
1 Page
Background: Color
Image
Set...
Thumbnail
Max. Width: 240
Max. Height: 160
Image
Max. Width: 640
Max. Height: 480
Show title
15 photos
Cancel
Export

Figure 5.49 Use the options in the Web Page tab of the Export Images dialog to set how your photos will appear on the Web page.

Glenn's Cacti
Refresh
Home
Print
Mail
Glenn's Cacti

Figure 5.50 To see how your Web page turned out, switch to the Finder, open your destination folder, and double-click the index.html file inside it. To view an image at full size, click its thumbnail.

Issues with iPhoto's Web Page Export

As you may have guessed, iPhoto's Web page export isn't particularly flexible. There are workarounds for some of its limitations, though not for others.

Issues with iPhoto's Web page export:

- iPhoto doesn't let you add descriptive text to your index.html thumbnail page, as it does when using HomePage. If you knew a little HTML, you could fairly easily add text to that index.html page using a text editor.
- Although iPhoto can place the title of each image under the thumbnails and on the page with the full-size image, it can't display comments at all.
- There's no way to have iPhoto generate full-size image pages with next and previous links on them. Users must return to the thumbnail page using the Web browser's Back button after viewing each large image. You could add these links manually, but that's more involved than adding a bit of descriptive text.
- Since title text is always black, stick with light background colors. To pick a background color, use the standard Mac OS X color panel. See "Changing Text Color" in Chapter 4, "Creating Books," for more information.
- If you select a background image instead of a color, the image is tiled underneath the thumbnails. Avoid using background images most of the time—they make for a cluttered presentation.
- To make your pages available, turn on Web Sharing in the Sharing preferences panel or upload your exported Web files manually to your Web server.

Alternative Web Export Tools

Other tools can generate significantly more flexible Web-based photo albums. Two of my favorites right now are Stone Table Software's Photo Framesite and iView Multimedia's iView MediaPro.

Photo Framesite is a one-trick-pony tool that generates a collection of Web pages with a frame of thumbnails down the left side; clicking one displays the full image in the large right-hand pane. It's $10 shareware and works well with iPhoto—just drag your images from iPhoto into Photo Framesite's window to add them. Photo Framesite offers a number of styles from which you can choose, and you can customize the templates to your liking. You can download a copy from `www.stonetablesoftware.com`.

The $50 shareware iView MediaPro does many things well (including extremely flexible slide shows), not the least of which is HTML export. It can generate both traditional sites with a page of thumbnails and framed sites with a thumbnail frame. You can customize the HTML, and it can also reduce the size and quality of exported images to make the site load quickly for users. Pick up a copy at `www.iview-multimedia.com`.

Finally, to add just a few more options within iPhoto itself, see the discussion of BetterHTMLExport in "Useful Export Plug-ins" at the end of this chapter.

Exporting to QuickTime Movies

Slide shows are great if people can gather in front of your computer, but what if you want to send someone a slide show in email or on CD? For that you'll want to take advantage of iPhoto's QuickTime movie export.

To export photos to a QuickTime movie:

1. Select an album or the individual photos you wish to publish.
2. Either choose Export from the File menu (Cmd E) or click the Share button and then share pane's Export button.
   iPhoto displays the Export Images dialog.
3. If it's not active, click the QuickTime tab (**Figure 5.51**).
4. Enter the maximum width and height for the images, how long each image displays, and select a background color.
5. If you want the music currently selected for use with slide shows to play with the movie, click the "Add currently selected music to movie" button.
6. Click Export, name your movie in the Save dialog that appears, choose a destination for it from the Where pop-up menu, and click Save.
   iPhoto builds the movie.
7. Switch to the Finder, locate your movie, and double-click it to see the results in QuickTime Player (**Figure 5.52**).

✔ Tips

- A background image won't show up in the final movie.
- When iPhoto resizes images, it does so proportionally with the limits you set.

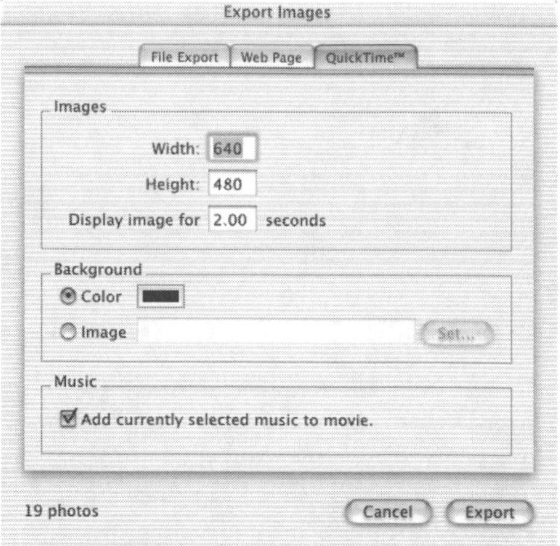

Export Images
File Export
Web Page
QuickTime™
Images
Width: 640
Height: 480
Display image for 2.00 seconds
Background
Color
Image
Set...
Music
Add currently selected music to movie.
19 photos
Cancel
Export

Figure 5.51 Use the options in the QuickTime tab of the Export Images dialog to configure your QuickTime movie.

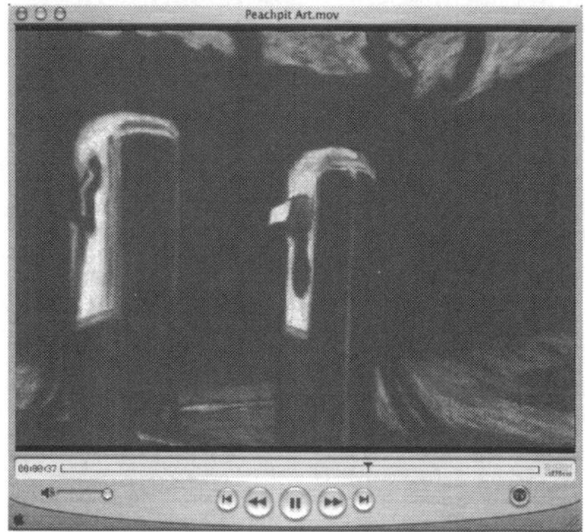

Peachpit Art.mov

Figure 5.52 To see what your movie looks like, double-click it in the Finder to open it in QuickTime Player.

Flipping through Movies

No matter how you create a QuickTime movie of still images, you can flip through the final movie in QuickTime Player one photo at a time (plus transitions) by using ← and → (the left and right arrow keys) while the movie is stopped.

Figure 5.53 To add a plug-in to iPhoto, select iPhoto in the Finder, choose Show Info to open its info window, choose Plugins from the pop-up menu, click Add, and select the desired plug-in in the open dialog.

Help
Open
Show Info
Show Package Contents
Move to Trash
Copy "iPhoto"

Figure 5.54 Alternatively, Control-click iPhoto and choose Show Package Contents.

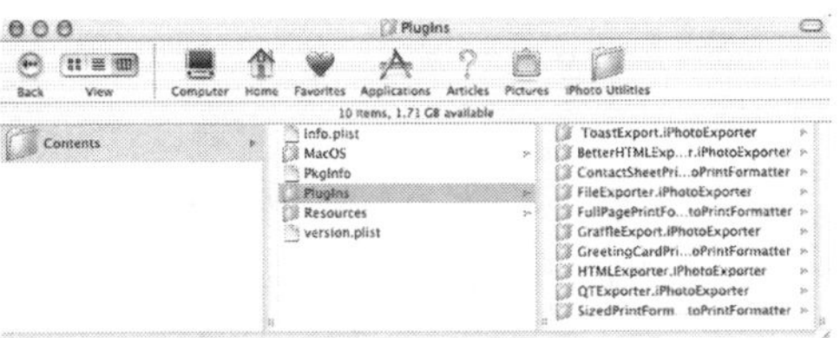

Figure 5.55 Mac OS X then opens a new Finder window showing the contents of the iPhoto application package. Copy the plug-in to the Plugins folder inside the Contents folder.

Beware Old Export Plug-ins!

It's important that any export plug-ins that you install be created explicitly for the current version of iPhoto. Some of those created for iPhoto 1.0 cause weird problems when loaded into iPhoto 1.1.1.

Installing Export Plug-ins

Programmers outside Apple can write plug-ins for iPhoto to give it more export functionality, and several have done so already. Before you can use them, though, you must install them.

To install a plug-in (I):

1. Download and unpack the plug-in.
2. Select iPhoto's icon in the Finder and choose Show Info (Cmd I) from the File menu to open the iPhoto Info window.
3. From the pop-up menu, choose Plugins to display the Plugins panel, where you can add, remove, and disable plug-ins (**Figure 5.53**).
4. Click Add, and select the desired plug-in (hint: it's the folder that contains another folder called Contents).

   iPhoto adds the plug-in to iPhoto, although it doesn't update the list in the Plugins panel until you close the iPhoto Info window and open it again. The next time you launch iPhoto, the plug-in appears as a tab in the Export Images dialog.

To install a plug-in (II):

1. Download and unpack the plug-in.
2. Control-click iPhoto's icon in the Finder and choose Show Package Contents from the contextual menu (**Figure 5.54**).

   Mac OS X opens a new Finder window showing what's in the iPhoto package.
3. Copy your plug-in to the PlugIns folder inside the Contents folder (**Figure 5.55**).

   The plug-in appears in the Export Images dialog the next time you launch iPhoto.

Useful Export Plug-ins

A few useful export plug-ins have appeared so far. Only the first two are compatible with iPhoto 1.1.1 now; look for an update for the OmniGraffle iPhoto Plugin before using it.

BetterHTMLExport

Simeon Leifer's free (donations welcome) BetterHTMLExport improves on iPhoto's Web page export (you can disable iPhoto's HTMLExporter in the iPhoto Info window's Plugins pane). BetterHTMLExport can show comments under thumbnails or images, control the quality of the exported images, and add next and previous links to the full image pages, plus you can edit the templates from which it generates Web pages (**Figure 5.56**). Download a copy from www.droolingcat.com/software/betterhtmlexport/.

iPhoto Toast Export Plugin

The free iPhoto Toast Export Plugin from El Gato Software lets you use Roxio's $89.95 Toast Titanium to burn selected photos (or your entire Photo Library) to CD or DVD for backup or sharing. Just set the appropriate disc format in Toast, select photos in iPhoto, choose Export from the File menu, and enter a name for the disc (**Figure 5.57**). Get it from www.elgato.com/toastexport/ and find more information about Toast at www.roxio.com/en/products/toast/.

OmniGraffle iPhoto Plugin

OmniGraffle, from the Omni Group, is a diagramming program for things like org charts and flow charts. The free OmniGraffle iPhoto Plugin lets you export photos as OmniGraffle documents, making it easy to do things like create org charts with pictures of people rather than just blank boxes (**Figure 5.58**). Find it, and the $59.95 OmniGraffle, at www.omnigroup.com.

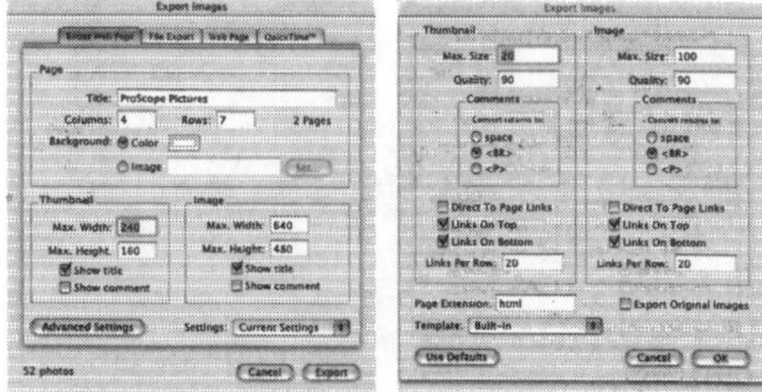

Figure 5.56 The essential BetterHTMLExport offers all the functionality of iPhoto's original Web export and much more, while retaining an interface similar to the original, as you can see in its export tab and Advanced Settings sheet above.

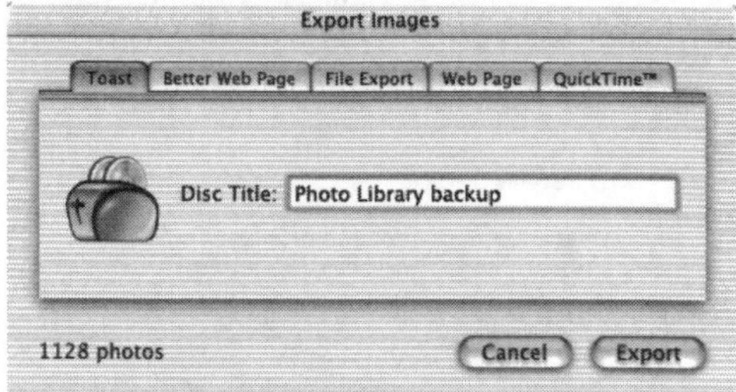
Export Images
Toast
Better Web Page
File Export
Web Page
QuickTime™
Disc Title:
Photo Library backup
1128 photos
Cancel
Export

Figure 5.57 The iPhoto Toast Export Plugin provides a simple way for people who own Roxio's Toast Titanium to burn photos to rewritable CD or DVD directly from within iPhoto. Great for backups!

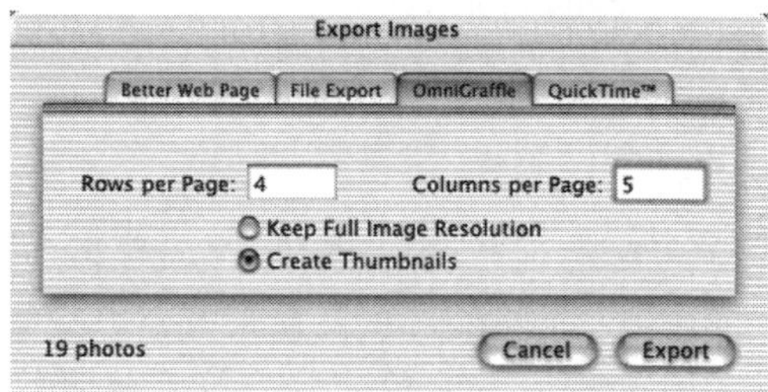
Export Images
Better Web Page
File Export
OmniGraffle
QuickTime™
Rows per Page:
4
Columns per Page:
5
Keep Full Image Resolution
Create Thumbnails
19 photos
Cancel
Export

Figure 5.58 With the OmniGraffle iPhoto Plugin, you can export photos to OmniGraffle documents and use them instead of blank boxes and shapes when making charts and diagrams.

TROUBLESHOOTING

The world of iPhoto is no more a perfect place than the real world. No one, iPhoto's developers least of all, wants problems, but realistically, bugs are simply a fact of life, especially in new software. iPhoto is new, so Apple hasn't had much time to find and stamp out these inevitable bugs. That's not to say that iPhoto is especially buggy; just that more mature programs tend to have their rough edges smoothed out.

One advantage iPhoto has in this respect is that it runs only under Mac OS X, which boasts a feature called protected memory. That means that if one program, such as iPhoto, crashes, no other program should be affected. Also on the positive side is the fact that iPhoto saves your changes frequently and automatically, so you're unlikely to lose much work even if it crashes.

Of course, most of the problems you might encounter won't result in a crash. It's more likely you'll have trouble importing photos from an unusual camera, printing a photo at the exact size you want, or convincing iPhoto to update a thumbnail after editing a photo in an external program. Those are the sorts of problems—and solutions— I'll focus on in this chapter.

General Problems and Solutions

Some problems you may experience in iPhoto aren't related to particular activities. Others are, and subsequent pages in this chapter will address issues with importing, editing, printing, and more.

iPhoto Crashes on Launch

If you run into a reproducible crash at launch, it may be caused by a corrupted file in your iPhoto Library folder.

1. In the Finder, move your iPhoto Library folder from the Pictures folder to the Desktop, and relaunch iPhoto.

   iPhoto creates a new, empty iPhoto Library folder.

2. If iPhoto still crashes, first replace your old iPhoto Library folder, and then download and reinstall iPhoto afresh. Reinstalling may solve the problem.

   or

   If iPhoto doesn't crash, then you know something in your iPhoto Library folder is causing the problem. Continue on.

3. Quit iPhoto, put your old iPhoto Library folder back in the Pictures folder, move the Library.cache file from the iPhoto Library folder to the Desktop and relaunch iPhoto (which creates a new Library.cache file automatically).

4. If iPhoto doesn't crash this time, delete the Library.cache file on the Desktop and keep working. Problem solved! (I don't think you lose any data by deleting that file, but Apple hasn't yet confirmed that.)

   or

   If iPhoto still crashes with the fresh Library.cache file, replace the old Library.cache file and repeat the process with other files in your iPhoto Library that could be corrupted. Obviously, this is a tedious process; it might be easier to move your iPhoto Library folder to the Desktop and import your photos into a clean iPhoto Library folder.

Performance Problems

iPhoto isn't a speed demon in the best of times, but you can speed it up. Some speed enhancing tricks are obvious (if expensive); others less so.

- Turn off title and keyword display in the organize pane.
- Delete some photos from iPhoto to reduce the number in your Photo Library. Make sure you have another copy of these photos before deleting, since iPhoto deletes its copies permanently.
- Quit other programs that are running. In my experience, it's usually one or two culprits. If you want to get your feet wet with Unix, double-click Terminal (it's in the Utilities folder in your Applications folder), type `top`, and press Return. In top's display, look at the %CPU column to see which programs are using the most CPU time and quit those first.
- Log out by choosing Log Out from the Apple menu (Cmd Shift Q) and log back in to quit everything that was running and provide a somewhat cleaner slate.
- Restart your Mac by choosing Restart from the Apple menu. In theory, this shouldn't make a difference under Mac OS X, but it's a habit left over from Mac OS 9, and it seems to help on occasion.
- Add more RAM to your Mac. Mac OS X works with 128 MB of RAM, but it likes a lot more, and RAM is cheap.
- Buy a faster Mac. That's always fun.

Flaky Behavior

Sometimes iPhoto just acts strangely, such as by drawing its window underneath the menu bar. I can't predict exactly how it might do so on your Mac, but you'll know it when you see it. I've come up with a few ways of resolving the behavior.

- Quit iPhoto and relaunch it.
- Log out by choosing Log Out from the Apple menu (Cmd Shift Q) and log back in.
- Restart your Mac by choosing Restart from the Apple menu.
- Switch to Thousands of colors in the Displays preferences panel (this may help with slide show problems).
- Quit iPhoto. Choose Find from the Finder's File menu (Cmd F), and search for files with "iPhoto." in their names. One of the results should be a preference file called "com.apple.iPhoto.plist". Drag it to the Trash and launch iPhoto again.
- Download a new copy of iPhoto and reinstall it.
- If you believe your Photo Library is corrupted or damaged, you can force iPhoto to rebuild it by holding down Command-Option-Shift while launching iPhoto. I wouldn't recommend doing this unless you believe you already have problems, but it could be useful in such a case.
- Quit iPhoto, move the Library.data and Library.cache files out of your iPhoto Library folder, and relaunch. If this doesn't make a difference, quit iPhoto and put those two files back in place.
- If all else fails, try this approach. You'll lose film rolls, keywords, photo titles, and albums, but you shouldn't lose photos. Select all the photos in the Photo Library and drag them to a folder in the Finder to copy all of your photos (you'll need as much free disk space as your iPhoto Library folder is large). Quit iPhoto, delete your iPhoto Library folder, launch iPhoto, and drag the folder of copies into the display pane to import them.

Too Many Photos?

iPhoto's online help says you can import roughly 1,000 to 2,000 photos into iPhoto, depending on how much RAM your Mac has. Unfortunately, even 2,000 photos isn't many for someone who has owned a digital camera for a few years. An Apple rep once told me that he knew someone who had imported 28,000 photos into iPhoto during testing, but reports on the Internet indicate that flaky behavior and slow performance may start well before that number. If you think you either have too many photos in iPhoto or have too many that you're planning to bring in, you have a few options.

- Use iPhoto Librarian or iPhoto Library Manager to create multiple iPhoto Library folders, each containing a smaller number of photos. See "iPhoto Directory Structure" in Chapter 1, "Importing Photos," for more details.
- Use another image cataloging program like iView MediaPro to catalog your full collection of photos. To use iPhoto's publishing tools on a relatively small number of pictures, select photos in the other program and drag them into iPhoto's display pane to import them. Keep in mind that iPhoto copies these photos, so you now have two copies of each imported photo.

Importing Problems and Solutions

For the most part, I've found importing into iPhoto to be trouble-free. However, because importing involves interacting with an unpredictable outside world of cameras, card readers, and files of varying formats, problems may crop up.

Camera or Card Reader Isn't Recognized

Mac OS X and iPhoto support many common digital cameras and card readers, but not all of them. And sometimes iPhoto may not recognize specific memory cards, even if it recognizes the card reader in general. Try the following workarounds.

- If you haven't yet purchased a camera or card reader, check the compatibility list Apple publishes on their iPhoto Web pages at `www.apple.com/iphoto/`.
- Use Software Update, accessible in System Preferences, to make sure you have the latest version of Mac OS X, since Apple continually adds support for more digital cameras and card readers.
- If your camera isn't compatible with Mac OS X and iPhoto, buy a card reader that supports the memory card used by your camera. It's often easier to use a card reader anyway, and they're cheap.
- iPhoto has had trouble with some large memory cards. People have resolved the issues by reformatting the card in the camera, using a memory card reader, or using smaller cards.

Nothing Appears After Import

In a few cases, after you import files from the hard drive, nothing appears in iPhoto. People who have run into this have come up with a few solutions.

- If the files you imported are in the iPhoto Library folder, iPhoto assumes they've already been imported and won't do so again. To solve the problem, move the files out of the iPhoto Library folder and try again.
- Instead of using the Import command in the File menu, drag the images (or a folder containing them) onto iPhoto's display pane. I've seen reports that this technique works better on occasion.

Damaged Photos Warning Appears During Import

Sometimes when you import photos, you might see a dialog box with this error message: "Unreadable Photo. Some files cannot be imported. They are either not photos, or damaged ones." You might see this dialog for several reasons.

- You're importing non-graphic files accidentally.
- iPhoto supports a few common graphic formats, like JPEG and TIFF, but it can't handle many other formats. If your files are in an unsupported format, try using GraphicConverter to convert the images to JPEG or TIFF.
- In particular, RAW images from Canon cameras aren't supported by iPhoto, but Canon has a free converter that turns them into TIFF files that iPhoto can import. It works only in Classic mode.

Download it from Canon's Web site at: `www.powershot.com/powershot2/customer/rimver120.html`. For a Mac OS X-native solution, use GraphicConverter.

- Sometimes the problem relates to a USB communications failure between your camera or card reader and your Mac. Try plugging the camera or card reader directly into one of the Mac's USB ports rather than into the keyboard's USB port or a port on a USB hub.
- iPhoto can display this error message if your hard drive is full. Since iPhoto duplicates every photo when importing from files, if you're importing hundreds of megabytes of photos, it's by no means unthinkable that you could run out of disk space. Clear some space and try importing again.
- If you're trying to import from a Kodak Picture CD, import only the contents of the Pictures folder. Selecting the entire CD imports unwanted graphics and other files that may generate this warning dialog.
- Photos taken with Apple's QuickTake 100 and QuickTake 150 digital cameras can be read only with special software loaded into Mac OS 9. Reboot into Mac OS 9, making sure the QuickTake Image extension is in the Extensions folder, and then use a utility like GraphicConverter or the free PixelPipe (available from `www.magendanz.com/pixelpipe.htm`) to convert the photos to standard JPEGs. Then you should be able to boot back into Mac OS X and import into iPhoto.
- It's possible that the image files are damaged in some way. See if you can open them in another program like Preview or GraphicConverter. If so, you may be able to run them through a conversion process that eliminates the corruption.

Duplicate Images After Import

Some people have reported seeing duplicate images in iPhoto after importing. The problem appears to be related to specific cameras, particularly from Kodak. You can avoid the problem in a few different ways.

- Use a card reader instead of connecting the camera directly.
- Import using Image Capture, then import those files into iPhoto.
- Get an even cooler digital camera that works properly with iPhoto.

Flaky Behavior After Import

If you import a file that is mis-named—a TIFF file with a .jpg filename extension, for example—iPhoto may display the pictures strangely when editing, refuse to let you order prints or use Apple's HomePage tool, or even crash. Delete the mis-named picture from your Photo Library, then rename it appropriately in the Finder before importing it again.

Editing Problems and Solutions

Most photo editing problems stem from using another program to edit the photos.

Photos Don't Open in an External Program

Although it is unlikely that you'll run into this problem, it could be frustrating. Here are a few reasons it could happen.

- If you have changed the name of the photo's file in the Finder, it may not open when double-clicked in iPhoto. The solution? Change the filename back to what iPhoto expects, and don't mess with any filenames within the iPhoto Library folder. It's a bad idea!
- Double-check to make sure iPhoto's preferences are set to open photos in an external program, that the program is present on your hard drive, and that you can launch it and open photos normally.

iPhoto Crashes When You Double-Click Photos

There are a few reasons iPhoto might crash when you double-click a photo to edit it within iPhoto.

- Changing the photo's filename in the Finder can cause this problem. Did I mention that it's a bad idea to change anything inside the iPhoto Library folder using the Finder?
- A corrupted photo can cause iPhoto to freak out. Editing and saving the original file in another application might eliminate the corruption, or you could delete the corrupt photo and import it again, assuming you have another copy.

iPhoto Doesn't Allow Editing

Some people have reported importing images from a CD that they later couldn't edit in iPhoto. As a workaround, try converting the images in GraphicConverter from JPEG to TIFF, for instance, and see if you can import and then edit those versions. My hope is that GraphicConverter will reset an attribute that tells iPhoto it can't edit the images.

Revert to Original Dimmed Out

In iPhoto 1.0 at least, the Revert to Original command in the File menu can be dimmed out when it shouldn't be. Here are two fixes.

- Using an external application to edit images increases the likelihood that the Revert to Original command won't be available after editing an image. As a workaround, crop the image in iPhoto before you edit in the other application to force iPhoto to start tracking changes (iPhoto copies the original image in a folder called "Originals" in the folder that holds the photo in the Finder).
- Drag the desired image onto the Show Image File AppleScript script to locate its file in the Finder. Quit iPhoto. Delete the photo you found, then move the file of the same name from the Originals folder up one level to replace the file you deleted. Then, in the Data folder at the same level, delete the two files whose numbers correspond to the image you're working with. Launch iPhoto, and force it to update the thumbnail using the technique below.

iPhoto Crashes Viewing a Thumbnail

Some people have reported editing a photo in an external program and then having iPhoto crash every time it tries to display the thumbnail for that photo in organize mode. I suspect this relates to corruption in the photo's thumbnail.

To delete a corrupted thumbnail (I):

1. Figure out which image causes the problem by zooming in so only one picture shows in the display pane in organize mode (arrange photos by film roll), then scroll through photos until iPhoto crashes, noting which photo showed just before the crash. Repeat the process to the point just before the crash, and then drag the last good photo onto the Show Image File AppleScript script to learn its filename.
2. From the Finder's File menu, choose Find to run Sherlock (Cmd F). Search for files whose names are one number higher than the last good photo to find the corrupted thumbnail, since it should be the next one in sequence.

   One of the files Sherlock finds will be in a folder called Thumbs. That's the thumbnail we think might be corrupted.
3. Drag that thumbnail to the Desktop, and replace it with a copy of another thumbnail from the Thumbs folder.
4. Launch iPhoto and see if the crash still occurs. If not, correct the replacement thumbnail using the technique mentioned next.

To delete a corrupted thumbnail (II):

1. In organize mode, zoom in so you can see only two images side by side. Now scroll down until just before iPhoto displays the corrupted thumbnail and crashes (this may require several tries).
2. Use the Show Image File AppleScript script to help you locate the files that correspond with the photos in the film roll containing the corrupted thumbnail. Don't worry about being too accurate, there's no harm in saving too many files.
3. Copy those files to another location in the Finder for later importing.
4. Back in iPhoto's Photo Library, click the film roll icon (make sure film rolls are showing) to select all the photos in that film roll containing the corrupted thumbnail, and deselect all those up to the corrupted one (which should be off-screen).
5. Delete the remaining selected photos, hopefully deleting the corrupted one in the process.
6. Reimport the photos you previously copied in the Finder. The actual files you want to import will be inside the folders named for days of the month and will themselves be named with sequential numbers.

Thumbnails Don't Reflect Changes

After you edit an image in an external program, its thumbnail in iPhoto 1.0 may not reflect your changes. To force iPhoto to update the thumbnail, select the photo, click the Edit button, make a change like red-eye correction, choose Undo from the Edit menu, and click the Organize button.

Beware Too Much Editing

One quick warning about editing. iPhoto saves edited photos using the lossy JPEG compression format, which throws away information in the image to keep file sizes small. That won't be a problem in normal usage, but every time you edit an image, you lose a little more quality. So don't edit photos an excessive number of times.

Printing Problems and Solutions

Many printing problems you'll experience will be specific to your particular printer and setup, so read your printer manual carefully and be sure to test before printing at the highest quality on expensive paper.

Prints Don't Appear Correctly on the Paper

You may have trouble getting prints to show up in exactly the right location on the paper. Try these solutions to the problem.

- Set the paper size appropriately in the Page Setup dialog. This is essential for unusual paper sizes.
- Make sure the margins are set correctly for your printer and paper combination.
- Verify that you load paper into your printer properly. This problem is common with unusual paper sizes.

Photos Print at Incorrect Sizes

Even if you ask iPhoto to print a standard size print, the image that comes out of the printer might not be the size you want. This can happen for a few reasons.

- Make sure your image is cropped to the appropriate aspect ratio. Otherwise, iPhoto shrinks the image proportionally to make it fit, adding borders in one dimension to accommodate the size change.
- Changing the layout to print multiple pages per sheet of paper in the Advanced Options of the Print dialog will likely result in unpredictable photo sizes.
- Changing the scale in the Page Setup dialog prevents a photo from printing at a specific size.

Poor Print Quality

The main complaint with printing occurs when print quality doesn't meet your expectations. Here's how you can address this problem.

- Make sure your inkjet cartridges aren't clogged. Once my black ink cartridge clogged and it took me an hour to figure out that the clog caused photos to print oddly. Your printer manual should tell you how to clear clogs.
- Change your ink cartridges. It's possible that one is low on a specific color and not yet reporting the problem.
- Use different paper. You'd be amazed how much better print quality is on paper designed for photo printing.
- Make sure your paper is loaded correctly to print on the printable side. It's usually whiter or glossier than the other side.
- Make sure you select the appropriate settings in the Print dialog for your printer to use high-quality mode.
- If iPhoto put a low resolution warning icon on the picture in the Print dialog's small preview, there isn't enough data in the image to print at the size you requested. Print at a smaller size. See "Dealing with Warning Icons" later in this chapter.
- Apple says that CMYK files, which you can create in some programs (but aren't going to come from a standard digital camera), don't print correctly in iPhoto. So don't bother trying to print them.
- Verify that the problems aren't inherent to the original image. If so, you may have to edit the image in PixelNhance or another program to correct the issue.

Print and Book Problems and Solutions

Only a few common problems have cropped up when working with prints and books.

No Order Prints, Order Book, or HomePage Buttons

If you don't see the Order Prints, Order Book, or HomePage buttons in your share pane, the reason may be related to not having the appropriate files (BookService, HomePageService, and PrintsService) in /System/Library/Services/. If those files are missing or have bad privileges, make a backup of the iPhoto Library folder in your Pictures folder, and reinstall iPhoto.

Photos Don't Upload

Some people have had trouble uploading photos to Apple's servers to have them printed or turned into a book. Here are a few things to try.

- Try again later. Many Internet problems come and go, so a second try an hour or a day later may succeed.
- See if the problem occurs uploading to the HomePage Web-publishing tool as well. If not, the problem may be limited to the specific servers used for prints or books.
- If possible, verify that you can upload a large file using a different program. If that fails, the problem is likely with your Internet connection. If it works, the problem is probably in iPhoto.
- Contact your Internet service provider's tech support department.
- Contact Apple by sending email to `internetservices@apple.com` or calling 1-800-709-2775.

Avoid Black-and-White in Books

Apple has warned that black-and-white photos don't print well in books due to the color printing process used. They haven't offered a workaround, so for the moment, stick to putting color photos in your books.

Pages Jump Around in Book Mode

When making large books with lots of photos and many locked pages, some people have experienced pages and images seemingly jumping around. One person eliminated the problem by arranging photos in organize mode first, and then working left to right in the book. For details of this method, see "Arranging Photos on Pages" in Chapter 4, "Creating Books."

Prints Are Too Dark

Some people have noticed that prints ordered via iPhoto come back darker than would be ideal. This may be because Mac and PC monitors have different color contrast settings, something called gamma. Macs usually use a gamma of 1.8, whereas PCs use a darker gamma of 2.2. The belief is that, Kodak serves more PC customers, and has tweaked its equipment so PC users don't think their prints look washed out.

You can't do color correction in iPhoto (for that, get PixelNhance), but you can adjust your monitor to use PC gamma settings when working with photos. Click System Preferences in the Dock, click the Displays preferences panel, click the Color tab, and click the Calibrate button to run the Display Calibrator Assistant. Then work through the several screens of the Display Calibrator Assistant, save the profile you create, and select it back in the Color tab of the Display preferences panel.

Understanding Color Management

You've probably noticed that iPhoto lacks tools for adjusting color saturation or amounts of any given color in a photo. Although many people feel that's likely to change in the next version, Apple's decision to leave color correction tools out entirely wasn't necessarily a bad one. Why? Color correction of any sort is devilishly difficult to do right. Color correction suffers from two basic problems, the fact that color is highly perceptual, and the fact that different devices render color in different ways.

Color Perception

Everyone sees color in different ways. My wife and I, for instance, frequently disagree on whether a given color is green or blue, and the fact that my opinion generally seems to match what others think as well doesn't change the fact that she is perceiving a different color. Add that to the fact that at least 10 percent of the population suffers from some level of color blindness.

The conditions in which color is perceived also make a huge difference, as you've probably realized if you ever purchased a shirt in a store lit with fluorescent lights and were surprised by how the shirt looked when you tried it on at home under incandescent lights. Similarly, when painting a room, you have to consider how the color will look in sunlight during the day and with artificial lighting at night. The differences can be striking.

The lesson here is that you cannot define color objectively—there is no right answer. Always keep that in mind and it will remove some of the stress about achieving the perfect color in your photos.

Rendering Color

Digital cameras, computer monitors, inkjet printers, and commercial photo processing equipment all use different methods of rendering color. Even with monitors, there's little common ground between normal CRT-based monitors and the increasingly popular LCD flat-panel monitors.

When you're trying to take a picture with your camera, look at it on your Mac, print a copy on your printer, and order a large print of the image from Kodak, you would like the colors in the image to match closely at each step. The engineers designing these devices have managed to make the color produced by each one match fairly well, but not perfectly. Here's how it works.

Imagine a three-dimensional graph, with the x-, y-, and z-axes representing the amount of red, green, and blue in every possible color. (Don't worry about this turning technical, that's as bad as it gets.) Now imagine an amorphous blob in the graph that represents the specific set of colors any given device can capture (for digital cameras) or display (for monitors or printers). That blob is called the "gamut," and every device has a gamut that's at least slightly different.

The problem with matching color across completely different types of devices is that each device can render only colors in the set represented by its gamut. When a color, say a specific light green, falls into an area where there's overlap between gamuts, each device does the right thing and renders the exact same light green. However, when a color falls outside the set of colors a device can render, it's a problem. There's no way the device can render a color outside its gamut, so it makes an educated guess about what color to render instead.

Color Matching Systems

Many efforts have been made to address this problem, but the one you're most likely to have heard about, being a Mac user, is Apple's ColorSync technology. The particular approach it uses to make educated guesses about which colors to render on different devices is immaterial; suffice to say that its goal is consistency. In theory, if you have chosen or set up a ColorSync profile for your monitor and your printer, for instance, it should help ensure that the colors you see on your monitor match those printed by your printer.

Without getting into too many details, you can calibrate your monitor by clicking System Preferences in the Dock, clicking the Displays preferences panel, clicking the Color tab, and clicking the Calibrate button to run and work through the Display Calibrator Assistant. Then, when you're printing, look for a ColorSync setting in the Color Management panel of the Print dialog. Whether it's present or not depends on your printer driver, but if the setting is present at all, it's usually the default. That's all there is to basic use of ColorSync, and on the whole, it works pretty well.

You may not be limited to ColorSync's educated guesses about how to render color (my Epson's Photo-Realistic mode sometimes produces better results), and in fact, none of the commercial photo processing companies, including Kodak, use it. Why not? Two reasons.

First, photos are displayed on monitors and on paper totally differently. Monitors emit light, causing photos to be extremely bright. Paper reflects light, so unless you shine a floodlight on a photo, you can't come close to the amount of light emanating from a monitor.

Second, color is highly perceptual, and Kodak and other photography companies have done incredible amounts of research to determine not so much how to match colors exactly, but how to print photographs that meet people's expectations.

In the end, the problem of matching color perfectly between devices is just too hard. Even with technologies like ColorSync, the differences between a photo on a light-emitting monitor and light-reflecting paper mean that the photo processing companies have a better chance of satisfying customers if they concentrate more on producing a photograph that looks desirable than on matching colors perfectly in an imperfect world where everyone sees color differently.

On Apple's part, hopefully you see why they decided to leave color correction tools out of these first versions of iPhoto. Color correction is complex, and the necessary tools are also generally complex (PixelNhance being a notable exception—see "Recommended Image Editing Programs" in Chapter 3, "Editing Photos"), so Apple didn't want to shackle a program as easy to use as iPhoto with difficult tools. I expect that to change to some extent in the future, but iPhoto will never compete with Adobe Photoshop's color correction tools.

Should You Correct Colors?

Now that you know how hard it is to achieve reliable, predictable results, should you bother using a tool like PixelNhance to color correct your photos? It all depends on how much you want to play. For those who don't like to fuss, no, don't bother. If you like fiddling with your photos so you can make them just right, then yes, go ahead. And for the majority of us who fall between those two poles, I recommend doing color correction only on the images you like the most and that will benefit from it the most.

Print and Book Ordering Problems and Solutions

Whenever a program like iPhoto has to interact with the outside world, as it does when you order prints or books, there's room for problems to arise.

Can't Enable 1-Click Ordering

A number of people have reported problems with enabling 1-Click ordering within iPhoto, even though they have a 1-Click account with Apple that works on Apple's Web sites. A lot of the early problems seemed to relate to people who had joined the Apple Developer Connection (ADC). Apple has said they're aware of the problem, but as of this writing people in the ADC continue to have problems. To fix the problem, try one of these solutions.

- Connect to `http://store.apple.com/`, click the Your Account link, and log in to your Apple Store account. Click the "Change Apple ID or Password" link, log in again, and then change your password (changing other data wouldn't hurt either). The goal here is to force the Apple database to be updated such that you can connect to it via iPhoto. (Also try the same procedure at `http://myinfo.apple.com/`.)
- Follow the above procedure, but instead of clicking "Change Apple ID or Password," click "Change 1-Click Settings." Again, make some changes and toggle 1-Click via the Web to see if that enables iPhoto to connect.
- If you can set up a new email address easily, create it and then add a new Apple ID that uses the new email address. This generally seems to work, but isn't an ideal solution, since then you have to keep track of an extra email address.

Errors During Ordering

You may encounter a few problems during ordering.

- You may see a confusing error message that says "The changes to your account information could not be saved." Ignore the message, and enter your credit card information again, making sure the card hasn't expired. If that doesn't work, try a different card.
- Different aspects of iPhoto may request access to your password keychain during ordering. That's fine.
- If you see an error dialog complaining that a network connection could not be established, verify that your Internet connection is working by checking in a Web browser or other program.
- iPhoto doesn't honor proxy settings, so if you have a firewall that blocks port 80, you'll have to turn that off to upload.

Order Doesn't Arrive or Is Damaged

There are three ways to learn more about your orders. Apple includes this information with each confirmation message.

- Check the status of your order at `www.apple.com/internetservices/yourorderstatus`. You need your Apple ID and password to sign in.
- Send an email query to Apple at `internetservices@apple.com`. Be sure to include the text of the confirmation message Apple sent you so they have your order details.
- Call Apple toll-free at 1-800-709-2775. Make sure you have your order details at hand. If you're not happy with what you ordered, you'll have to call this number.

iPhoto Support
AppleCare
Hello Adam
New
Knowledge Base
Get Answers to Your Questions
Documentation

Figure 6.1 Start with Apple's iPhoto support pages for general help and pointers to other resources.

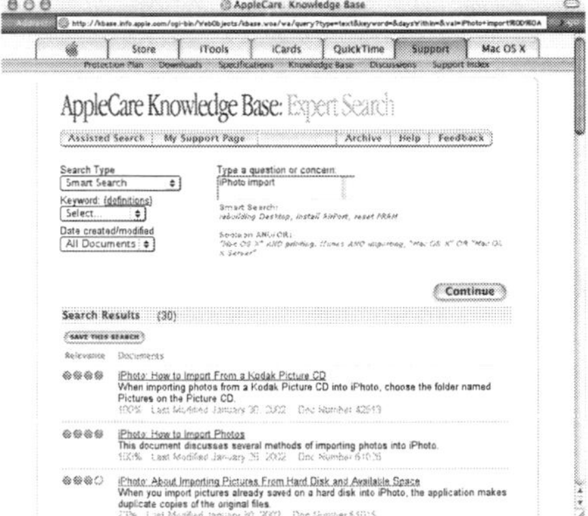
AppleCare Knowledge Base: Expert Search
Search Results (30)

Figure 6.2 For detailed troubleshooting and help articles, search in Apple's Knowledge Base.

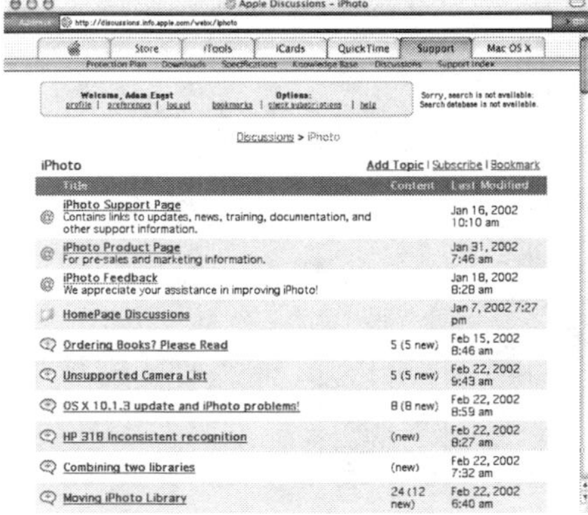
iPhoto
iPhoto Support Page
iPhoto Product Page
iPhoto Feedback
HomePage Discussions
Ordering Books? Please Read
Unsupported Camera List
OS X 10.1.3 update and iPhoto problems!
HP 318 Inconsistent recognition
Combining two libraries
Moving iPhoto Library

Figure 6.3 If all else fails, ask for help on Apple's iPhoto discussion boards.

Help Resources

I'm sure other problems and solutions will become known after I finish writing. Along with iPhoto's online help (choose iPhoto Help from the Help menu), a variety of Internet resources also provide assistance.

Places to look for more help:

- Check Apple's iPhoto support pages at `www.info.apple.com/usen/iphoto/` (**Figure 6.1**).
- Search for "iPhoto" in Apple's Knowledge Base at `http://kbase.info.apple.com/` (**Figure 6.2**). Narrow your search by adding terms, so if you're having trouble importing, search for "iPhoto import" or something similar. I far prefer the Knowledge Base's Expert Search, shown here, to the Assisted Search.
- Try asking a question on Apple's iPhoto Web-based discussion board at `http://discussions.info.apple.com/webx/iphoto` (**Figure 6.3**). In my experience, these discussions are good for straightforward questions; harder questions tend to go unanswered. When posting, state your problem clearly and include relevant information while at the same time keeping the question concise.
- Check out this book's Web site at `http://iphoto.tidbits.com/`.
- For order-related problems, send email to `internetservices@apple.com` or call 1-800-709-2775. Make sure you have your order details at hand.
- Subscribe to *TidBITS*, the free weekly newsletter I publish. It contains tons of useful information on all sorts of topics, including digital photography. Visit `www.tidbits.com` or send an email message to `tidbits-on@tidbits.com`.

Understanding Resolution

Understanding how the dimensions of a digital photo relate to what comes out of a printer is hard. That's why iPhoto merely alerts you with a warning icon when a photo won't print well at a specific size. Read these two pages to learn why iPhoto displays warning icons; the next page offers some specific solutions.

Pixels and Dots

Every digital photo is made up of a rectangular grid of points, called pixels, each of which can display one of 16 million colors or several hundred shades of grey. For instance, photos from my camera are 1600 pixels wide by 1200 pixels high. Monitors also display rectangular grids of pixels, often 1024 pixels wide by 768 pixels high.

Not all of a 1600 x 1200 photo can fit on a 1024 x 768 monitor when every pixel in the image is mapped to a pixel on the monitor. To display a photo so it fits entirely in a window, iPhoto removes pixels on the fly, a process called downsampling.

You can't perform the same one-to-one mapping when it comes to print, though, because most printers (which have only four or six colors) can't display a pixel's exact color in a single dot. Instead, they use collections of single-colored dots to fool the eye into seeing that color. For this reason and other more complex ones, the main fact to grok is that, in general, the more pixels in the image, the better it will look printed.

This fact is particularly relevant when you're printing images at large sizes. For instance, why does an image that looks fine when printed at 4" x 6" appear fuzzy at 8" x 10" ?

Imagine a blanket knitted from yarn. If you stretch it to make it larger, you can see through the holes between the threads.

Roll 39 - 7 (100%)

Figure 6.4 The original image at 100 percent.

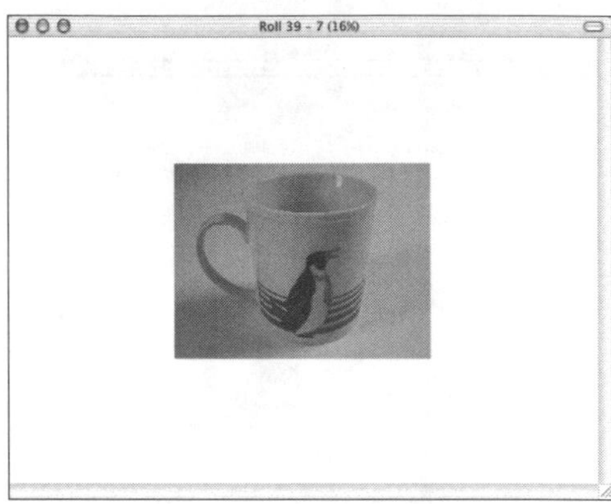
Roll 39 - 7 (16%)

Figure 6.5 Shrink the image to 16 percent of original size and the loss of detail caused by downsampling makes it hard to see the stripes on the penguin's tie.

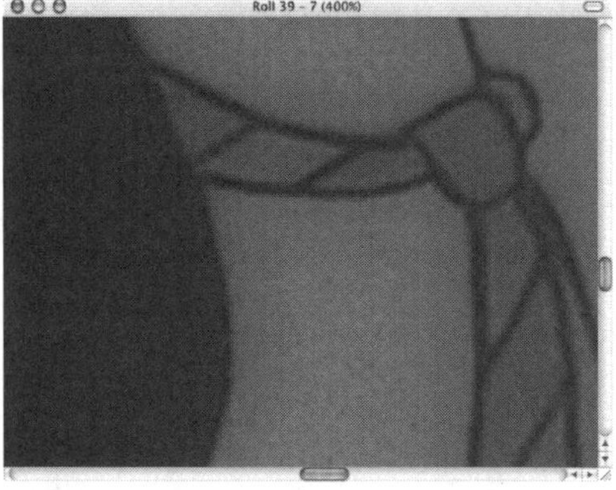
Roll 39 - 7 (400%)

Figure 6.6 Expand the image to 400 percent of the original and the fuzziness added by interpolation becomes evident.

Figure 6.7 The original 1600 x 1200 pixel image, with a small area to crop selected.

Figure 6.8 Crop the image to 247 x 185 pixels and display it at the same size, and you can see how the horse looks much fuzzier due to all the interpolation necessary to expand it to the desired size.

Expanding a photo to print at a larger size works similarly, except the printer fills in each hole with dots of roughly the same color as the dots surrounding the hole, a process called interpolation. The more pixels in the image, the smaller the holes that need to be filled, and the less interpolation is necessary.

Downsampling vs. Interpolation

Downsampling onscreen works well, since it's easy to remove similarly colored pixels without changing the image much. Even though the photo loses pixels and thus some detail, quality doesn't suffer much (**Figure 6.4** and **Figure 6.5** on the previous page). Along with the fact that onscreen images are extremely bright because monitors *emit* light, whereas paper *reflects* light, minimal downsampling helps explain why photos look good on monitors at full size.

Interpolation, particularly on a printer, is different. There's no way to avoid the fact that expanding a photo requires adding dots that didn't exist before, and because those dots exist only by virtue of the dots around them, they make the image look fuzzier (**Figure 6.4** and **Figure 6.6** on the previous page). Interpolation simply cannot add details to the image that weren't originally present. Scale an image too large, and iPhoto warns you that so much interpolation will be needed that you won't like the result.

Cropping Implies Interpolation

Cropping exacerbates the problem because it removes pixels, making the photo smaller and requiring more interpolation to expand the image back up to the desired size.

To see this, compare the original image in **Figure 6.7** with **Figure 6.8**, which shows a heavily cropped version of the same image, displayed at the same size as the original. Notice how the cropped horse is fuzzier.

Dealing with Warning Icons

Now that you have the background on how image dimensions relate to print sizes from the previous two pages, let's return to practicalities. You want to print a photo in a book, on your printer, or via Kodak's online print service, and iPhoto is displaying a warning icon on the book page thumbnail, on the preview in the Print dialog, or next to a specific size you want in the Order Prints window. What can you do to resolve this situation?

Ways of handling warning icons:

- You can simply print at a smaller size. When printing photos and ordering prints, try a smaller size (**Figure 6.9**); with a book, choose a different page design or rearrange the photos so the offending one prints at a smaller size (**Figure 6.10**).
- If the photo is too small because you cropped it, you can select it, choose Revert to Original from the File menu, and crop it again to a larger size. I'd recommend you do this primarily if you think you're right on the edge of receiving the warning icon.
- This solution would definitely take more effort, but you can also increase the size of your image using GraphicConverter or Adobe Photoshop. These programs will do interpolation as well, but the way they do it might look better than iPhoto's method.

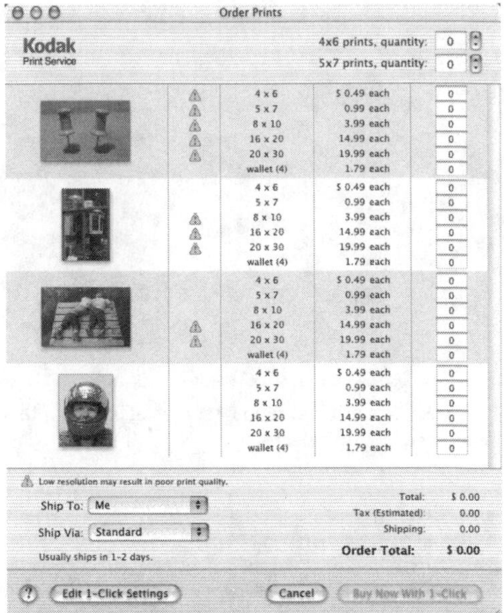
Order Prints
Kodak
Print Service
4x6 prints, quantity: 0
5x7 prints, quantity: 0
4 x 6 $ 0.49 each
5 x 7 0.99 each
8 x 10 3.99 each
16 x 20 14.99 each
20 x 30 19.99 each
wallet (4) 1.79 each
Low resolution may result in poor print quality.
Ship To: Me
Ship Via: Standard
Usually ships in 1-2 days.
Total: $ 0.00
Tax (Estimated): 0.00
Shipping: 0.00
Order Total: $ 0.00
Edit 1-Click Settings
Cancel
Buy Now With 1-Click

Figure 6.9 Note how the four images I've chosen to order prints of here have warning icons applied to different print sizes. The first image (364 x 242 pixels) can print well only at wallet size. The second (849 x 1274 pixels) won't print well at 8" x 10" or larger. The third image (1600 x 1066 pixels) drops out at 16" x 20". And the final image (1920 x 2560 pixels), will print fine at any size. Not showing here is an uncropped 1600 x 1200 image from my camera, which can also print well at all sizes.

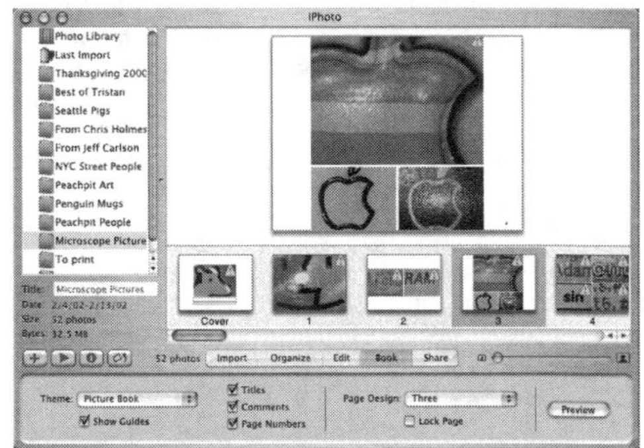
iPhoto
Photo Library
Last Import
Best of Tristan
Seattle Pigs
NYC Street People
Peachpit Art
Penguin Mugs
Peachpit People
Microscope Pictures
To print
Cover
Import
Organize
Edit
Book
Share
Theme: Picture Book
Show Guides
Titles
Comments
Page Numbers
Page Design: Three
Lock Page
Preview

Figure 6.10 Note how all of these photos, which were taken with a 50X lens using a ProScope USB microscope at 640 x 480 pixels, show low resolution warning icons except the two smaller photos of the Command key's Apple logo in the three-up page design. A 640 x 480 image needs to be quite small to print acceptably.

INDEX

E

F

INDEX

Q

R

S

T

U

V

W

Y

Z